FIFTH EDITION

BASIC

GRAMMAR
in CONTEXT

SANDRA N. ELBAUM
JUDI P. PEMÁN

The cover photo shows the
Ann W. Richards Congress
Avenue Bridge over Lady Bird
Lake in Austin, Texas.

HEINLE
CENGAGE Learning

Australia • Brazil • Japan • Korea • Mexico • Singapore • Spain • United Kingdom • United States

Grammar in Context, Basic
Student Book
Sandra N. Elbaum and Judi P. Pemán

Publisher: Sherrise Roehr

Acquisitions Editor: Tom Jefferies

Development Editor: Sarah Sandoski

Senior Technology Development Manager:
 Debie Mirtle

Director of Global Marketing: Ian Martin

Director of US Marketing: Jim McDonough

Product Marketing Manager: Katie Kelley

Marketing Manager: Caitlin Driscoll

Content Project Manager: Andrea Bobotas

Senior Print Buyer: Susan Spencer

Project Manager: Chrystie Hopkins

Production Services: Nesbitt Graphics, Inc.

Interior Design and Cover Design:
 Muse Group, Inc.

© 2010 Heinle, Cengage Learning

Library of Congress Control Number: 2010923821

ISBN 13: 978-1-4240-7908-7

ISBN 10: 1-4240-7908-X

Heinle

20 Channel Center Street

Boston, Massachusetts 02210

USA

Cengage Learning is a leading provider of customized learning solutions with office locations around the globe, including Singapore, the United Kingdom, Australia, Mexico, Brazil, and Japan. Locate our local office at international.cengage.com/region

Cengage Learning products are represented in Canada by Nelson Education, Ltd.

Visit Heinle online at **elt.heinle.com**

Visit our corporate website at **www.cengage.com**

Printed in the United States of America.
1 2 3 4 5 6 7 8 9 10 — 14 13 12 11 10

Contents

Unit 11

Acknowledgments

Many thanks to Dennis Hogan, Sherrise Roehr, and Tom Jefferies from Heinle Cengage for their ongoing support of the *Grammar in Context* series. We would especially like to thank our development editor, Sarah Sandoski, for her patience, sensitivity, keen eye to detail, and invaluable suggestions.

And many thanks to our students at Truman College, who have increased our understanding of our own language and taught us to see life from another point of view. By sharing their observations, questions, and life stories, they have enriched our lives enormously.

This new edition is dedicated to the millions of displaced people in the world. The U.S. is the new home to many refugees, who survived unspeakable hardships in Burundi, Rwanda, Sudan, Burma, Bhutan, and other countries. Their resiliency in starting a new life and learning a new language is a tribute to the human spirit.—*Sandra N. Elbaum and Judi P. Pemán*

Heinle would like to thank the following people for their contributions:

Elizabeth A. Adler-Coleman
Sunrise Mountain High
    School
Las Vegas, NV

Dorothy Avondstondt
Miami Dade College
Miami, FL

Judith A. G. Benka
Normandale Community
    College
Bloomington, MN

Carol Brutza
Gateway Community College
New Haven, CT

Lyn Buchheit
Community College of
    Philadelphia
Philadelphia, PA

Charlotte M. Calobrisi
Northern Virginia
    Community College
Annandale, VA

Gabriela Cambiasso
Harold Washington College
Chicago, IL

Jeanette Clement
Duquesne University
Pittsburgh, PA

Allis Cole
Shoreline Community College
Shoreline, WA

Fanshen DiGiovanni
Glendale Community
    College
Glendale, CA

Antoinette B. d'Oronzio
Hillsborough Community
    College-Dale Mabry
    Campus
Tampa, FL

Maha Edlbi
Sierra College
Rocklin, CA

Rhonda J. Farley
Cosumnes River College
Sacramento, CA

Jennifer Farnell
University of Connecticut
    American Language
    Program
Stamford, CT

Gail Fernandez
Bergen Community College
Paramus, NJ

Irasema Fernandez
Miami Dade College
Miami, FL

Abigail-Marie Fiattarone
Mesa Community College
Mesa, AZ

John Gamber
American River College
Sacramento, CA

Marcia Gethin-Jones
University of Connecticut
    American Language
    Program
Stamford, CT

Kimlee Buttacavoli Grant
The Leona Group, LLC
Phoenix, AZ

Shelly Hedstrom
Palm Beach Community
    College
Lake Worth, FL

Linda Holden
College of Lake County
Grayslake, IL

Sandra Kawamura
Sacramento City College
Sacramento, CA

Bill Keniston
Normandale Community
    College
Bloomington, MN

Michael Larsen
American River College
Sacramento, CA

Bea C. Lawn
Gavilan College
Gilroy, CA

Rob Lee
Pasadena City College
Pasadena, CA

Oranit Limmaneeprasert
American River College
Sacramento, CA

Linda Louie
Highline Community
    College
Des Moines, WA

Melanie A. Majeski
Naugatuck Valley
    Community College
Waterbury, CT

Maria Marin
De Anza College
Cupertino, CA

Michael I. Massey
Hillsborough Community
    College-Ybor City
    Campus
Tampa, FL

Marlo McClurg-Mackinnon
Cosumnes River
    College
Sacramento, CA

Michelle Naumann
Elgin Community College
Elgin, IL

Debbie Ockey
Fresno, CA

Lesa Perry
University of Nebraska at
    Omaha
Omaha, NE

Herbert Pierson
St. John's University
Queens, NY

Dina Poggi
De Anza College
Cupertino, CA

Steven Rashba
University of Bridgeport
Bridgeport, CT

Mark Rau
American River College
Sacramento, CA

Maria Spelleri
State College of Florida
    Manatee-Sarasota
Venice, FL

Eva Teagarden
Yuba College
Marysville, CA

Colin S. Ward
Lone Star College-North
    Harris
Houston, TX

Robert Wachman
Yuba College
Yuba City, CA

Nico Wiersema
Texas A&M International
    University
Laredo, TX

Susan Wilson
San Jose City College
San Jose, CA

A word from the authors

When we started teaching many years ago, grammar textbooks used a series of unrelated sentences with no context. We knew instinctively that there was something wrong with this technique. It ignored the fact that language is a tool for communication, and it missed an opportunity for some important collateral learning to take place. As we gained teaching experience, we noticed that when we embedded the grammar into topics that taught students life skills, this captured their interest, sparked their curiosity, and motivated them to understand the grammar better and use it more effectively.

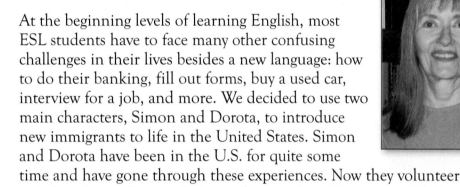

At the beginning levels of learning English, most ESL students have to face many other confusing challenges in their lives besides a new language: how to do their banking, fill out forms, buy a used car, interview for a job, and more. We decided to use two main characters, Simon and Dorota, to introduce new immigrants to life in the United States. Simon and Dorota have been in the U.S. for quite some time and have gone through these experiences. Now they volunteer to help others adjust to their new lives in the U.S.

Like the other books in the *Grammar in Context* series, a reading (a narrative or a dialogue) introduces the grammar and is followed by grammar charts using sentences from the context of the reading. What sets *Basic* apart is specific attention to vocabulary and listening activities geared to beginning levels of ESL.

At the end of *Grammar in Context Basic*, students should have a good introduction to the most common grammatical structures of the English language, a solid vocabulary base, and an understanding of the practicalities of American life. Students will then be ready for more in-depth study and practice of each structure as found in *Grammar in Context 1, 2,* and *3.*

Enjoy using *Grammar in Context Basic!*

–Sandra N. Elbaum and Judi P. Pemán

> For
> Cassia, Laila, Gentille, Chimene, Joseph, Joy, and Ange

Welcome to *Grammar in Context*

Basic

Grammar in Context presents grammar in interesting contexts that are relevant to students' lives and then recycles the language and context throughout every activity. Learners gain knowledge and skills in both the grammar structures and topic areas.

The new edition of *Grammar in Context* engages learners with updated readings, clear and manageable grammar explanations, and a new full-color design.

New To This Edition!

Full-color design makes grammar more visually contextualized and even easier to study and teach from.

Listening Activities allow students the opportunity to improve listening comprehension.

High-interest, informative readings present grammar in context, in the form of journal entries, dialogues, and Web articles, illustrating the grammatical structure in an informative and meaningful way.

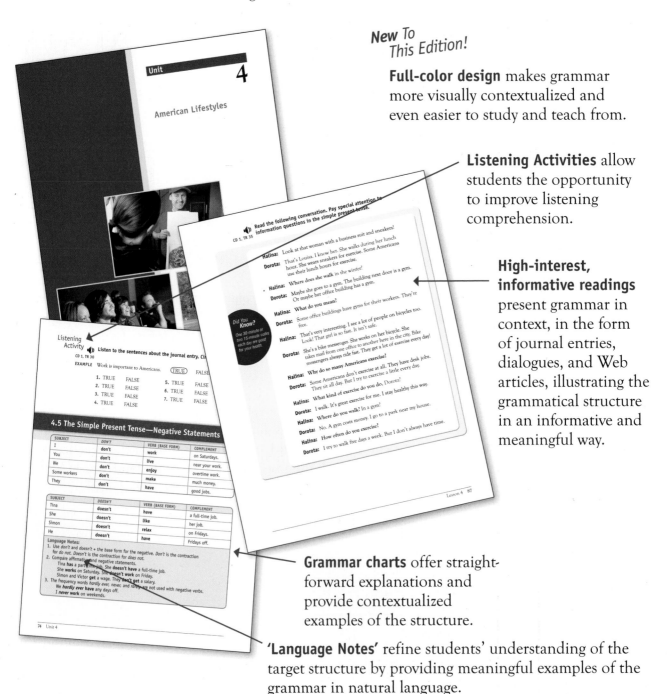

Grammar charts offer straight-forward explanations and provide contextualized examples of the structure.

'Language Notes' refine students' understanding of the target structure by providing meaningful examples of the grammar in natural language.

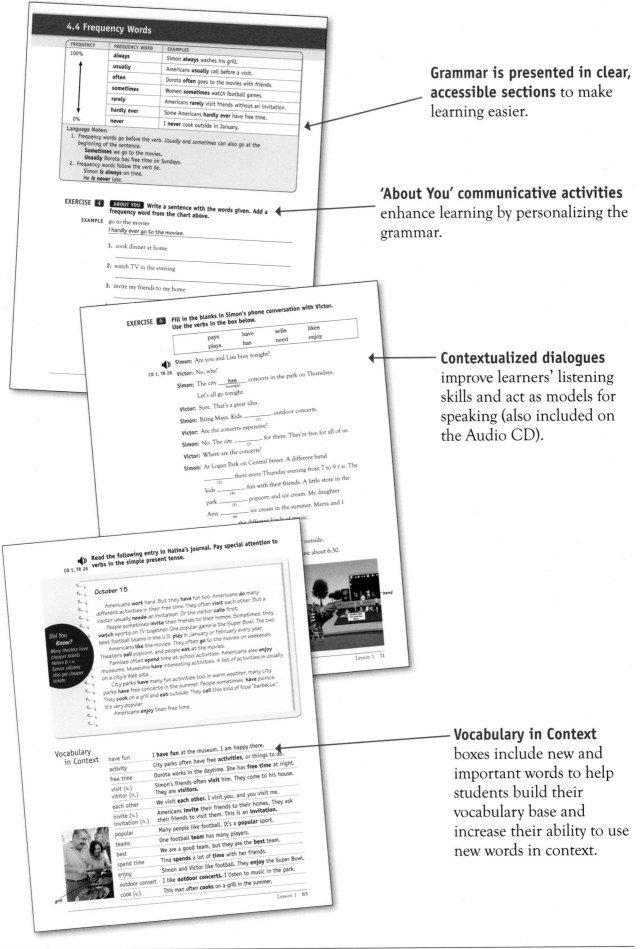

4.4 Frequency Words

FREQUENCY	FREQUENCY WORD	EXAMPLES
100%	always	Simon **always** washes his grill.
	usually	Americans **usually** call before a visit.
	often	Dorota **often** goes to the movies with friends.
	sometimes	Women **sometimes** watch football games.
	rarely	Americans **rarely** visit friends without an invitation.
	hardly ever	Some Americans **hardly ever** have free time.
0%	never	I **never** cook outside in January.

Language Notes:
1. Frequency words go before the verb. *Usually* and *sometimes* can also go at the beginning of the sentence.
   Sometimes we go to the movies.
   Usually Dorota has free time on Sundays.
2. Frequency words follow the verb *be*.
   Simon **is always** on time.
   He **is never** late.

EXERCISE 4 **ABOUT YOU** Write a sentence with the words given. Add a frequency word from the chart above.

EXAMPLE go to the movies
I hardly ever go to the movies.

1. cook dinner at home
_____

2. watch TV in the evening
_____

3. invite my friends to my home
_____

Grammar is presented in clear, accessible sections to make learning easier.

'About You' communicative activities enhance learning by personalizing the grammar.

EXERCISE 6 Fill in the blanks in Simon's phone conversation with Victor. Use the verbs in the box below.

pays	have	sells	likes
plays	has	need	enjoy

Simon: Are you and Lisa busy tonight?

CD 1, TR 28 **Victor:** No, why?

Simon: The city ___has___ concerts in the park on Thursdays.
(example)
Let's all go tonight.

Victor: Sure. That's a great idea.

Simon: Bring Maya. Kids ___(1)___ outdoor concerts.

Victor: Are the concerts expensive?

Simon: No. The city ___(2)___ for them. They're free for all of us.

Victor: Where are the concerts?

Simon: At Logan Park on Central Street. A different band ___(3)___ there every Thursday evening from 7 to 9 P.M. The kids ___(4)___ fun with their friends. A little store in the park ___(5)___ popcorn and ice cream. My daughter Amy ___(6)___ ice cream in the summer. Marta and I the different kinds of music.

Contextualized dialogues improve learners' listening skills and act as models for speaking (also included on the Audio CD).

Read the following entry in Halina's journal. Pay special attention to verbs in the simple present tense.
CD 1, TR 26

October 15

Americans **work** hard. But they **have** fun too. Americans **do** many different activities in their free time. They often **visit** each other. But a visitor usually **needs** an invitation. Or the visitor **calls** first.

People sometimes **invite** their friends to their homes. Sometimes, they **watch** sports on TV together. One popular game is the Super Bowl. The two best football teams in the U.S. **play** in January or February every year.

Americans **like** the movies. They often **go** to the movies on weekends. Theaters **sell** popcorn, and people **eat** at the movies. Americans also **enjoy** museums. Museums **have** interesting activities. A list of activities is usually on a city's Web site.

Families often **spend** time at school activities.

City parks **have** many fun activities too. In warm weather, many city parks **have** free concerts in the summer. People sometimes **have** picnics. They **cook** on a grill and **eat** outside. They **call** this kind of food "barbecue." It's very popular.

Americans **enjoy** their free time.

Did You Know?
Many theaters have cheaper tickets before 6 P.M. Senior citizens also get cheaper tickets.

outside.
use about 6:30.

band

Lesson 1 71

Vocabulary in Context

have fun	I **have fun** at the museum. I am happy there.
activity	City parks often have free **activities**, or things to do.
free time	Dorota works in the daytime. She has **free time** at night.
visit (v.) visitor (n.)	Simon's friends often **visit** him. They come to his house. They are **visitors**.
each other	We visit **each other**. I visit you, and you visit me.
invite (v.) invitation (n.)	Americans **invite** their friends to their homes. They ask their friends to visit them. This is an **invitation**.
popular	Many people like football. It's a **popular** sport.
teams	One football **team** has many players.
best	We are a good team, but they are the **best** team.
spend time	Tina **spends** a lot of **time** with her friends.
enjoy	Simon and Victor like football. They **enjoy** the Super Bowl.
outdoor concert	I like **outdoor concerts**. I listen to music in the park.
cook (v.)	This man often **cooks** on a grill in the summer.

grill

Lesson 1 65

Vocabulary in Context boxes include new and important words to help students build their vocabulary base and increase their ability to use new words in context.

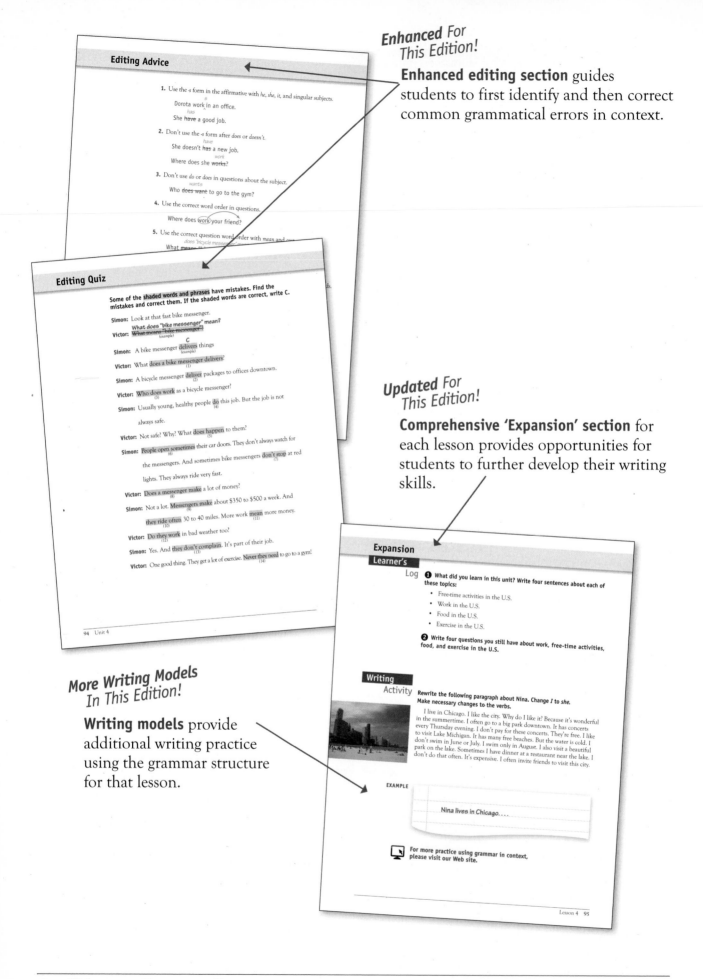

Enhanced For This Edition!

Enhanced editing section guides students to first identify and then correct common grammatical errors in context.

Editing Advice

1. Use the *-s* form in the affirmative with *he, she, it,* and singular subjects.
   s
   Dorota work in an office.
   has
   She ~~have~~ a good job.

2. Don't use the *-s* form after *does* or *doesn't.*
   have
   She doesn't ~~has~~ a new job.
   work
   Where does she ~~works~~?

3. Don't use *do* or *does* in questions about the subject.
   wants
   Who ~~does want~~ to go to the gym?

4. Use the correct word order in questions.
   Where does work your friend?

5. Use the correct question word order with *mean* and *cost.*
   does "bicycle messenger"
   What mean "bicycle messenger"?

Editing Quiz

Some of the shaded words and phrases have mistakes. Find the mistakes and correct them. If the shaded words are correct, write C.

Simon: Look at that fast bike messenger.

Victor: What does "bike messenger" mean?
~~What means "bike messenger"?~~
(example)

Simon: A bike messenger delivers things
C
(example)

Victor: What does a bike messenger delivers?
(1)

Simon: A bicycle messenger deliver packages to offices downtown.
(2)

Victor: Who does work as a bicycle messenger?
(3)

Simon: Usually young, healthy people do this job. But the job is not
(4)
always safe.

Victor: Not safe? Why? What does happen to them?
(5)

Simon: People open sometimes their car doors. They don't always watch for
(6)
the messengers. And sometimes bike messengers don't stop at red
(7)
lights. They always ride very fast.

Victor: Does a messenger make a lot of money?
(8)

Simon: Not a lot. Messengers make about $350 to $500 a week. And
(9)
they ride often 30 to 40 miles. More work mean more money.
(10)   (11)

Victor: Do they work in bad weather too?
(12)

Simon: Yes. And they don't complain. It's part of their job.
(13)

Victor: One good thing. They get a lot of exercise. Never they need to go to a gym!
(14)

94 Unit 4

Updated For This Edition!

Comprehensive 'Expansion' section for each lesson provides opportunities for students to further develop their writing skills.

Expansion
Learner's
Log

❶ What did you learn in this unit? Write four sentences about each of these topics:

- Free-time activities in the U.S.
- Work in the U.S.
- Food in the U.S.
- Exercise in the U.S.

❷ Write four questions you still have about work, free-time activities, food, and exercise in the U.S.

Writing
Activity

Rewrite the following paragraph about Nina. Change *I* to *she.* Make necessary changes to the verbs.

I live in Chicago. I like the city. Why do I like it? Because it's wonderful in the summertime. I often go to a big park downtown. It has concerts every Thursday evening. I don't pay for these concerts. They're free. I like to visit Lake Michigan. It has many free beaches. But the water is cold. I don't swim in June or July. I swim only in August. I also visit a beautiful park on the lake. Sometimes I have dinner at a restaurant near the lake. I don't do that often. It's expensive. I often invite friends to visit this city.

EXAMPLE

Nina lives in Chicago. . . .

For more practice using grammar in context, please visit our Web site.

Lesson 4 95

More Writing Models In This Edition!

Writing models provide additional writing practice using the grammar structure for that lesson.

Additional resources for each level:

FOR THE STUDENT:

New To This Edition!

- **Online Workbook** features additional exercises that learners can access in the classroom, language lab, or at home.

- **Audio CD** includes dialogues, Listening Activities, and all readings from the student book.

- Student Web site features additional practice: http://elt.heinle.com/grammarincontext.

FOR THE TEACHER:

New To This Edition!

- **Online Lesson Planner** is perfect for busy instructors, allowing them to create and customize lesson plans for their classes, then save and share them in a range of formats.

Updated For This Edition!

- **Assessment CD-ROM with Exam*View*®** lets teachers create and customize tests and quizzes easily and includes many new contextualized test items.

- **Teacher's Edition** offers comprehensive teaching notes including suggestions for more streamlined classroom options.

- Instructor Web site includes a printable Student Book answer key.

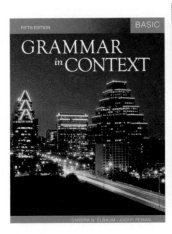 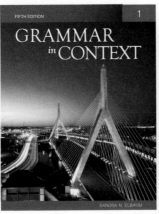 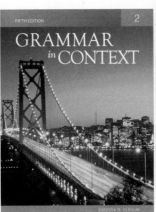 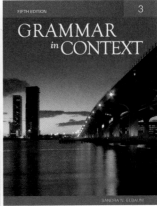

It is nice to meet you!

Simon and Marta, with Tina, Amy, and Ed

Halina and Peter, with Anna

Dorota

Shafia and Ali

Victor and Lisa, with Maya

Sue and Rick

Welcome to the U.S.

Grammar
Subject Pronouns

Be—**Affirmative Statements**

Context
Help for New Immigrants

We Are Here to Help

Before
You Read

Circle *yes* or *no*.

1. Many things are new for me in this country.   YES   NO
2. People help me with new things.   YES   NO

Read the following conversation. Pay special attention to *is, am,* **and** *are.*

Dorota: Welcome! My name **is** Dorota. I **am** from Poland, but I **am** a citizen of the U.S. now. My first language **is** Polish. This **is** Simon. He **is** from Mexico. We **are** here to help you.

Simon: Hi. My name **is** Simon. I **am** from Mexico, but I **am** a citizen now. Spanish **is** my first language. We **are** both here to help you.

Dorota: You **are** new in this country. You **are** immigrants. Life **is** different here. Many things **are** different for you— the supermarket **is** different, the laundromat **is** different, the doctor's office **is** different, and the bank **is** different. Everything **is** new for you. Maybe you **are** confused.

Simon: We **are** here to help you in new places. The laundromat and supermarket **are** the first places to go.

Did You
Know?

Some supermarkets and laundromats are open 24 hours a day.

Vocabulary in Context

citizen	Dorota is a **citizen** of the United States.
help (v.) helpful (adj.)	Dorota and Simon **help** immigrants. They are **helpful**.
both	Dorota and Simon are **both** citizens.
immigrant	I am from Colombia. I am new to the U.S. I am an **immigrant**.
life	**Life** in the U.S. is new for me.
different	Simon and Dorota are from **different** countries.
supermarket	We buy food in a **supermarket**.
laundromat	The **laundromat** is a place to wash clothes.
bank	He needs money. He is at the **bank**.
everything	**Everything** is new—the bank, the supermarket, and the laundromat.
confused	I am new here. Everything is different. I am **confused**.

🔊 **Listen to the sentences about the conversation.**
Circle *true* or *false*.

EXAMPLE   Dorota and Simon are in the supermarket now.   TRUE   (FALSE)

1. TRUE   FALSE   **4.** TRUE   FALSE

2. TRUE   FALSE   **5.** TRUE   FALSE

3. TRUE   FALSE   **6.** TRUE   FALSE

1.1 Subject Pronouns

EXERCISE 1   **Fill in the blanks with the correct subject pronoun.**

EXAMPLE   ___*We*___ are immigrants.

1. Dorota is from Poland. _____ is here to help.
2. _____ am new to this country.
3. Simon is from Mexico. _____ is from Mexico City.
4. You and I are new here. _____ are confused.
5. The bank is near my house. _____ is big.
6. Simon and Dorota are citizens now. _____ are helpful.
7. **Halina:** Thank you for your help.

   Simon: _____ are welcome.

1.2 *Be*—Affirmative Statements

SUBJECT	FORM OF *BE*	COMPLEMENT
I	am	a citizen.
Dorota		from Poland.
She	is	helpful.
Simon		from Mexico.
He		in the U.S.
The supermarket	is	different.
It		big.
We		here to help.
You		new here.
Dorota and Simon	are	American citizens.
They		helpful.

Language Note: We use a form of *be* to:
1. describe the subject *(helpful, big)*
2. tell where the subject is from *(from Mexico, from Poland)*
3. classify the subject *(a citizen)*
4. show location *(here, in the U.S.)*

EXERCISE 2   **Fill in the missing words: *am*, *is*, or *are*.**

EXAMPLE   The laundromat ____is____ different.

1. I _____ new here.
2. You _____ a citizen.
3. We _____ here to help you.
4. Some things _____ different in the U.S.
5. He _____ confused.
6. Simon and Dorota _____ helpful.
7. Dorota _____ from Poland.

EXERCISE 3   **Dorota is talking to Halina, a new immigrant. Fill in the blanks with the correct form of *be*.**

CD 1, TR 03

Halina: Hi, Dorota. I ____*am*____ Halina.
(example)

Dorota: You _____ new.
(1)

Halina: Yes. I _____ from Poland.
(2)

Dorota: I _____ from Poland too. Many people here _____
(3)   (4)

from Poland. I _____ here to help you. Simon _____
(5)   (6)

here to help you too. He _____ from Mexico.
(7)

Halina: Many things _____ new for me.
(8)

Dorota: Yes. Life _____ different here. But Simon and
(9)

I _____ both here to help you.
(10)

Halina: Thank you.

EXERCISE 4 **ABOUT YOU** Check (✓) the items that are true for you.

EXAMPLES   ✓   I am new to the U.S.

        _____ I am a citizen of the U.S.

1. _____ I am new to the U.S.
2. _____ I am new at this school.
3. _____ Life is different in a new country.
4. _____ I am confused about life in the U.S.
5. _____ I am a citizen of the U.S.
6. _____ I am an immigrant.
7. _____ Americans are helpful.
8. _____ I am from Mexico.
9. _____ Spanish is my native language.
10. _____ My family is in the U.S.

EXERCISE 5 **ABOUT YOU** Fill in the blanks.

EXAMPLE   I am a citizen of _____ Peru _____.

1. My name is _____.
2. I am from _____.
3. _____ is my native language.
4. I am confused about _____.
5. _____ is a helpful person for me.
6. _____ is different for me now.

Grammar

Contractions (Short Forms)

Singular and Plural

This/That/These/Those

Context

Using a Laundromat

Help at the Laundromat

Before
  You Read **Circle *yes* or *no*.**

1. I use the laundromat.   YES   NO

2. I wash some things by hand.   YES   NO

Read the following conversation. Pay special attention to contractions with *be*.

Dorota and a new immigrant, Shafia, are at the laundromat.

Dorota: **We're** at the laundromat.

Shafia: The **laundromat's** new for me.
I'm confused.

Dorota: Don't worry. **We're** together.
I'm here to help you.

Shafia: Thanks. My clothes are dirty.

Dorota: These are the washing machines. The small machines are for small items—clothes, towels, and sheets. Those big machines are for big items, like blankets. Coins are necessary for the machines.

Shafia: Those machines are different.

Dorota: Yes. **They're** dryers.

Shafia: **It's** hot inside the laundromat.

Dorota: **You're** right.

Shafia: **It's** easy to wash clothes in a laundromat.

Dorota: Yes, it is.

Shafia: These two washers[1] are empty. **I'm** ready to wash my clothes.

Vocabulary in Context

don't worry	**Don't worry.** I'm here to help you.
together	Dorota is with Shafia. They're **together**.
right	**A:** It's hot here. **B:** Yes, you're **right**.
item	These machines are for small **items**.
clothes	These are my **clothes**.
necessary	It's **necessary** to wash clothes.
empty	The dryer is **empty**.
dirty/clean	Your clothes are **dirty**. My clothes are **clean**.

[1]*Washer* is another word for "washing machine."

Listening
   Activity 🔊 **Listen to the sentences about the conversation.**
      CD 1, TR 05 **Circle _true_ or _false_.**

EXAMPLE The laundromat is new for Shafia.   (TRUE)   FALSE

1. TRUE	FALSE		**4.** TRUE	FALSE
2. TRUE	FALSE		**5.** TRUE	FALSE
3. TRUE	FALSE			

1.3 Contractions (Short Forms)

LONG FORM		CONTRACTION (SHORT FORM)	EXAMPLES
I am	→	I'm	**I'm** here to help.
She is	→	She's	**She's** from Poland.
He is	→	He's	**He's** from Mexico.
It is	→	It's	**It's** hot in here.
Life is	→	Life's	**Life's** different.
Everything is	→	Everything's	**Everything's** new.
Dorota is	→	Dorota's	**Dorota's** from Poland.
The laundromat is	→	The laundromat's	The **laundromat's** hot.
You are	→	You're	**You're** very helpful.
We are	→	We're	**We're** together.
They are	→	They're	**They're** at the laundromat.

Language Notes:
1. To make a contraction (short form), we put an apostrophe (') in place of the missing letter.
2. We can make a contraction with a subject pronoun + _am, is,_ and _are_.
3. We can make a contraction with a singular subject + _is_.
4. Do not make a contraction with a plural noun + _are_.
   The dryers are empty.

EXERCISE 1 Write the contraction for the words in parentheses ( ).

EXAMPLE (I am) _____I'm_____ new here.

1. (Simon is) _____ from Mexico.
2. (He is) _____ a citizen of the U.S. now.
3. (Dorota is) _____ from Poland.
4. (She is) _____ a citizen too.
5. (They are) _____ both very helpful.
6. (The laundromat is) _____ big.
7. (It is) _____ hot in the laundromat.
8. (You are) _____ confused.
9. (I am) _____ confused too.
10. (We are) _____ both confused.

EXERCISE 2 Shafia and Halina are new immigrants. This is their conversation. Fill in the blanks with *am, is,* or *are.* Make a contraction, where possible.

CD 1, TR 06

Shafia: I _'m_____ from India. You _'re_____ from Russia, right?
(example)   (example)

Halina: No. I _____ from Warsaw. It _____ in Poland.
(1)   (2)

Shafia: I _____ new here. I _____ confused.
(3)   (4)

Halina: We _____ both confused. Life _____ different here.
(5)   (6)

Shafia: Yes. Many things _____ new here. The bank _____
(7)   (8)

new for me. The school _____ new for me.
(9)

Halina: Simon and Dorota are citizens now. Simon _____ from
(10)

Mexico. He _____ helpful. Dorota _____ from Poland.
(11)   (12)

She _____ helpful too.
(13)

Shafia: They _____ both very helpful to new immigrants.
(14)

Halina: You _____ right.
(15)

1.4 Singular and Plural

Singular means one. **Plural** means more than one. A plural noun usually ends in *-s*.

SINGULAR	PLURAL
one machine	five machine**s**
one coin	six coin**s**
one towel	three towel**s**
one blanket	two blanket**s**

EXERCISE 3 **Write the plural form of the words.**

EXAMPLE sheet ___sheets___

quarter

dime

nickel

1. quarter _____
2. dime _____
3. dryer _____
4. nickel _____
5. machine _____

6. towel _____
7. item _____
8. blanket _____
9. coin _____
10. dollar _____

dollar

1.5 *This, That, These, Those*

This and **that** are singular. **These** and **those** are plural.

	SINGULAR	PLURAL
Near $\longrightarrow$	**This** is a laundromat.	**These** are quarters.
Not near Far $\longrightarrow$	**That** is a big machine.	**Those** are the dryers.

Language Note: Only *that is* has a contraction—***that's.***
  That's a big machine.
Pronunciation Note: It's hard for many students to hear the difference between *this* and *these*. Listen to your teacher pronounce the sentences above.

EXERCISE 4   Fill in the blanks with *this is, that's, these are,* or *those are.*

EXAMPLE   _____That's_____ the change[2] machine.

1. _____ a dollar.

2. _____ coins.

3. _____ quarters.

4. _____ the big washing machines.

5. _____ an empty machine.

6. _____ dryers.

EXERCISE 5   Circle the correct word.

EXAMPLE   The (*sheet* / (*sheets*)) are white.

1. The blankets (*is* / *are*) big.
2. (*These* / *This*) are the dryers.
3. (*They're* / *They*) hot.
4. (*Quarter* / *Quarters*) are necessary for the machine.
5. (*That* / *Those*) machines are empty.

[2]Four quarters is *change* for one dollar.

Grammar

Be—Negative Statements

Adjectives

Expressions with *It*

Singular and Plural—
Spelling Rules

Context
Buying Food

Help at the Supermarket

Before
You Read   **Circle *yes* or *no*.**

1. I'm confused in an American supermarket.   YES   NO

2. Prices are the same in every supermarket.   YES   NO

Read the following conversation. Pay special attention to negative forms of *be*.

CD 1, TR 07

Dorota: We're at the supermarket now. It's early. The supermarket **isn't** crowded. The parking lot**'s not** crowded.

Halina: This is my first time in an American supermarket. I**'m not** sure what to do.

Dorota: It's not hard to use the supermarket. I'm here to help you.

Halina: Thanks. The prices **aren't** on the products.

Dorota: The prices are on the shelves, under the products. A bar code is on each package. Prices **aren't** the same every week. Some things are on sale each week. Look—bananas are on sale this week. They're usually 69¢ a pound. This week they**'re not** 69¢ a pound. They're 29¢ a pound.

bar code

Halina: Look! These cookies are free.

Dorota: The samples are free, but the bags of cookies **aren't**. (*ten minutes later*) We're finished. This checkout is empty.

Halina: The cashier**'s not** here.

Dorota: It's an automatic checkout.

Vocabulary in Context

early	It's 8 A.M. It's **early**.
crowded	The store is empty. It isn't **crowded**.
sure	I'm confused. I'm not **sure** what to do.
hard	It's not **hard** to use the supermarket. It's easy.
price	The **price** is 29¢ a pound.
product	The supermarket has many **products**: milk, fruit, meat.
shelf/shelves	The prices are on the **shelves**.
bar code	A **bar code** is on each product.
package	The cookies are in **packages**.
the same	Prices aren't **the same** every week.
on sale	Bananas are **on sale** this week. They're only 29¢ a pound.
pound	Americans use **pounds**, not kilograms.
free	The packages of cookies aren't **free**. They're $2.79.
sample	The **samples** are free.
cashier	The **cashiers** are at the checkouts.
automatic checkout	The **automatic checkout** is fast.

Listening Activity

CD 1, TR 08

Listen to the sentences about the conversation. Circle _true_ or _false_.

EXAMPLE Simon and Dorota are at the supermarket.   TRUE   (FALSE)

1. TRUE	FALSE		**4.** TRUE	FALSE
2. TRUE	FALSE		**5.** TRUE	FALSE
3. TRUE	FALSE		**6.** TRUE	FALSE

1.6 *Be*—Negative Statements

Compare long forms and contractions (short forms).

NEGATIVE LONG FORMS	NEGATIVE SHORT FORMS	
I **am not** sure.	I**'m not** sure.	*
You **are not** confused.	You**'re not** confused.	You **aren't** confused.
She **is not** a cashier.	She**'s not** a cashier.	She **isn't** a cashier.
He **is not** at home.	He**'s not** at home.	He **isn't** at home.
The store **is not** small.	The store**'s not** small.	The store **isn't** small.
It **is not** crowded.	It**'s not** crowded.	It **isn't** crowded.
That **is not** the price.	That**'s not** the price.	That **isn't** the price.
We **are not** in the laundromat.	We**'re not** in the laundromat.	We **aren't** in the laundromat.
They **are not** on sale.	They**'re not** on sale.	They **aren't** on sale.
The cookies **are not** free.	**	The cookies **aren't** free.

Language Notes:
 *1. We cannot make a contraction for *am not*.
 **2. We cannot make a contraction for a plural noun + *are*.

Compare affirmative and negative statements with *be*.

AFFIRMATIVE	NEGATIVE
We **are** at the supermarket.	We **aren't** at home.
The milk **is** fresh.	It **isn't** old.
I **am** new here.	I**'m not** sure about many things.
The samples **are** free.	The cookies in packages **aren't** free.
You **are** from the U.S.	You**'re not** confused.
Halina **is** a new immigrant.	Dorota **isn't** a new immigrant.

EXERCISE **1** **Fill in the blanks with a negative form of the <u>underlined</u> verbs. Use contractions if possible.**

EXAMPLE   The supermarket <u>is</u> big. It ___isn't___ small.

1. The date <u>is</u> on packages. The date _____ on fruit.

2. We<u>'re</u> at the supermarket. We _____ at the laundromat.

3. Bananas <u>are</u> 29¢ this week. They _____ 29¢ every week.

4. I<u>'m</u> in the supermarket. I _____ in the laundromat.

(continued)

Lesson 3   17

5. The store <u>is</u> empty. It _____ crowded.

6. You<u>'re</u> helpful. You _____ confused.

7. Prices <u>are</u> on the shelves. They _____ on the products.

8. The sample cookies <u>are</u> free. The packages of cookies _____ free.

9. That<u>'s</u> a bar code. That _____ the price.

EXERCISE **2** **Check (✓) the true statements. Change the false statements to the negative form and add a true statement. Answers may vary.**

EXAMPLES _____ Supermarkets are dirty. *Supermarkets aren't dirty. They're clean.*

✓ Cashiers are helpful.

bag

parking lot

1. _____ I'm confused about supermarkets.

2. _____ Life in the U.S. is easy.

3. _____ Supermarkets are small.

4. _____ Americans are helpful.

5. _____ Supermarkets are crowded in the morning.

6. _____ Prices are the same every week.

7. _____ Supermarkets are hot.

8. _____ Bags are free.

1.7 Adjectives

An adjective gives a description of a noun.

EXAMPLES			EXPLANATION
Subject	*Be*	**Adjective**	An adjective can follow the verb *be*.
The parking lot	is	**empty.**	subject + *be* + (*not*) + adjective
The store	isn't	**crowded.**	
The samples	are	**free.**	
Those are **free** samples.			An adjective can come before a noun.
These are **big** packages.			adjective + noun

Language Note: Descriptive adjectives are always singular. Only the noun is plural.
    one **free** sample
    two **free** samples			

EXERCISE **3** **In each of the conversations below, fill in the blanks with an adjective from the box.**

CD 1, TR 09

Vocabulary for Conversation A

new	early	helpful	different
crowded	easy	big	

Conversation A: Halina and Dorota are at the supermarket.

Halina: I'm _____ new _____ to this country. Everything is _____ for me.
(example)   (1)

Dorota: Don't worry. I'm here with you.

Halina: You're very _____.
(2)

Dorota: This is the supermarket. It's _____
(3)

to shop in a supermarket.

Halina: The supermarket and the parking lot

aren't _____. Why not?
(4)

Dorota: It's only 10 A.M. It's _____.
(5)

Halina: This supermarket is _____. In my country, stores are small.
(6)

Dorota: Look! Bananas are on sale this week; they're only 29¢ a pound. That's a good price.

Vocabulary for Conversation B

small	open	different
hot	big	

Conversation B: Simon is showing a new immigrant, Victor, the laundromat.

Simon: This is the laundromat.

Victor: It's _____ in here.
(1)

Simon: Yes, it is. But the door is _____.
(2)

Victor: Some machines are _____ and some are _____.
(3)   (4)

Simon: The big machines are for big items, like blankets.

Victor: All of these machines are the same, but those are _____.
(5)

Simon: These are washing machines. Those machines are dryers.

Victor: In my country, sometimes my wife is the washer and the air is the dryer!

1.8 Expressions with *It*

EXAMPLES	EXPLANATION
It's hot in the laundromat. **It**'s cold outside.	Use *it* with weather or temperature.
It's 10 A.M. **It**'s early. **It** isn't late.	Use *it* with time.
It's easy **to wash** clothes at the laundromat. **It** isn't **hard.** It's early. **It**'s a good time **to shop**.	Use *it* with impersonal expressions: *it's easy, it's hard, it's good.* An infinitive (*to* + the base form of a verb) often follows.

EXERCISE **4** **Fill in the blanks with one of the words from the list below. Answers may vary.**

early	important	necessary	crowded
hard	good	hot	easy

EXAMPLE It's _____ **easy** _____ to shop in a supermarket.

1. It's _____. It's only 8 A.M. The supermarket isn't
   _____ at this hour.

2. It's _____ in the laundromat. Open the door.

3. It isn't _____ to wash clothes in a washing machine.

4. It's _____ to wash my clothes every week.

5. It's _____ to take coins to the laundromat.

6. It's _____ to learn about the supermarket and the
   laundromat.

EXERCISE **5** **ABOUT YOU** **Fill in the blanks to make true statements.**

EXAMPLE It's good _to have friends._ _____

1. It's important _____

2. It's necessary _____

3. It's good _____

4. It isn't easy _____

1.9 Singular and Plural—Spelling Rules

SINGULAR	PLURAL	RULE
coin dime dollar	coin**s** dime**s** dollar**s**	Add **-s** to form the plural of most nouns.
dish watch box dress	dish**es** watch**es** box**es** dress**es**	Add **-es** to make the plural of nouns that end in *sh, ch, x,* and *ss.*
family baby	famil**ies** bab**ies**	Change final *y* to *i* and add **-es** when a word ends in a consonant + *y*.
day toy	day**s** toy**s**	Add only **-s** when a word ends in a vowel + *y*.
shelf life	shel**ves** li**ves**	Take away final *f* or *fe*. Add **–ves**.

Pronunciation Note: Sometimes we need to pronounce an extra syllable. Listen to your teacher pronounce these words.

    price—prices   noise—noises   page—pages

EXERCISE 6 **Fill in the blanks with the plural form of the noun in parentheses ( ).**

EXAMPLES   The _____**cars**_____ are in the parking lot.

                    (car)

1. The _____ are under the _____.

       (price)   (shelf)

2. The _____ are in a blue box.

       (match)

3. It's Saturday and many _____ are at the

                        (family)

    supermarket.

4. The soap for washing _____ costs $1.89.

                     (dish)

5. The _____ are on sale this week.

       (banana)

6. Some _____ are in the supermarket today.

       (baby)

Editing Advice

1. Use the correct form of *be*.

       are
   You ~~is~~ at the laundromat.

2. Every sentence has a subject.

       It's
   ~~Is~~ 10:15 A.M.

       It's
   ~~Is~~ important to know English.

               He is
   This is Simon. ~~Is~~ from Mexico.

3. Don't confuse *this* and *these*.

       These
   ~~This~~ are big machines.

4. In a contraction, put the apostrophe in place of the missing letter.

       You're
   ~~Your'e~~ late.

                  isn't
   The supermarket ~~is'nt~~ crowded.

5. Use an apostrophe, not a comma, in a contraction.

       I'm
   ~~I,m~~ at the supermarket.

6. Don't make adjectives plural.

             big
   These are ~~bigs~~ machines.

7. Don't use *a* before a plural noun.

   This is a small machine. Those are ~~a~~ big machines.

8. Don't confuse *your* and *you're*.

       You're
   ~~Your~~ at the supermarket.

9. Don't confuse *he* and *she*.

             She's
   Dorota is from Poland. ~~He's~~ from Warsaw.

Editing Quiz

Some of the shaded words and phrases have mistakes. Find the mistakes and correct them. If the shaded words are correct, write C.

Dorota and Shafia are in the laundromat.

Dorota: We're here to wash clothes.
~~We,re~~
(example)

Shafia: C
It's easy to wash clothes in a laundromat.
(example)

Dorota: Yes, it is. But is hot in here.
(1)

Shafia: Your right.
(2)

Dorota: The door is'nt open.
(3)

Shafia: This are my blankets.
(4)

Dorota: Theyr'e big. Those machines is for bigs items, and this machines
(5) *(6)* *(7)* *(8)*

are for small items. These are a quarters for the machines.
(9) *(10)*

Shafia: Thanks. Your'e helpful.
(11)

Dorota: I,m here to help. Simon's helpful too. But is at the bank today.
(12) *(13)*

She's with Victor.
(14)

Expansion

Learner's Log

Write three sentences about each of the following topics. Use affirmative and negative sentences with *be*.

- An American laundromat
- An American supermarket
- Items in an American supermarket

Activity

Rewrite the following paragraph. Change the singular nouns and pronouns to plurals. Change other necessary words, too.

This is a green apple. It's on sale. It's very big. It's only 75¢ a pound. That's a red apple. It isn't on sale. It's not very big. It's $1.39 a pound. This is a free sample of the green apple. It's not very fresh. That's a free sample of the red apple. It's fresh. This red apple is good. That green apple isn't good today.

Granny Smith Apples
75¢/lb.

Red Delicious Apples
$1.39/lb.

EXAMPLE

These are green apples. . . .

For more practice using grammar in context, please visit our Web site.

Time and Money

Grammar

Possessive Nouns

Possessive Adjectives

Context

Time

My Clock Is Fast

Before You Read

Circle *yes* or *no*.

1. I wear a watch every day.   YES   NO
2. I have a clock in every room of my house.   YES   NO

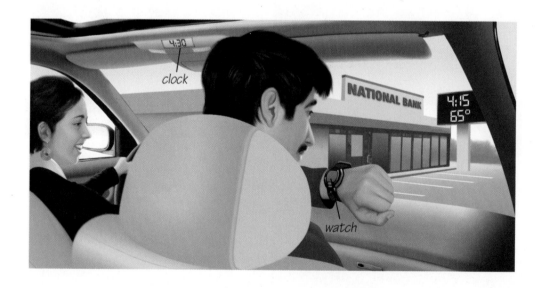

Read the following conversation. Pay special attention to possessive forms.

CD 1, TR 10

*Victor and Dorota are in **Dorota's** car.*

Victor: Hi, Dorota. I'm surprised to see you. It's **Simon's** turn to help me.

Dorota: Yes, it is. But he's with **his** kids today. **His** wife, Marta, is at the hospital. **Her** father is sick. So I'm here to help you with the bank.

Victor: It's late. Look at **your** clock. It's 4:30. The bank is closed.

Dorota: No, it isn't. **My** clock is fast. It's only 4:15.

Victor: So **your** clock is broken.

Dorota: No, it isn't. **My** clock is always fast. And **my** watch is always fast. That way I'm always on time.

Victor: I'm confused. **Your** clock is fast, and that's OK with you?

Dorota: Yes. I'm never late. Time is important for Americans. **Their** ideas about time are different from **our** ideas about time.

(five minutes later)

Dorota: We're here now. Oh, no. The bank is closed. Today is a holiday. It's Columbus Day.

Vocabulary in Context

surprised	Simon isn't here today. Victor is **surprised** to see Dorota.
turn	It's Simon's **turn** to help.
kid, son, daughter	Simon and Marta have **kids.** They have a **son** and two **daughters.**
wife	Simon has a **wife.** Her name is Marta.
clock	Look at the **clock.** It's 4:30.
fast	Your clock is **fast.** It's only 4:15.
watch	My **watch** is fast. It isn't 4:30. It's 4:15.
broken	My clock isn't **broken.** It's fast.
on time	You're **on time.** You're not late.
holiday	It's a **holiday** today. The schools and banks are closed.

Listen to the sentences about the conversation. Circle *true* or *false*.

EXAMPLE   The bank is closed today.   (TRUE)   FALSE

   1. TRUE   FALSE   4. TRUE   FALSE
   2. TRUE   FALSE   5. TRUE   FALSE
   3. TRUE   FALSE   6. TRUE   FALSE

2.1 Possessive Nouns

EXAMPLES	EXPLANATION
Simon's wife is at the hospital. **Marta's** father is sick.	Use noun + **'s** to show relationship.
Dorota's clock is fast.	Use noun + **'s** to show ownership.

EXERCISE 1   Fill in the blanks with *Marta's, Simon's,* or *Dorota's*.

EXAMPLE   __Dorota's__ clock is fast.

   1. _____ wife is Marta.
   2. _____ father is sick.
   3. Today it's _____ turn to help, but he's with the kids.
   4. _____ language is Polish.
   5. _____ language is Spanish. He's from Mexico.

EXERCISE 2   Fill in the blanks. Put the words in the correct order. Add an apostrophe (') + s.

EXAMPLE   (kids/Simon) _____Simon's kids_____ aren't in school today.

   1. (Victor/daughter) _____ isn't with him.
   2. (children/Simon) _____ are at home.
   3. (father/Marta) _____ is sick.
   4. This is (Dorota/car) _____.

2.2 Possessive Adjectives

Compare subject pronouns and possessive adjectives.

EXAMPLES	SUBJECT PRONOUN	POSSESSIVE ADJECTIVE
I am late. **My** watch is slow.	I	my
You are late. **Your** watch is slow.	you	your
He is late. **His** watch is slow.	he	his
She is late. **Her** watch is slow.	she	her
We are late. **Our** clock is slow.	we	our
They are late. **Their** clock is slow.	they	their

EXERCISE **3** **Fill in the blanks with *my, your, his, her, our,* or *their*.**

EXAMPLE   You are with ___your___ kids.

1. She is with _____ kids.
2. They are with _____ kids.
3. I am with _____ kids.

4. He is with _____ kids.
5. We are with _____ kids.

EXERCISE **4** **ABOUT YOU Circle *true* or *false*.**

1. My watch is fast.   TRUE   FALSE
2. Time is important to me.   TRUE   FALSE
3. Money is important to me.   TRUE   FALSE
4. I am with my classmates. Their language is different from my language.   TRUE   FALSE
5. My teacher's name is hard for me to say.   TRUE   FALSE

EXERCISE **5** **Simon and Dorota are on the telephone. Fill in the blanks with *my, your, his, her, our,* or *their*.**

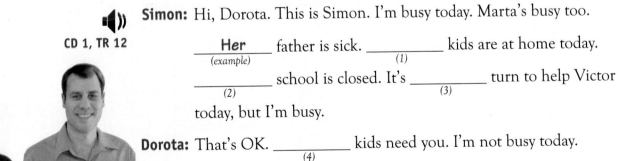

CD 1, TR 12

Simon: Hi, Dorota. This is Simon. I'm busy today. Marta's busy too.

___Her___ father is sick. _____ kids are at home today.
(example)   (1)

_____ school is closed. It's _____ turn to help Victor
(2)   (3)

today, but I'm busy.

Dorota: That's OK. _____ kids need you. I'm not busy today.
(4)

Grammar

Be—Yes/No **Questions**

Irregular Plural Forms

Context

Being on Time

Time Is Money

Before
You Read

Circle *yes* or *no*.

1. I'm usually on time.   YES   NO

2. My doctor is usually on time.   YES   NO

🔊 **Read the following conversation. Pay special attention to *yes/no* questions.**

CD 1, TR 13

Simon comes to the bank to help Victor.

Simon: **Am I late?** I'm sorry. Traffic is bad today.

Victor: You're not late. It's only 10:15.

Simon: Oh, I'm 15 minutes late, then. I'm sorry.

Victor: Fifteen minutes is nothing.

Simon: In the U.S., people are usually on time.

Victor: Really? **Are you serious?**

Simon: Yes, I am.

Victor: I'm surprised. **Are people on time for everything?**

Simon: For most things. They're on time for appointments.

Victor: **Is this an appointment?**

Simon: Yes, it is. I'm here to help you with the bank.

Victor: I'm confused. My doctor is never on time. She's always late.

Simon: That's different. Doctors are always late.

Victor: **Is it necessary to be on time with friends?**

Simon: It's not necessary, but it's polite.

Victor: Look. The time and temperature are on a clock outside the bank. **Is time always on your mind?**

Simon: Yes, it is. "Time is money." Time is always on our minds.

Did You **Know?**

Americans use Fahrenheit (F) for temperature. Other countries use Celsius (C).

Vocabulary in Context

traffic	I'm late. **Traffic** is bad today.
usually	Students are **usually** on time for class.
serious	Are you **serious?** Is it true?
appointment	Victor has a 10 A.M. **appointment** with Simon.
never	Some people are **never** on time.
polite	It's **polite** to say "please" and "thank you."
outside/inside	Victor is **outside** the bank. He isn't **inside** the bank.
on (my, your, etc.) mind	Time is always **on my mind.** I think about it a lot.
always	Some people are **always** late.
temperature	The **temperature** is 69 degrees today.

FAHRENHEIT	CELSIUS
0	– 18
10	–12
20	–7
30	–1
40	4
50	10
60	16
70	21
80	27
90	32
100	38
212	100

Listening Activity

CD 1, TR 14

Listen to the questions about the conversation. Circle the correct answer.

EXAMPLE Is traffic bad today? (Yes, it is.)   No, it isn't.

1. Yes, he is.   No, he isn't.
2. Yes, they are.   No, they aren't.
3. Yes, they are.   No, they aren't.
4. Yes, it is.   No, it isn't.
5. Yes, they are.   No, they aren't.

2.3 Be—Yes/No Questions

Put the form of *be* before the subject to ask a question.

BE	SUBJECT	COMPLEMENT	SHORT ANSWER
Am	I	late?	No, you aren't.
Is	traffic	bad?	Yes, it is.
Is	Simon	on time?	No, he isn't.
Are	you	serious?	Yes, I am.
Are	they	at the bank?	Yes, they are.

Language Note:
You can use a contraction for a negative answer. Don't use a contraction for an affirmative answer.

Am I late?	Am I on time?
No, you aren't. OR No, you're not.	Yes, you are. (NOT: Yes, you're.)

Compare statements and questions with *be*.

STATEMENTS	QUESTIONS
I am late.	**Am I** very late?
Time is important.	**Is time** always on your mind?
People are on time.	**Are people** always on time?
It is necessary to be on time.	**Is it** necessary to be on time with friends?

Pronunciation Note: A *yes/no* question has rising intonation. Listen to your teacher pronounce the statements and the questions above.
Punctuation Note: Put a question mark (?) at the end of a question.

EXERCISE 1 Fill in the correct form of *be* and the noun or pronoun in parentheses ( ) to make a question.

EXAMPLES (Simon and Victor) <u>Are Simon and Victor</u> at the supermarket?
No, they aren't.

(they) <u>Are they</u> at the bank? Yes, they are.

1. (the bank) _____ open? Yes, it is.

2. (I) _____ late? No, you're not.

3. (it) _____ necessary to be on time? No, it isn't.

4. (Simon and Victor) _____ inside the bank?
   No, they aren't.

5. (we) _____ on time? Yes, we are.

6. (Simon) _____ polite? Yes, he is.

EXERCISE 2   Answer with a short answer, based on the conversation on page 31.

EXAMPLE   Is the bank open? _____Yes, it is._____

1. Is Simon on time? _____
2. Are Simon and Victor at the bank? _____
3. Is Simon with Dorota? _____
4. Are doctors usually on time? _____
5. Is it necessary to be on time with friends? _____
6. Are Americans usually late for appointments? _____

EXERCISE 3   **ABOUT YOU**   Answer with a short answer. You may work with a partner.

EXAMPLE   Are you usually on time?
Yes, I am.

1. Are you surprised about some things in this country?
2. Is your apartment big?
3. Are you a serious student?
4. Are you an immigrant?
5. Are you an American citizen?
6. Is this class easy for you?
7. Is English hard for you?
8. Are your classmates from your native country?
9. Is this your first English class?
10. Is your dictionary new?

EXERCISE 4   Fill in the blanks.

Conversation A:

🔊
CD 1, TR 15

Victor: _____Am I_____ on time?
            (example)

Dorota: Yes, you _____.
                              (1)

Victor: _____ at the bank?
              (2)

Dorota: Yes, we _____. We're here to learn about the bank.
                            (3)

Victor: _____ open?
              (4)

Dorota: No, it _____. It's only 8:48. We're a few minutes
                          (5)
early.

---

34   Unit 2

Conversation B:

Simon: Hello?

Marta: Hi, Simon.

Simon: _____ in the car?
_____(1)_____

Marta: No, I _____. I'm at the supermarket now.
_____(2)_____

Simon: It's 9 P.M. _____ open now?
_____(3)_____

Marta: Yes, it _____. This store is open 24 hours a day.
_____(4)_____

Simon: _____ with Halina?
_____(5)_____

Marta: No, I'm not. I'm alone.

Simon: We need bananas. _____ on sale?
_____(6)_____

Marta: Yes, they _____. They're only 29¢ a pound this
_____(7)_____
week.

Simon: Buy bread too. _____ also on sale?
_____(8)_____

Marta: No, it _____.
_____(9)_____

2.4 Irregular Plural Forms

SINGULAR	PLURAL	EXPLANATION
child person	children people	Sometimes the plural form is a different word.
man woman	men women	Sometimes the plural form has a vowel change.
Pronunciation Note: You hear the difference between *woman* and *women* in the first syllable. Listen to your teacher pronounce the singular and plural forms.		

EXERCISE 5   Fill in the blanks with the singular or plural form of the noun in parentheses ( ).

EXAMPLE   The _____men_____ are at the bank.
                          (man)

1. One _____ is behind me. Two _____ are in front of me.
             (person)   (person)

2. One _____ is with two _____.
             (woman)   (child)

3. One _____ is small.
             (child)

4 One _____ is behind me.
           (man)

5. Five _____ are in line.
             (woman)

6. Three _____ are near the door.
              (man)

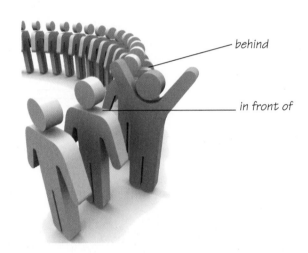

behind

in front of

EXERCISE 6   Fill in the blanks with *is* or *are*.

EXAMPLE   The people at the bank _____are_____ helpful.

1. This child _____ with her mother.

2. Those children _____ with their father.

3. The woman _____ busy.

4. One person _____ alone.

5. The people in the bank _____ busy.

6. That man _____ polite.

Grammar
Be—Information Questions

Articles *A* and *An*

Context
Getting Cash

At the ATM

Before
You Read

Circle *yes* or *no*.

1. I have a bank account.   YES   NO

2. I have an ATM card.   YES   NO

security guard

cash

Read the following conversation. Pay special attention to information questions.

Dorota and Victor are at the bank.

Dorota: Hi, Victor. **How are you?**

Victor: Fine, thanks. **Where are we?**

Dorota: We're at the First Community Bank.

Victor: **What time is it?**

Dorota: It's 7:30 P.M. The bank is closed now.

Victor: **Who's that woman inside?**

Dorota: She's a security guard.

Victor: **When is the bank open?**

Dorota: This bank is open from 9 to 4, Monday through Thursday. It's open from 9 to 7 on Friday and 9 to 1 on Saturday.

Victor: **Why are we here, then?**

Dorota: I need cash. I'm out of cash for the supermarket. The ATM is always open.

Victor: **What's an ATM?**

Dorota: An ATM is an Automatic Teller Machine. It's a machine for cash.

Victor: **What's that?**

Dorota: This is my bank card. It's the key to open the door and use the ATM.

Victor: Is it easy to get cash?

Dorota: Yes, it is. But a PIN is necessary. And cash in your account, of course!

Victor: **What's a PIN?**

Dorota: It's a Personal Identification Number.

Victor: **What's your PIN?**

Dorota: That's a secret!

Did You Know?

You can do your banking online. You can see your monthly statement or pay bills.

Vocabulary in Context

through	The bank is open Monday **through** Saturday.
ATM	The **ATM** is always open.
out of	I'm **out of** money.
security guard	The **security guard** is in the bank.
cash	We are at the bank. It's easy to get **cash** at an ATM.
PIN	A **PIN** is a Personal Identification Number.
account	I have a bank **account.**
of course	**A:** Is the ATM always open?
	B: Yes, **of course.**
secret	No one knows my PIN. It's a **secret.**

Listening Activity

CD 1, TR 17

Listen to the following questions about the conversation. Circle the correct answer.

EXAMPLE   Where are Victor and Dorota?

(At the bank.)   At the supermarket.

1. Yes, it's late.   It's 7:30.
2. 24 hours a day   Monday through Saturday
3. from 9 to 4   24 hours a day
4. It's a machine for cash.   It's at the bank.
5. at 10:15   to get cash
6. 924   It's a secret.

2.5 *Be*—Information Questions

Information questions begin with *where, when, why, who, what, whose,* and *how.* Observe the word order in an information question.

QUESTION WORD(S)	*BE*	SUBJECT + . . . ?	ANSWER
Where	are	we?	We're at the ATM.
What	is	that?	It's a machine.
What time	is	it?	It's 10:15.
Why	are	we here?	We're here to get cash.
When	is	the bank open?	It's open Monday through Saturday.
Who	is	that woman?	She's a security guard.
Whose money	is	this?	It's Dorota's money.
How	are	you?	I'm fine, thanks.
How old	is	Simon's son?	He's 15. OR He's 15 years old.

Language Note: You can make a short form (contraction) with most information words and *is.*
  What's an ATM? **When's** the bank open? **Why's** he here?

Compare statements and information questions.

STATEMENTS	QUESTIONS
The bank is open.	When **is the bank** open?
We are at the ATM.	Why **are we** at the ATM?
You are a student.	How old **are you?**
I am at a bank.	Where **am I?**
She is inside the bank.	Why **is she** inside the bank?
Dorota is from Poland.	Who **is Dorota?**
That is Dorota's money.	Whose money **is that?**
It is late.	What time **is it?**

Pronunciation Note: Information questions have a falling intonation. Listen to your teacher pronounce the statements on the left and the questions on the right.

EXERCISE 1 Fill in the blanks with a question word in this conversation between Dorota and Victor.

CD 1, TR 18

Dorota: _____How_____ are you?
(example)

Victor: I'm fine. _____ are we?
(1)

Dorota: We're at the bank.

Victor: _____ 's that?
(2)

Dorota: It's an ATM.

Victor: _____ are we here?
(3)

Dorota: To learn about the bank.

Victor: _____'s that woman?
(4)

Dorota: She's the security guard.

Victor: _____ is the bank open?
(5)

Dorota: Monday through Thursday, from 9 A.M. to 4 P.M., Friday from 9 A.M. to 7 P.M., and Saturday from 9 A.M. to 1 P.M.

Victor: _____ is it?
(6)

Dorota: It's 8:45. We're early.

EXERCISE 2 Complete the question.

EXAMPLE It's late. What time _____ **is it** _____?

1. We're late. Why _____?
2. The ATM is near here. Where _____?
3. That woman is in the bank. Who _____?
4. That money is Dorota's. Whose _____ this?
5. Simon's 42 years old. How _____ Marta?

EXERCISE 3 **ABOUT YOU** Answer the questions. Write a sentence.

EXAMPLE What time is it now? _____ **it's 4:30 now.**

1. Where are you from? _____
2. Who's your English teacher? _____
3. Where's your English teacher from? _____
4. Where's your school? _____
5. When's the school open? _____

2.6 Articles *A* and *An*

Use *a* or *an* before a singular noun.

EXAMPLES	EXPLANATION
What's this? It's **a** bank. Who's that woman? She's **a** security guard.	Use **a** before a consonant sound.
What's that? It's **an** ATM. What's this? It's **an** envelope.	Use **an** before a vowel sound. The vowels are *a, e, i, o,* and *u*.
Quarters and dimes are coins. What are those? They're pennies.	Do not use **a** or **an** before a plural noun. *Wrong:* Quarters and dimes are *a* coins. *Wrong:* Those are *a* pennies.
adjective **adjective + noun** ↓ ↓ ↙ The bank is big. It's **a** big bank.	Use **a** or **an** only if a noun follows the adjective. *Wrong:* The bank is *a* big.

EXERCISE **4** **Fill in the blanks with *a* or *an*.**

EXAMPLES This is _____*a*_____ bank.

That's _____*an*_____ envelope.

1. I'm _____ immigrant.

2. I'm _____ new immigrant.

3. This is _____ PIN.

4. This is _____ easy PIN.

5. A quarter is _____ coin.

6. Simon isn't _____ old man.

7. Dorota's from Poland. Poland is _____ Eastern European country.

8. She's _____ busy person.

EXERCISE **5** **Fill in the blanks with the correct form of *be* and *a* or *an* where necessary.**

Victor: What's that?

CD 1, TR 19 **Dorota:** It 's an_____ ATM.

         (example)

Victor: What's an ATM?

Dorota: It _____ machine for cash.

     (1)

Victor: What are these?

Dorota: These _____ envelopes
(2)
for checks.

Victor: What _____ check?
(3)

Dorota: Look. This _____ check. It _____ paycheck.
(4)   (5)

Victor: What _____ those?
(6)

Dorota: Those _____ drive-up ATMs.
(7)

Victor: Americans _____ busy people. They _____ always
(8)   (9)
in their cars.

Dorota: It _____ easy way to use the bank.
(10)

EXERCISE 6 **Add the adjective in parentheses ( ) to the sentence. Change _a_ to _an_ or _an_ to _a_ if needed.**

EXAMPLE First Community is a bank. (old)
First Community is an old bank. _____

1. That's an ATM. (new)

_____

2. Columbus Day is a holiday. (American)

_____

3. This is a number. (identification)

_____

4. This is a way to get cash. (easy)

_____

5. That's an envelope. (big)

_____

6. That's a clock. (old)

_____

Editing Advice

1. *People* is a plural word. Use a plural verb.

   are
   The new people ~~is~~ late.

2. Use the correct possessive adjective.

   her
   She is with ~~his~~ father.

   their
   They are with ~~they~~ mother.

3. Don't confuse *you're* and *your*.

   your
   What's ~~you're~~ name?

   You're
   ~~Your~~ never late.

4. Use the correct word order in a question.

   are you
   Why ~~you are~~ late?

   the supermarket big
   Is ~~big the supermarket~~?

5. Use *a* or *an* before a singular noun.

   a   *an*
   This is ‸ bank. It's ‸ old bank.

6. Don't use *a* or *an* with plural nouns.

   Victor and Dorota are ~~an~~ immigrants.

7. Use *a*, not *an*, before a vowel sound.

   an
   She is ~~a~~ immigrant.

8. Use the correct plural form.

   children
   The ~~childs~~ are happy.

9. Use the correct possessive form with nouns.

   's
   Dorota‸ clock is fast.

Editing Quiz

Some of the shaded words and phrases have mistakes. Find the mistakes and correct them. If the shaded words are correct, write *C*.

Victor and Simon are at the bank.

Victor: Where are we? *C*
(example)

Simon: We're at the bank. What time it is? is it
(example)

Victor: It's 9:15. Why we are here?
(1)

Simon: To learn about the ATM.

Victor: What's a ATM?
(2)

Simon: It's machine for cash.
(3)

Victor: Where's Dorota today? Why she isn't here?
(4)   (5)

Simon: His son is home. She's with him.
(6)   (7)

Victor: Is small her son?
(8)

Simon: No, he's not. He's an big boy.
(9)   (10)

Victor: How old is Dorota son?
(11)

Simon: He's 18 years old. He's a college student.
(12)

Victor: Oh, look. The bank's closed today.
(13)

Simon: Don't worry. I have a card to use the ATM.
(14)

Victor: Who is those people in the bank? The bank is closed but those
(15)

mens are inside.
(16)

Simon: They're a security guards.
(17)

Victor: Your right.
(18)

Expansion

Learner's Log

1 Write three sentences about each topic. Your sentences can be affirmative or negative.

- Time in the United States
- ATM machines

2 Write three questions you still have about ATM machines or time in the U.S.

Writing Activities

1 Write five sentences about Marta and her daughter Amy in the picture. Use affirmative and negative sentences. Use possessives where possible.

EXAMPLE

Dr. Shem is with someone now.

2 Write five questions about your sentences above. Use *yes/no* questions and information questions with the verb *be*.

EXAMPLES   Where is Doctor Shem?

Is he with Marta and Amy now?

 For more practice using grammar in context, please visit our Web site.

Filling Out Forms

Grammar
Imperatives—Affirmative

Imperatives—Negative

Context
Applications

Getting a Social Security Card

Before You Read

Circle *yes* or *no*.

1. I have a Social Security card.   YES   NO

2. I write the month before the day.
   (Example: October 27 or 10/27)   YES   NO

SOCIAL SECURITY ADMINISTRATION			
Application for a Social Security Card			Form Approved OMB No. 0960-0066

(Form image: Application for a Social Security Card — Form SS-5 (10-2003) EF (12-2004) Destroy Prior Editions, Page 5)

■)) **Read the following conversation. Pay special attention to imperative forms.**

Dorota:	I have something for you. **Look.**
Halina:	What is it?
Dorota:	It's an application. It's for a Social Security card.
Halina:	I'm not sure what to do.
Dorota:	**Don't worry.** It's easy. **Let** me help.
Halina:	OK. I have a pencil.
Dorota:	No, no. **Don't use** a pencil. **Use** a blue or black pen.
Halina:	OK.
Dorota:	Here's a pen. **Fill out** all the information. **Print** the information, but **sign** your name in Box 16.
Halina:	I'm finished.
Dorota:	What's your date of birth?
Halina:	11/6/70.
Dorota:	Is your birthday in November?
Halina:	No. It's in June.
Dorota:	**Don't write** 11/6. **Write** the month, then the day. That's the American way.
Halina:	OK. 6/11/70.
Dorota:	**Don't write** 70. **Write** 1970.
Halina:	I'm finished. What's next?
Dorota:	**Don't forget** to **sign** your name. **Make** a copy of your birth certificate. Then **go** to the Social Security office. **Take** your birth certificate and another identity document with you.

Did You
Know?

Identity documents include:

- *Driver's license*
- *Marriage certificate*
- *Passport*
- *School ID (identification) card*

Vocabulary in Context

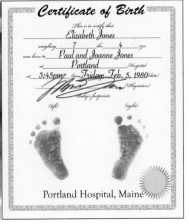

application	This is an **application** for a Social Security card.
let	**Let** me help you.
fill out	**Fill out** the application with a pen.
information	The application has a lot of questions. Write the **information** on the line.
print	**Print** the information like this: Halina Laski
sign	**Sign** your name. *Halina Laski*
birthday/date of birth	My **birthday/date of birth** is June 11, 1980.
forget	Don't **forget** your Social Security number.
birth certificate	A new baby has a **birth certificate.**
identity document	My driver's license is one **identity document.**

Listening Activity

CD 1, TR 21

Listen to these instructions about how to fill out a Social Security card application. Circle *true* or *false*.

EXAMPLE Don't use a pencil.   (TRUE)   FALSE

1. TRUE	FALSE		**4.** TRUE	FALSE	
2. TRUE	FALSE		**5.** TRUE	FALSE	
3. TRUE	FALSE		**6.** TRUE	FALSE	

3.1 Imperatives—Affirmative

Use the base form of the verb for the imperative.

EXAMPLES	EXPLANATION
Use a pen. **Write** your date of birth. **Look** at this.	Use the imperative to give instructions or suggestions. Use the imperative to get someone's attention.
Help me, *please.* *Please* **help** me.	Add *please* to be more polite.

EXERCISE 1 **Fill in the blanks with one of the verbs from the box below.**

Fill	Use	Take	Sign
Go	Write	Make	Help

EXAMPLE ___Make___ a copy of your birth certificate.

1. I'm confused. _____ me, please.

2. _____ out the application today.

3. _____ a pen.

4. _____ the month before the day.

5. _____ to the Social Security office today.

6. _____ your birth certificate with you.

7. _____ your name in Box 16.

3.2 Imperatives—Negative

EXAMPLES	EXPLANATION
Don't worry. **Don't write** 11/6 for June 11. **Don't be** late.	Use *don't* + the base form for the negative. *Don't* is the contraction for *do not*.

EXERCISE 2 **Fill in the blanks with the negative imperative of a verb from the box below.**

put	print	be	forget
worry	use	go	

EXAMPLE It's not hard. _____Don't worry_____. I can help you.

1. Take your papers with you. _____.

2. Stay here. _____ to the Social Security office now.

3. Here's a black pen. _____ a red pen.

4. Be on time. _____ late.

5. Stop. _____ one more word on the application.

6. Sign your name in Box 16. _____ it.

EXERCISE 3 **Fill in the blanks with an affirmative or negative imperative. Use the verbs from the box below. Answers may vary.**

use	put	make
forget	write	take

EXAMPLE _____Don't make_____ the application dirty.

1. _____ a pencil to fill out your application.

2. _____ to sign your application at the end.

3. _____ two forms of ID with you to the Social Security office.

4. _____ all four numbers for the year (*1970*, not *70*).

5. _____ the day first in your date of birth.

Read the following conversation. Pay special attention to *let's* + the base form.

CD 1, TR 23

Halina and Shafia are students at the same school.

Halina: College is expensive in the U.S.

Shafia: Yes, it is.

Halina: **Let's go** to the financial aid office at the college tomorrow. **Let's get** an application.

Shafia: That's not necessary. **Let's go** on the Internet and get an application.

Halina: Are the applications online?

Shafia: Yes. They're available online.

Halina: You're right. Here's the financial aid Web site. The application is here.

Shafia: **Let's fill out** the application online. It's easy. Enter your Social Security number.

Halina: That's an easy question.

Shafia: Don't use dashes.

Halina: OK.

Shafia: Now enter your first and last name. Next, create a password.

Halina: OK. Don't look at my password. What about this question? What's a middle initial?

Shafia: I don't know. **Let's call** Dorota.

Halina: It's after 10 P.M. **Let's not call** now. **Let's not bother** her. **Let's look up** the words in the dictionary.

Shafia: Good idea.

Did You **Know?**

Many Americans have a middle name. For example, Nicole Anne Jackson and Brian Robert Goldberg.

000–00–0000

dashes

Vocabulary in Context

expensive	College is **expensive** in the U.S. It's a lot of money for many students.
available	Dorota isn't **available** now. She's busy.
financial aid	**Financial aid** is money to help pay for college.
online	The application is available **online.** It's on the Internet.
dash	Write your Social Security number. Don't use **dashes.**
enter	**Enter** your name on line 3 of the application.
create a password	**Create a password.** It's a secret number or word.
what about	**What about** this question? What is it?
middle initial	My name is Dorota R. Nowak. My **middle initial** is R.
bother	Let's not **bother** her. She's busy.
look up	**Look up** the word in the dictionary.

Listening Activity

🔊 CD 1, TR 24 **Listen to the sentences about the conversation. Circle *true* or *false.***

EXAMPLE Halina needs a financial aid application. (TRUE) FALSE

1. TRUE FALSE **4.** TRUE FALSE

2. TRUE FALSE **5.** TRUE FALSE

3. TRUE FALSE **6.** TRUE FALSE

3.3 *Let's*—Affirmative and Negative

EXAMPLES	EXPLANATION
Let's go to the office. **Let's get** an application.	Use *let's* + the base form to make a suggestion. *Let's* is the contraction for *let us*.
Let's not call now.	Use *let's not* + the base form to make the negative.

Fill in the blanks with *let's* **or** *let's not* **and one of the verbs from the box below.**

walk	fill it out	go
get	call	drive

EXAMPLE   _____Let's go_____ to the financial aid office today.

1. _____ to the financial aid office. It's not far.

2. _____. It's very cold today. _____ there.

3. It's not necessary to go to the office. _____
   an application online.

4. This application is easy. _____ now.

5. What's a "middle initial"? Where's the telephone?
   _____ Dorota now.

6. It's late. _____ her now. Let's call tomorrow.

3.4 Subject and Object Pronouns

Compare subject pronouns and object pronouns.

EXAMPLES	EXPLANATION
I am confused. Help **me**. **You** are not alone. I am here to help **you**. **He** is at home. Call **him**. **She** is at home. Call **her**. **It** is your date of birth. Write **it**. **We** are busy. Don't bother **us**. **They** are confused. Help **them**.	**Subject Pronoun** **Object Pronoun** I me you you he him she her it it we us they them Put the subject pronoun before the verb. Put the object pronoun after the verb.
I am finished ***with*** it. This application is ***for*** you. This question is ***about*** me.	Use the object pronoun after a preposition. Some prepositions are: *with, for, about, to,* *on, in, of, at,* and *from*.

EXERCISE 2 Fill in the blanks with an object pronoun.

EXAMPLE   I'm confused. Please help ___me___.

1. Dorota is helpful. Let's call _____.
2. I'm busy. Don't bother _____.
3. We are confused. Please help _____.
4. I'm confused too. Don't ask _____.
5. Simon is busy. Don't bother _____.
6. I'm busy. Your father is here. Ask _____ for help.
7. Dorota and Simon are helpful. Let's ask _____.
8. The application is necessary. Let's fill _____ out.
9. This is my password. Don't look at _____.
10. Are you confused? Don't worry. I'm here to help _____.

EXERCISE 3 Fill in the blanks with the object or subject pronoun.

EXAMPLE   We are with them. ___They___ are with ___us___.

1. I am with you. _____ are with _____.
2. She is with him. _____ is with _____.
3. They are with us. _____ are with _____.
4. You are with me. _____ am with _____.
5. She is with them. _____ are with _____.

EXERCISE 4 Fill in the blanks with the object or subject pronoun.

CD 1, TR 25

Shafia: What's that?

Halina: ___It___'s an application for financial aid. College is expensive
            (example)

in the U.S. We're immigrants. It's very expensive for _____.
                                                          (1)

Shafia: It's expensive for Americans too. But it's easy for _____
                                                                    (2)

to fill out the application. It isn't easy for _____. This
                                                  (3)

question is hard. I'm confused about _____.
                                         (4)

Let's call Dorota.

Halina: _____'s late. It's after 10 P.M. Maybe _____'s
(5)   (6)

asleep. Let's call _____ tomorrow.
(7)

Shafia: Or call Simon.

Halina: _____'s busy. His wife's father is sick. She's with
(8)

_____ in the hospital. Simon's with his kids. He's with
(9)

_____ all day.
(10)

Shafia: Let's read the application together. Maybe _____ can do
(11)

_____ together.
(12)

Halina: Let's try.

Editing Advice

1. Use *not* after *let's* to make the negative.

   not
   Let's ~~don't~~ be late.

2. Don't use *to* after *don't*.

   Don't ~~to~~ write on this line.

3. Don't use *to* after *let's*.

   Let's ~~to~~ eat now.

4. Don't forget the apostrophe in *let's*.

   Let's
   ~~Lets~~ go home.

5. Use the subject pronoun before the verb.

   They
   ~~Them~~ are good students.

6. Use the object pronoun after the verb or preposition.

   him   *them*
   Don't bother ~~he.~~   Look at ~~they.~~

Editing Quiz

Some of the shaded words and phrases have mistakes. Find the mistakes and correct them. If the shaded words are correct, write C.

Shafia: Let's ~~to~~ call Dorota for help with the application. *She* is always
(example)   *C*
                                                           (example)

        helpful to us.
              (1)

Halina: Dorota is busy today. Her brother is sick. She's with he. Let's don't
                                                              (2)   *(3)*

        bother her now.

Shafia: Maybe Simon is available. Let's call him.
                                      (4)   *(5)*

Halina: Don't to call him now. Marta's father is sick. Dorota and Simon
              (6)

        are busy today.

Shafia: You're right. Let's not to bother they.
                              (7)   *(8)*

Halina: Lets try to fill out the application together. The application is
          (9)

        online. Let's print her.
                        (10)

Shafia: Make two copies: one for you and one for I.
        (11)   *(12)*   *(13)*

Halina: OK.

Expansion

Learner's

Log   **❶ Write three imperative sentences about each of these topics. Use affirmatives and negatives.**

- How to fill out a Social Security card application
- How to fill out a financial aid application

❷ Write three questions you still have about Social Security cards or financial aid for students.

Writing Activities

❶ Rewrite these instructions. Put the sentences in the correct order.

How to Get a Social Security Card

Make a copy of your birth certificate.
Take or send all your documents to the Social Security office.
Get an application online or from a Social Security office.
Find another identity document.
Don't forget to sign the form.
Fill out all the necessary information.
Print the information.

❷ Rewrite the following paragraph. Change all the underlined nouns to object pronouns.

This is a financial aid application. Read <u>the financial aid application</u> carefully. Write your name and Social Security number on <u>the financial aid application</u>. Dashes are always in a Social Security number. Don't write <u>the dashes</u> on the application. Some questions are hard. Ask about <u>hard questions</u>. Dorota is helpful. Ask <u>Dorota</u> for help. The man at the financial aid office is helpful too. Ask <u>the man</u> for help.

EXAMPLE

> This is a financial aid application.
>
> Read it carefully. . . .

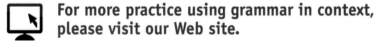 For more practice using grammar in context, please visit our Web site.

American Lifestyles

Grammar

The Simple Present Tense—Affirmative Statements

Spelling of the -s Form

Uses of the Simple Present Tense

Frequency Words

Context

Free-time Activities

Having Fun

Before
You Read

1. What are your free-time activities?

2. What is your favorite summer activity?

Read the following entry in Halina's journal. Pay special attention to verbs in the simple present tense.

CD 1, TR 26

October 15

Americans **work** hard. But they **have** fun too. Americans **do** many different activities in their free time. They often **visit** each other. But a visitor usually **needs** an invitation. Or the visitor **calls** first.

People sometimes **invite** their friends to their homes. Sometimes, they **watch** sports on TV together. One popular game is the Super Bowl. The two best football teams in the U.S. **play** in January or February every year.

Americans **like** the movies. They often **go** to the movies on weekends. Theaters **sell** popcorn, and people **eat** at the movies.

Families often **spend** time at school activities. Americans also **enjoy** museums. Museums **have** interesting activities. A list of activities is usually on a city's Web site.

City parks **have** many fun activities too. In warm weather, many city parks **have** free concerts in the summer. People sometimes **have** picnics. They **cook** on a grill and **eat** outside. They **call** this kind of food "barbecue." It's very popular.

Americans **enjoy** their free time.

Did You Know?

Many theaters have cheaper tickets before 6 P.M. Senior citizens also get cheaper tickets.

Vocabulary in Context

have fun	I **have fun** at the museum. I am happy there.
activity	City parks often have free **activities**, or things to do.
free time	Dorota works in the daytime. She has **free time** at night.
visit (v.) visitor (n.)	Simon's friends often **visit** him. They come to his house. They are **visitors.**
each other	We visit **each other.** I visit you, and you visit me.
invite (v.) invitation (n.)	Americans **invite** their friends to their homes. They ask their friends to visit them. This is an **invitation.**
popular	Many people like football. It's a **popular** sport.
teams	One football **team** has many players.
best	We are a good team, but they are the **best** team.
spend time	Tina **spends** a lot of **time** with her friends.
enjoy	Simon and Victor like football. They **enjoy** the Super Bowl.
outdoor concert	I like **outdoor concerts.** I listen to music in the park.
cook (v.)	This man often **cooks** on a grill in the summer.

grill

Lesson 1 65

Listening
Activity 🔊 **Listen to the sentences about the journal entry. Circle *true* or *false*.**

CD 1, TR 27

EXAMPLE Americans like the movies.   (TRUE)   FALSE

1. TRUE	FALSE	**5.** TRUE	FALSE
2. TRUE	FALSE	**6.** TRUE	FALSE
3. TRUE	FALSE	**7.** TRUE	FALSE
4. TRUE	FALSE		

4.1 The Simple Present Tense—Affirmative Statements

A simple present tense verb has two forms: the base form and the -s form.

SUBJECT	VERB (BASE FORM)	COMPLEMENT
I	**like**	concerts.
You	**have**	a grill.
We	**watch**	football games.
Americans	**enjoy**	movies.
They	**buy**	popcorn at the movies.

SUBJECT	VERB (-*S* FORM)	COMPLEMENT
Simon	**enjoys**	the Super Bowl.
He	**likes**	sports.
Dorota	**has**	a lot of friends.
She	**visits**	them on weekends.
My family	**spends**	a lot of time in the park.
Our team	**plays**	every Saturday.
It	**has**	good players.

Language Notes:
1. *Have* is an irregular verb. The -*s* form is *has*.
2. *Family* and *team* are singular nouns. Use the -*s* form of the verb with these nouns.

EXERCISE 1 Fill in the blanks with the correct form of the simple present tense. Use the verb in parentheses ( ).

EXAMPLE Simon __enjoys__ movies on the weekends.
(enjoy)

1. His kids _____ activities in parks.
(like)

2. Simon's family _____ fun together.
(have)

3. His daughter often _____ her friends to play.
(invite)

4. We _____ a lot of time with our friends.
(spend)

5. Americans _____ before a visit to a friend's house.
(call)

6. I _____ museums with my friends.
(visit)

7. The best teams _____ in the Super Bowl.
(play)

4.2 Spelling of the -s Form

EXAMPLES	EXPLANATION
visit—visit**s** like—like**s** see—see**s**	Add **-s** to most verbs to make the -s form.
kiss—kiss**es** wash—wash**es** watch—watch**es** fix—fix**es**	Add **-es** to base forms with *ss*, *sh*, *ch*, or *x* at the end. Pronounce an extra syllable.
do—do**es** go—go**es**	Add **-es** to *do* and *go*. The pronunciation of *does* is /dʌz/.
worry—worr**ies** try—tr**ies**	If the base form ends in a consonant + *y*, change *y* to *i* and add **-es.**
pay—pay**s** play—play**s**	If the base form ends in a vowel + *y*, do not change the *y*. Just add **-s.**

EXERCISE 2 Fill in the blanks with the -s form of the verb in parentheses ( ).

EXAMPLE The team __plays__ football.
(play)

1. Each football team _____ to be the best.
(try)

2. Simon's son, Ed, _____ football on TV.
(watch)

(continued)

football
player

3. He _____ football games on TV.
   (enjoy)

4. He sometimes _____ to football games.
   (go)

5. A football player sometimes _____ before a big game.
   (worry)

6. Simon _____ the grill after a barbecue.
   (wash)

7. He _____ a lot of time outside in summer.
   (spend)

8. Simon _____ a lot of things with his family.
   (do)

4.3 Uses of the Simple Present Tense

EXAMPLES	EXPLANATION
American movie theaters **sell** popcorn. Americans **like** the movies.	Use the simple present tense for facts.
We **go** to the movies once a month. Every week we **visit** our friends.	Use the simple present for repeated actions.

EXERCISE **3** **Write a sentence with the correct form of the verb in the simple present tense. Use the ideas in the reading. Answers will vary.**

EXAMPLE   Americans / like
           Americans like outdoor concerts.

1. American museums / have

   _____

2. A park / have

   _____

3. Two teams / play

   _____

4. People / invite

   _____

5. A movie theater / sell

   _____

6. Americans / cook

   _____

7. On weekends, American families / enjoy

   _____

4.4 Frequency Words

FREQUENCY	FREQUENCY WORD	EXAMPLES
100%	**always**	Simon **always** washes his grill.
	usually	Americans **usually** call before a visit.
	often	Dorota **often** goes to the movies with friends.
	sometimes	Women **sometimes** watch football games.
	rarely	Americans **rarely** visit friends without an invitation.
	hardly ever	Some Americans **hardly ever** have free time.
0%	**never**	I **never** cook outside in January.

Language Notes:
1. Frequency words go before the verb. *Usually* and *sometimes* can also go at the beginning of the sentence.

   Sometimes we go to the movies.

   Usually Dorota has free time on Sundays.
2. Frequency words follow the verb *be*.

   Simon *is* **always** on time.

   He *is* **never** late.

EXERCISE **4** **ABOUT YOU** Write a sentence with the words given. Add a frequency word from the chart above.

EXAMPLE go to the movies

I hardly *ever go to the movies.*

1. cook dinner at home

_____

2. watch TV in the evening

_____

3. invite my friends to my home

_____

4. visit my friends without an invitation

_____

5. spend time at museums

_____

6. work on Saturdays

_____

EXERCISE 5 **Complete the sentences in Dorota's talk about American customs. Put the words in the correct order.**

_____Americans often invite_____ each other to dinner at their homes.
(example: Americans/invite/often)

_____ a guest for a specific
(1 an American/invite/usually)

day and time. "Let's have dinner sometime" is not an invitation.

_____ on time. It isn't polite
(2 a dinner guest/come/always)

to be more than 15 minutes late. _____
(3 guests/bring/usually)

something for the host or hostess. _____ flowers.
(4 they/bring/sometimes)

At dinner, _____ something nice
(5 guests/say/often)

about the food. _____ for more
(6 guests/ask/sometimes)

food. This is not polite in some countries. But it's OK in the U.S.

EXERCISE 6 Fill in the blanks in Simon's phone conversation with Victor. Use the verbs in the box below.

pays	have	sells	likes
plays	has	need	enjoy

🔊
CD 1, TR 28

Simon: Are you and Lisa busy tonight?

Victor: No, why?

Simon: The city ___**has**___ concerts in the park on Thursdays.
(example)
Let's all go tonight.

Victor: Sure. That's a great idea.

Simon: Bring Maya. Kids _____ outdoor concerts.
(1)

Victor: Are the concerts expensive?

Simon: No. The city _____ for them. They're free for all of us.
(2)

Victor: Where are the concerts?

Simon: At Logan Park on Central Street. A different band
_____ there every Thursday evening from 7 to 9 P.M. The
(3)
kids _____ fun with their friends. A little store in the
(4)
park _____ popcorn and ice cream. My daughter
(5)
Amy _____ ice cream in the summer. Marta and I
(6)
_____ the different kinds of music.
(7)

Victor: We _____ chairs, right?
(8)

Simon: Yes, but I _____ some chairs for outside.
(9)
Don't worry about that. Be at our house about 6:30.

Victor: Thanks, Simon.

See you tonight!

—band

Grammar

The Simple Present Tense— Negative Statements

Time Expressions with the Simple Present Tense

Infinitives with Simple Present Tense Verbs

Context
Work

Working in the U.S.

Before
You Read

1. What's a good job?
2. What's a hard job?

🔊 **Read the following entry in Halina's journal. Pay special attention to the negative forms of the simple present tense.**

October 23

Work is very important to Americans. They often ask each other about their jobs. But they **don't ask** each other about salary or wages.

Americans usually work five days a week. Most people get paid every two weeks. Most office workers and teachers **don't work** on Saturdays and Sundays. But many people have other days off. Workers in stores and restaurants hardly ever have days off on weekends. Stores and restaurants are very busy on weekends.

Full-time work is usually eight hours a day, or 40 hours a week. But many Americans work more. Some people complain. They **don't like** to work so many hours. But others want to make more money. People with wages get extra money for each hour of overtime work.

Sometimes a day off **doesn't mean** free time. Many people **don't relax** on their days off. Some people get part-time jobs on these days. High-school and college students often have part-time jobs.

Today, the average American worker **doesn't expect to keep** the same job for a long time. Young people change jobs often. Older people **don't like** to change jobs often.

Did You Know?

In 2009, the federal minimum wage was $7.25 an hour.

Vocabulary in Context

make money	He **makes** $55,000 a year.
wage/salary	My **wages** are $8 an hour. His **salary** is $40,000 a year.
get paid	I **get paid** on Friday. I take my money to the bank.
day off	Tuesday is my **day off.** I don't work on Tuesdays.
full-time	Simon has a **full-time** job. He works 40 hours a week.
part-time	Tina has a **part-time** job. She works after school.
complain	She doesn't like her job. She **complains** about it a lot.
overtime/extra	I like to work **overtime.** For **extra** work, I get **extra** pay.
relax	We **relax** on Sundays. We don't work. We go to the park.
mean	"Weekend" **means** Saturday and Sunday.
average	The **average** American worker changes jobs often.
expect	He **expects** to keep his job for five years.
job/work	I like my **job.** The **work** is interesting.
keep	I have a good job. I want to **keep** my job for a long time.

Listening
Activity 🔊 **Listen to the sentences about the journal entry. Circle *true* or *false*.**

CD 1, TR 30

EXAMPLE Work is important to Americans.   (TRUE)   FALSE

1. TRUE   FALSE   5. TRUE   FALSE
2. TRUE   FALSE   6. TRUE   FALSE
3. TRUE   FALSE   7. TRUE   FALSE
4. TRUE   FALSE

4.5 The Simple Present Tense—Negative Statements

SUBJECT	*DON'T*	VERB (BASE FORM)	COMPLEMENT
I	**don't**	**work**	on Saturdays.
You	**don't**	**live**	near your work.
We	**don't**	**enjoy**	overtime work.
Some workers	**don't**	**make**	much money.
They	**don't**	**have**	good jobs.

SUBJECT	*DOESN'T*	VERB (BASE FORM)	COMPLEMENT
Tina	**doesn't**	**have**	a full-time job.
She	**doesn't**	**like**	her job.
Simon	**doesn't**	**relax**	on Fridays.
He	**doesn't**	**have**	Fridays off.

Language Notes:
1. Use *don't* and *doesn't* + the base form for the negative. *Don't* is the contraction for *do not*. *Doesn't* is the contraction for *does not*.
2. Compare affirmative and negative statements.
   Tina **has** a part-time job. She **doesn't have** a full-time job.
   She **works** on Saturday. She **doesn't work** on Friday.
   Simon and Victor **get** a wage. They **don't get** a salary.
3. The frequency words *hardly ever, never,* and *rarely* are not used with negative verbs.
   We ***hardly ever* have** any days off.
   I ***never* work** on weekends.

EXERCISE 1 Fill in the blanks with the negative form of the verb in parentheses ( ).

EXAMPLE Tina _____doesn't have_____ a full-time job.
(have)

1. Young people _____ one job for a long time.
(keep)

2. Dorota _____ about her job.
(complain)

3. Some workers _____ a lot of money.
(make)

4. You and I _____ the same days off.
(have)

5. Simon _____ about his salary.
(talk)

6. A day off _____ free time for Simon. He's always busy.
(mean)

EXERCISE 2 Write a negative sentence with the words given.

EXAMPLES Simon works on Saturday. (on Wednesday)
Simon doesn't work on Wednesday.

Simon works on Saturday. (Many Americans)
Many Americans don't work on Saturday.

1. Simon gets paid every two weeks. (every week)

_____

2. *Salary* means money for a year of work. (money for an hour of work)

_____

3. Some people complain about long work hours. (Dorota and Simon)

_____

4. I get Mondays and Tuesdays off. (weekends off)

_____

5. Halina works part-time. (40 hours a week)

_____

6. Many Americans work overtime. (You and I)

_____

4.6 Time Expressions with the Simple Present Tense

SUBJECT	VERB (+ COMPLEMENT)	TIME EXPRESSION
My sister She	works doesn't work	eight hours a day. five days a week. every day. on the weekends.
My friend and I We	have a day off don't have a day off	twice a week. once a month. on Tuesdays.
Those workers They	get paid don't get paid	every two weeks. once a week. every Friday.

Language Note: Time expressions with 2 or more words usually go at the end of the sentence. They don't go after the subject.

EXERCISE 3 **ABOUT YOU** Write a sentence about you or someone you know. Use the simple present tense—affirmative or negative—and an expression of time. Add extra information where possible.

EXAMPLE   take the bus

I take the bus twice a day. OR

My sister doesn't take the bus. She drives to work every day.

1. relax

_____

2. work

_____

3. have a day off

_____

4. drive

_____

5. complain about work

_____

6. get paid

_____

7. work overtime

_____

4.7 Infinitives with Simple Present Tense Verbs

We often use the infinitive (*to* + the base form) after simple present tense verbs. The infinitive form is always the same. We can use infinitives after the following verbs: *want, need, like, expect,* and *try.*

SUBJECT	VERB	INFINITIVE FORM	COMPLEMENT
I	like don't like	**to relax**	on the weekends.
He	wants doesn't want	**to take**	a day off.
She	expects doesn't expect	**to have**	a day off.
We	try don't try	**to do**	good work.
They	need don't need	**to work**	on Saturday.

EXERCISE 4 Fill in the blanks with the simple present tense, affirmative or negative, and the infinitive. Use the words in parentheses ( ).

EXAMPLES   Americans _____*don't like to talk*_____ about their salaries.
(not/like/talk)

I _____*expect to get*_____ extra money for overtime work.
(expect/get)

1. Some people _____ about their jobs.
(like/complain)

2. Simon _____ his job.
(not/want/leave)

3. We _____ a day off this week.
(need/take)

4. Americans _____ every day.
(not/expect/work)

5. Dorota _____ on Sundays.
(not/like/work)

6. Simon always _____ a good job.
(try/do)

7. Halina _____ a new job.
(need/find)

EXERCISE 5 **Write each sentence again. Add the verb in parentheses ( ).**

EXAMPLES Victor takes a day off on Sunday. (want)
Victor wants to take a day off on Sunday.

He doesn't take a day off on Friday (want)
He doesn't want to take a day off on Friday.

1. Many Americans get a second job. (try)

   _____

2. The workers don't work on Sundays. (expect)

   _____

3. I don't complain about my job. (want)

   _____

4. Simon doesn't work overtime. (need)

   _____

EXERCISE 6 **Fill in the blanks with the simple present tense. Use the negative form of the verbs in parentheses ( ).**

Dorota: We have a day off tomorrow. Let's go to the museum.

CD 1, TR 31 **Halina:** I'm sorry. But I ____don't have____ time. I need to look for
                                        (example: have)
a new job.

Dorota: You have a job.

Halina: I know. But I _____ it. I _____
                                (1 like)   *(2 work)*
enough hours. And the job _____ enough money.
                                            (3 pay)
My boss _____ my work. It's not a good job for me.
                        (4 like)

Dorota: There's a job in my company. But it's only part-time.

Halina: Thanks, Dorota, but I _____ to work part-time.
                                            (5 want)
I need a full-time job.

Dorota: The Web is one place to look. But most people

_____ their jobs on Web sites. They hear about
        (6 find)
them from other people. So ask all of your friends.

EXERCISE **7** **ABOUT YOU** Write true sentences about work in your hometown or country. Use the simple present tense of the verbs in parentheses ( ), affirmative or negative. Read your sentences to the class.

EXAMPLE   The average worker in my hometown ___doesn't work___ every day.
                                              (work)

1. A worker _____ two days off every week.
            (get)

2. Most people _____ more than eight hours a day at work.
              (spend)

3. A company _____ extra money for overtime work.
             (pay)

4. People _____ overtime.
          (like/work)

5. Most people _____ about their jobs.
              (complain)

6. Workers _____ low wages.
           (get)

7. Companies _____ wages in cash.
             (pay)

8. The average worker _____ a part-time job on days off.
                      (take)

9. Workers _____ four weeks off each year with pay.
           (expect/get)

10. People _____ on vacation on their weeks off.
            (go)

11. The average worker _____ jobs often.
                       (change)

12. The average worker _____ the same job for a
                       (keep)
    long time.

13. Teachers _____ a lot of money.
             (make)

14. Most women in my hometown _____.
                             (work)

15. Most high school students _____ after school.
                             (work)

Grammar
**The Simple Present Tense—*Yes/No*
Questions**

Context
American Food

Eating Customs

Before
You Read

Circle *yes* or *no*.

1. I like American food.   YES   NO
2. I often eat in restaurants.   YES   NO

🔊 **Read the following conversation. Pay special attention to *yes/no* questions in the simple present tense.**

Halina: It's 1:30. It's early. **Do Americans** usually **have** lunch at this time?

Dorota: One-thirty is late. Lunch hours often begin at 11 A.M. Americans usually have an hour for lunch. **Do you want to order** a sandwich, Halina?

Halina: Yes, I do. I'm hungry. Look. That man has a very big salad.

Dorota: Some people eat a salad for lunch.

Halina: **Does it have** meat?

Dorota: I don't think so. Maybe the man's a vegetarian. Some people don't eat meat.

Halina: **Do Americans** often **eat** in restaurants?

Dorota: Yes, they do. They're very busy. They don't have time to cook every meal. Sometimes they eat in restaurants. Sometimes they order their food from restaurants.

Halina: **Do restaurants deliver** food to your home?

Dorota: Yes, some do. And many restaurants have "takeout" food. They prepare the food for you. You take it home to eat. Supermarkets have prepared food too. It's in the deli section. They have hot and cold food. Some supermarkets have tables, and people eat there. But most people take home prepared food. Prepared food is very popular.

Halina: **Does prepared food cost** more?

Dorota: Yes, it does. But it's very convenient.

Did You **Know?**

About 7.3 million Americans are vegetarians. Almost 60 percent are women.

Vocabulary in Context

order	Halina wants to **order** a sandwich. She asks for a big sandwich.
hungry	She's **hungry.** She wants to eat.
vegetarian	He's a **vegetarian.** He doesn't eat meat.
meal	I eat three **meals** a day: breakfast, lunch, and dinner.
deliver	That restaurant **delivers** pizza. Someone brings it to your house.
takeout	Let's order **takeout.** We take the food home to eat.
prepared food	**Prepared food** is very popular. It's ready to eat.
deli	Let's go to the **deli** section. They have sandwiches there.
convenient	Prepared food is **convenient.** It's fast and easy.

Listening Activity

CD 1, TR 33

Listen to the statements about the conversation. Circle *true* or *false*.

EXAMPLE   Americans often eat lunch in restaurants.   (TRUE)   FALSE

1. TRUE   FALSE   **5.** TRUE   FALSE

2. TRUE   FALSE   **6.** TRUE   FALSE

3. TRUE   FALSE   **7.** TRUE   FALSE

4. TRUE   FALSE

4.8 The Simple Present Tense—*Yes/No* Questions

DO	SUBJECT	VERB (BASE FORM)	COMPLEMENT	SHORT ANSWER
Do	you	**like**	American food?	Yes, I do.
Do	we	**have**	time to cook?	No, we don't.
Do	vegetarians	**eat**	meat?	No, they don't.
Do	they	**enjoy**	salad?	Yes, they do.

DOES	SUBJECT	VERB (BASE FORM)	COMPLEMENT	SHORT ANSWER
Does	Simon	**go**	to a restaurant for lunch?	Yes, he does.
Does	Dorota	**eat**	lunch at 2 P.M.?	No, she doesn't.
Does	this restaurant	**have**	takeout food?	Yes, it does.

EXERCISE **1** **Fill in the blanks with *do* or *does*. Then write a short answer to each question, based on the conversation on page 81.**

EXAMPLE _____Does_____ the man in the restaurant have a salad?

Yes, he does.

1. _____ the man's salad have meat?

   _____

2. _____ Halina want a salad for lunch?

   _____

3. _____ many Americans eat lunch in restaurants?

   _____

4. _____ American workers have two hours for lunch?

   _____

5. _____ some restaurants deliver to your home?

   _____

6. _____ the deli section have hot and cold food?

   _____

7. _____ vegetarians eat meat?

   _____

EXERCISE **2** **Complete the conversation with the correct question from the box.**

Do you work Monday through Friday?	Do you deliver the pizzas?
Does Joe's Pizza have pizza for vegetarians too?	Does the job pay well?
	Do you use your car?

EXAMPLE **Victor:** I have a new part-time job. I work for Joe's Pizza.

Simon: _Do you deliver the pizzas?_____

Victor: Yes, I do. I deliver them all over the city.

1. **Simon:** _____

   Victor: No, I don't. I work on the weekends.

2. **Simon:** _____

   Victor: Yes, I do. I put a sign on my car. It says "Joe's Pizza."

3. **Simon:** _____

   Victor: No, it doesn't. But people often give me extra money for the delivery.

   Simon: We call that money a "tip."

4. **Simon:** _____

   Victor: Yes, It does. Many people order a pizza with no meat.

EXERCISE **3** Complete each short conversation with a *yes/no* question in the simple present tense. Use the words in parentheses ( ).

EXAMPLE A: Many Americans eat lunch outside the home. (eat in restaurants)

B: _Do they eat lunch in restaurants?_ _____

1. A: Victor likes meat. (like salads)

 B: _____

2. A: Halina buys food at a supermarket. (buy prepared food)

 B: _____

3. A: That restaurant has takeout food. (have vegetarian food)

 B: _____

4. A: You go to lunch early. (go at 11:00 A.M.)

 B: _____

5. A: Halina and Dorota want to order some lunch. (want to order sandwiches)

 B: _____

6. A: This restaurant delivers pizza. (deliver sandwiches)

 B: _____

7. A: Americans eat prepared food. (eat it in the supermarket)

 B: _____

EXERCISE **4** **ABOUT YOU** Find a partner. Ask and answer *yes/no* questions with the words given. Your partner adds more information where possible. Then tell the class about your partner's answers.

EXAMPLE you/like to eat in restaurants
Student 1: Do you like to eat in restaurants?
Student 2: Yes, I do. I like to eat in Chinese restaurants.
Student 1: Maria likes to eat in Chinese restaurants.

1. you / like pizza

2. you / like to cook

3. you / eat dinner with your family

4. you / sometimes order takeout food

5. you / eat lunch at home

6. someone / cook for you

7. restaurants in your country / deliver

8. supermarkets in your country / have deli sections

9. most people in your country / eat meat

EXERCISE 5 Shafia and Ali are at Halina and Peter's house for dinner. Fill in the blanks in their conversation to make a *yes/no* question in the simple present tense. Use the words in parentheses ( ).

CD 1, TR 34

Shafia: Halina, this is a delicious[1] meal. _____Do you cook_____
(example: you/cook)

like this every day? _____ time?
(1 you/have)

Halina: Um . . . not really. _____ good?
(2 the food/taste)

Ali: The salad is very good. _____ lemon in it?
(3 it/have)

Halina: Well . . . yes. But . . .

Shafia: I like the carrots. Something is different about them.

_____ orange juice in them?
(4 they/have)

Halina: Yes, I think so.

Ali: _____ Halina?
(5 you/like to cook)

Peter: Tell them about the meal, Halina.

Halina: Well . . . it's all from the supermarket!

Shafia: Of course. But you're the cook. And it's all delicious.

Halina: No, I'm not the cook. It's all prepared food.

Ali: _____ hot food like this?
(6 the supermarket/prepare)

Halina: Yes, it does.

Shafia: _____ prepared food often?
(7 you and Peter/eat)

Halina: No, we don't. But sometimes it's very convenient..

[1]*Delicious* food is very good food.

Lesson 4

Grammar
**The Simple Present Tense—
Information Questions**

**The Simple Present Tense—
Subject Questions**

Context
Staying Healthy

Exercise

Before
You Read

1. Do you exercise every day?

2. What kind of exercise do you do?

Read the following conversation. Pay special attention to information questions in the simple present tense.

Halina: Look at that woman with a business suit and sneakers!

Dorota: That's Louisa. I know her. She walks during her lunch hour. She wears sneakers for exercise. Some Americans use their lunch hours for exercise.

Halina: **Where does she walk** in the winter?

Dorota: Maybe she goes to a gym. The building next door is a gym. Or maybe her office building has a gym.

Halina: **What do you mean?**

Dorota: Some office buildings have gyms for their workers. They're free.

Halina: That's very interesting. I see a lot of people on bicycles too. Look! That girl is so fast. It isn't safe.

Dorota: She's a bike messenger. She works on her bicycle. She takes mail from one office to another here in the city. Bike messengers always ride fast. They get a lot of exercise every day!

Halina: **Why do so many Americans exercise?**

Dorota: Some Americans don't exercise at all. They have desk jobs. They sit all day. But I try to exercise a little every day.

Halina: **What kind of exercise do you do,** Dorota?

Dorota: I walk. It's great exercise for me. I stay healthy this way.

Halina: **Where do you walk?** In a gym?

Dorota: No. A gym costs money. I go to a park near my house.

Halina: **How often do you exercise?**

Dorota: I try to walk five days a week. But I don't always have time.

Did You **Know?**

One 30-minute or two 15-minute walks each day are good for your health.

Vocabulary in Context

exercise (n.) exercise (v.)	Louisa walks for **exercise.** Some Americans don't **exercise** a lot.
wear/sneakers	I walk for exercise. I **wear sneakers.**
during	She often walks **during** her lunch hour.
gym	I go to a **gym.** I exercise there.
next door	We work in an office building. The building **next door** is a gym.
ride a bicycle/ bike	I **ride** my **bike** (**bicycle**) to work.
messenger	A **messenger** takes information from place to place.
at all	My father has no free time. He doesn't exercise **at all.**
desk job	He has a **desk job.** He works at a desk all day.
stay healthy	Dorota exercises a lot. She **stays healthy** that way.
cost	The gym is expensive. It **costs** $100 a month.

Listening Activity

CD 1, TR 36

Listen to the sentences about the conversation. Circle *true* or *false*.

EXAMPLE   All Americans exercise.   TRUE   (FALSE)

1.	TRUE	FALSE	**4.**	TRUE	FALSE
2.	TRUE	FALSE	**5.**	TRUE	FALSE
3.	TRUE	FALSE	**6.**	TRUE	FALSE

4.9 The Simple Present Tense—Information Questions

QUESTION WORD(S)	DO	SUBJECT	VERB (BASE FORM)	ANSWER
How often	**do**	you	**ride** your bike?	Three times a week.
Why	**do**	we	**exercise?**	Because we want to stay healthy.
Where	**do**	they	**work?**	Near the gym.
When	**do**	Simon and Marta	**walk?**	In the morning.
What	**do**	they	**do** for exercise?	They walk.
Who	**do**	you	**see** at the gym?	All my friends.

QUESTION WORD(S)	*DOES*	SUBJECT	VERB (BASE FORM)	ANSWER
What kind of exercise	**does**	Marta	**do?**	She rides a bike.
What	**does**	"bike"	**mean?**	It means bicycle.
How much	**does**	that bike	**cost?**	It costs about $200.
How many days	**does**	Dorota	**exercise?**	Five days a week.

Language Notes:
1. When we ask *how often*, we want a number of times.
2. We use *because* with answers to *why* questions.
3. Compare statements and questions:
   Marta **rides** a bike. How often **does** Marta **ride** a bike?
   You **walk** fast. Why **do** you **walk** fast?

EXERCISE 1 **Fill in the correct question word in each short conversation. Use** *what, who, when, where, how, why, what kind of, how many, how often,* **or** *how much.* **The underlined words are the answers to the questions.**

EXAMPLE **A:** _____How often_____ does she ride her bicycle?

B: She rides her bicycle <u>every day</u>.

1. **A:** _____ does "healthy" mean?

   B: It means <u>not sick</u>.

2. **A:** _____ do they walk every day?

   B: <u>Because it's good exercise</u>.

3. **A:** _____ hours do they walk every day?

   B: They walk <u>for one hour</u> every day.

4. **A:** _____ shoes does Louisa have?

   B: She has <u>sneakers</u>.

5. **A:** _____ do good sneakers cost?

   B: They cost <u>about $100</u>.

6. **A:** _____ do some people get to work?

   B: <u>They ride their bicycles</u>.

7. **A:** _____ does Dorota walk in the park?

   B: She tries to walk <u>five days a week</u>.

8. **A:** _____ does Louisa exercise?

   B: She exercises <u>during her lunch hour</u>.

EXERCISE 2 Write questions with the words given. Write an answer to each question. Use the ideas from the conversation on page 87.

EXAMPLE what / Halina / ask Dorota

<u>What does Halina ask Dorota?</u>

<u>She asks Dorota about exercise in the U.S.</u>

1. what kind of exercise / Dorota / do

_____

_____

2. where / Dorota / exercise

_____

_____

3. when / Louisa / exercise

_____

_____

4. how often / Dorota / exercise

_____

_____

5. why / people / need to exercise

_____

_____

6. what / "bike" / mean

_____

_____

EXERCISE 3 Complete each short conversation with a question. Use the words in parentheses ( ).

EXAMPLE **A:** Dorota walks for exercise. (how often)

B: <u>How often does she walk?</u>

1. A: She wears sneakers to work. (why)

B: _____

2. A: She has a day off each week. (when)

B: _____

3. A: I have some new shoes. (what kind of)

B: _____

4. A: She goes to the gym in the winter. (how often)

B: _____

5. A: Halina sees some bikes in the street. (how many)

B: _____

6. A: Bike messengers ride fast. (why)

B: _____

4.10 The Simple Present Tense—Subject Questions

Do not use *do/does* when the question word is the subject.

QUESTION WORD(S)	VERB (BASE FORM OR -S FORM)	COMPLEMENT	SHORT ANSWER
Who	**wants**	a new bike?	Tina does.
Who	**works**	in that company?	We do.
What kind of people	**exercise**	here?	Office workers do.
Which company	**has**	a gym for workers?	My company does.
How many people	**wear**	sneakers to exercise?	Everybody does.
Whose friend	**exercises**	at lunch time?	Dorota's friend does.
What	**happens**	at the gym?	People exercise.

Language Notes:
1. *Who* questions are singular. Answers can be singular or plural.
2. *How many* questions are plural. Answers can be singular or plural.

EXERCISE **4** Write a question about each statement. Use the question words in parentheses ( ) as subjects.

EXAMPLE Somebody needs a job. (who)

Who needs a job?

1. Somebody wants to exercise. (who)

_____

2. Some jobs pay well. (what kinds of)

_____

3. Some people ride their bicycles to work. (how many)

_____

4. Some people work three days a week. (who)

_____

(continued)

5. Some workers exercise during their lunch hours. (which)

_____

6. Some people in my company exercise before work. (how many)

_____

7. Someone's company has a gym for the workers. (whose)

_____

8. Something happens after lunch. (what)

_____

EXERCISE **5**   **Write an information question to complete each short conversation below. The underlined words are the answers. Some questions may vary.**

EXAMPLE   **A:** <u>What kind of shoes do people wear at the gym?</u>

B: People wear <u>sneakers</u>.

1. A: _____

B: <u>Because they want to stay healthy</u>.

2. A: _____

B: <u>Dorota's</u> friend does.

3. A: _____

B: Some office workers exercise <u>after work in the evening</u>.

4. A: _____

B: A bike messenger <u>takes mail from one office to another</u>.

5. A: _____

B: <u>That bike costs over $500</u>.

6. A: _____

B: Louisa exercises <u>five days a week</u>.

7. A: _____

B: <u>A bike messenger</u> works on a bicycle.

8. A: _____

B: Halina and Dorota see <u>only one</u> bike messenger.

Editing Advice

1. Use the *-s* form in the affirmative with *he*, *she*, *it*, and singular subjects.

               s
      Dorota work in an office.

          has
      She ~~have~~ a good job.

2. Don't use the *-s* form after *does* or *doesn't*.

               have
      She doesn't ~~has~~ a new job.

                 work
      Where does she ~~works~~?

3. Don't use *do* or *does* in questions about the subject.

           wants
      Who ~~does want~~ to go to the gym?

4. Use the correct word order in questions.

      Where does work your friend?

5. Use the correct question word order with *mean* and *cost*.

          does "bicycle messenger" mean
      What ~~means "bicycle messenger"~~?

            does that bike cost
      How much ~~costs that bike~~?

6. Don't separate the subject and verb with time expressions of 2 or more words.

      He three days a week goes to the gym.

7. Use the correct word order with frequency words.

      He goes always to the gym.

      He usually is tired.

Editing Quiz

Some of the shaded words and phrases have mistakes. Find the mistakes and correct them. If the shaded words are correct, write C.

Simon: Look at that fast bike messenger.

Victor: ~~What means "bike messenger"?~~ *What does "bike messenger" mean?*
(example)

Simon: A bike messenger delivers things
                          C
                      (example)

Victor: What does a bike messenger delivers?
                          (1)

Simon: A bicycle messenger deliver packages to offices downtown.
                                  (2)

Victor: Who does work as a bicycle messenger?
              (3)

Simon: Usually young, healthy people do this job. But the job is not
                                          (4)

always safe.

Victor: Not safe? Why? What does happen to them?
                              (5)

Simon: People open sometimes their car doors. They don't always watch for
              (6)

the messengers. And sometimes bike messengers don't stop at red
                                                    (7)

lights. They always ride very fast.

Victor: Does a messenger make a lot of money?
              (8)

Simon: Not a lot. Messengers make about $350 to $500 a week. And
                      (9)

they ride often 30 to 40 miles. More work mean more money.
      (10)   *(11)*

Victor: Do they work in bad weather too?
              (12)

Simon: Yes. And they don't complain. It's part of their job.
                      (13)

Victor: One good thing. They get a lot of exercise. Never they need to go to a gym!
                                                          (14)

Expansion

Learner's Log

❶ What did you learn in this unit? Write four sentences about each of these topics:

- Free-time activities in the U.S.
- Work in the U.S.
- Food in the U.S.
- Exercise in the U.S.

❷ Write four questions you still have about work, free-time activities, food, and exercise in the U.S.

Writing Activity

Rewrite the following paragraph about Nina. Change *I* to *she*. Make necessary changes to the verbs.

I live in Chicago. I like the city. Why do I like it? Because it's wonderful in the summertime. I often go to a big park downtown. It has concerts every Thursday evening. I don't pay for these concerts. They're free. I like to visit Lake Michigan. It has many free beaches. But the water is cold. I don't swim in June or July. I swim only in August. I also visit a beautiful park on the lake. Sometimes I have dinner at a restaurant near the lake. I don't do that often. It's expensive. I often invite friends to visit this city.

EXAMPLE

Nina lives in Chicago. . . .

 For more practice using grammar in context, please visit our Web site.

Driving

Lesson 1

Grammar
Modals—*Can* and *Should*

Have To

Context
Driving in the U.S.

Getting a Driver's License

Before
You Read   **Circle *yes* or *no*.**

1. Can you drive?   YES   NO

2. Do you have a driver's license from this state?   YES   NO

CD 2, TR 01

🔊 **Read the following conversation. Pay special attention to affirmative and negative forms of *can*, *should*, and *have to*.**

Simon's son, Ed, wants to learn to drive. He is 15 years old.

Ed: Dad, I want to get my driver's license.

Simon: You **have to get** a learner's permit first.

Ed: You **can help** me with that.

Simon: I **can help** you with the rules. But in this state, drivers under age 18 **have to take** a driver's education class at school. It's the law.

Ed: A class takes a long time. I **can learn** faster with you.

Simon: No, you **can't**. It takes a long time to learn to drive. You **shouldn't be** in a hurry. First, you **have to pass** two tests: a vision test and a written test. The written test is about the rules of driving in this state. You **have to study** 30 hours in the classroom. It's the law.

Ed: And then I **can get** my license. I **don't have to wait** anymore, right?

Simon: No. You **can get** a learner's permit. Then you **have to practice** in the car. In this state, you **have to practice** at least 50 hours, but you **should practice** much more. And you **have to wait** three months. Then you **can take** the driving test.

Ed: Then I **can get** my license. And I **can drive** with my friends, right?

Simon: Not exactly.

Ed: What do you mean?

Simon: Drivers under the age of 17 in this state **have to drive** with an adult driver at night. You **can have** only one other teenager in the car. And you **can't drive** at all from 11 P.M. to 6 A.M. It's not safe during those hours.

Ed: I don't like that. Are you sure?

Simon: Yes, I am. These rules are for your safety. This law saves a lot of lives every year. You **can go** online and check the rules of the state there.

Vocabulary in Context

learner's permit	A **learner's permit** lets a new driver practice.
law	Stop at a stop sign. This is the **law.**
takes time	It **takes** a long **time** to be a good driver.
in a hurry	Ed wants his license now. He's **in a hurry.**
pass a test	When you **pass** the **tests,** you can get the permit.
vision test	A **vision test** checks a person's eyes.
written test	We use pencil and paper for a **written test.**
rule	Teenagers can't drive between 11 P.M. and 6 A.M. That's the **rule.**
practice (v.) practice (n.)	Ed's new at driving. He has to **practice.** He needs a lot of **practice.**
at least	He has to practice **at least** 50 hours. He can practice 50 hours or more.
under/over	Ed is 15 years old. He's **under** age 16. Ed's sister Tina is 17. She's **over** age 16.
teenager/adult	Ed is a **teenager.** Simon is an **adult.**
safety (n.) save (v.)	The rules are for your **safety.** They **save** many lives each year.

Listening Activity

CD 2, TR 02

Listen to the sentences about the conversation. Circle *true* **or** *false.*

EXAMPLE All states in the U.S. have the same laws about driving.   TRUE   (FALSE)

1. TRUE   FALSE   5. TRUE   FALSE
2. TRUE   FALSE   6. TRUE   FALSE
3. TRUE   FALSE   7. TRUE   FALSE
4. TRUE   FALSE

5.1 Modal: *Can*—Affirmative and Negative

We use *can* to show ability, permission, or possibility.

SUBJECT	CAN	VERB (BASE FORM)	COMPLEMENT
I She Simon It We You They	**can cannot can't**	help	him.

Language Notes:
1. We write *cannot* as one word. The contraction for *cannot* is *can't*.
2. *Can* doesn't have an **-s** ending.
3. We often use *can't* with rules or laws.
   You **can't** park at a bus stop. It's against the law.

Pronunciation Note: In affirmative statements, we usually pronounce *can* /kən/. In negative statements, we pronounce *can't* /kænt/. It is hard to hear the final **t**, so we use the vowel sound and stress to tell the difference between *can* and *can't*. Listen to your teacher pronounce these sentences:

  I *can* go. [accent on *go*]
  I *can't* go. [accent on *can't*]

EXERCISE **1** **Fill in the blanks with *can* or *can't*. Use the ideas from the conversation on page 99.**

EXAMPLE   Ed ___can't___ drive now.

1. Simon _____ help Ed with the rules.
2. Ed _____ get his driver's license now.
3. People _____ find the rules on the state Web site.
4. Ed _____ take the driver's education class now.
5. Simon _____ help Ed practice in the car now.
6. Ed _____ get a learner's permit without a driver's education class.
7. Teenagers under 17 _____ drive alone at night in Ed's state.
8. Teenagers under 17 _____ have more than one other teenager in the car.

5.2 Modal: *Should*—Affirmative and Negative

We use *should* when we give advice or make a suggestion.

SUBJECT	*SHOULD*	VERB (BASE FORM)	COMPLEMENT
I He She We You They	**should** **should not** **shouldn't**	take	the test today.

EXERCISE 2 **Give advice in each conversation. Use *should* or *shouldn't* and the words in parentheses ( ).**

EXAMPLE **A:** I have my written test tomorrow.

B: ___You should read___ the rule book again tonight.
<u>(you/read)</u>

1. **A:** My car is dirty.

   B: _____ it today!
   <u>(you/wash)</u>

2. **A:** Ed wants to learn to drive.

   B: _____ in a hurry.
   <u>(he/be)</u>

3. **A:** Ed wants to be a safe driver.

   B: _____ a lot with a good driver.
   <u>(he/practice)</u>

4. **A:** I'm very tired today and I have driving practice.

   B: _____ today. Wait until tomorrow.
   <u>(you/drive)</u>

5. **A:** Ed doesn't know the driving laws in his state.

   B: _____ them before the written test.
   <u>(he/learn)</u>

6. **A:** Many cars are on the roads from 4 to 7 P.M.

   B: _____ during those hours.
   <u>(new drivers/drive)</u>

7. **A:** I don't have the book of driving rules, and I need to study it tonight.

   B: _____ online. The information is on the state Web site.
   <u>(you/look)</u>

5.3 *Have To*—Affirmative and Negative

Have to shows necessity.

SUBJECT	HAVE TO	VERB (BASE FORM)	COMPLEMENT
She He Ed	has to doesn't have to	pass	the test now.
I You We They	have to don't have to		

Language Notes:
1. In the affirmative, *have to* shows laws or strong necessity.
   Ed **has to** get a learner's permit.
2. In the negative, *have to* means not necessary.
   Simon **doesn't have to** work on Saturday.

Pronunciation Note: In normal speech, we pronounce *have to* /hæftə/. We pronounce *has to* /hæstə/. Listen to your teacher pronounce the following sentences in normal speech.

We *have to* take the test.   She *has to* drive to work.

EXERCISE **3**   **Fill in the blanks with the affirmative or negative form of *have to*. Use the verbs in parentheses ( ) and the ideas from the conversation on page 99.**

EXAMPLE   Ed _____ *has to take* _____ a driver's education class.
   (take)

1. Simon _____ a learner's permit.
   (get)

2. All drivers _____ the vision and written tests.
   (pass)

3. Ed _____ at least 50 hours before the driving test.
   (practice)

4. People over age 18 _____ a driver's education class.
   (take)

5. Drivers over age 18 _____ with an adult driver at night.
   (be)

6. All drivers _____ a driver's license.
   (have)

7. Simon _____ Ed the driving rules. Ed can learn them at school.
   (teach)

EXERCISE 4 **ABOUT YOU** Write true sentences about driving in your country. Fill in the blanks with the affirmative or negative form of *have to.*

EXAMPLES We ___**have to get**___ a permit before the driving test.
(get)

We ___**don't have to finish**___ high school to get a driver's license.
(finish)

1. Drivers under age 18 _____ a driver's education class.
(take)

2. New drivers _____ a vision test.
(pass)

3. Young drivers _____ with an adult driver.
(practice)

4. New drivers _____ all the answers right on the
(get)
written test.

5. Young drivers _____ driving at 11 P.M.
(stop)

6. New drivers _____ at least three months before the
(practice)
driving test.

EXERCISE 5 Look at the following road signs from Ed's rule book. Write two sentences about each road sign. Use *can, should,* or *have to,* affirmative and/or negative. Answers may vary.

EXAMPLE Drivers can't go over 65 miles per hour.

Drivers have to go at least 45 miles per hour.

1. _____

_____

2. _____

_____

3. _____

_____

4. _____

_____

5. _____

_____

6. _____

_____

7. _____

_____

8. _____

_____

EXERCISE 6 **ABOUT YOU** Write about drivers in your country. Use the words given. Answers will vary.

EXAMPLES   They can _learn to drive at age 15._

They can't _drive without a permit._

1. They can _____

2. They can't _____

3. They should _____

4. They shouldn't _____

5. They have to _____

6. They don't have to _____

EXERCISE 7 **Read the following conversations. Fill in the blanks with the affirmative or negative form of *can, should,* or *have to* and the verb in parentheses ( ). Some answers may vary.**

EXAMPLE **A:** I don't have a car.

B: Don't worry. You _____ can use _____ my car today.
(use)

1. **A:** I don't like to drive.

   B: That's OK. You _____ the bus.
   (take)

2. **A:** Where are your car keys?

   B: They're in the car.

   A: You _____ your keys in the car.
   (leave)

3. **A:** Today is a holiday. Do you want to go to a movie?

   B: No, I'm sorry. I _____ the driving rules
   (study)
   for my test on Friday.

   A: You _____ it today. It's Monday. You have
   (do)
   three more days before the test.

4. **A:** Your car is very dirty. You _____ it.
   (wash)

   B: I know, but I _____ it today. I'm too busy.
   (wash)

5. **A:** Let's walk to work today.

   B: We don't have time. We _____ at work
   (be)
   in 30 minutes.

6. **A:** My son wants to get his driver's license. But he's only 15.

   B: Then he _____ a driver's training class first.
   (take)
   But don't worry. He _____ for it.
   (pay)
   He _____ the class free in school.
   (take)

7. **A:** My written test is tomorrow and I don't know the rules of the road.

   B: You _____ to study until the night before the test.
   (wait)
   You _____ all the rules in one night. It's not possible.
   (learn)

8. **A:** There's a good program on TV now about driver safety.

   B: We _____ it.
   (watch)

   A: Good idea!

EXERCISE 8 Fill in the blanks in the conversations with the correct verbs from the box.

CD 2, TR 03

Conversation A: Ed is asking Simon about his friend from Mexico.

doesn't have to get	should study	can drive
has to take	has to get	can use

Ed: Dad, one of my friends has an international driver's license.

He _____ **can use** _____ it to drive in this state, right?
(example)

Simon: Yes, he can. But he _____ with an international
(1)

license for only three months. Then he _____
(2)

a new driver's license in this state.

Ed: What about a learner's permit?

Simon: He _____ a learner's permit. But he
(3)

_____ the rules of the road for this state. Then he
(4)

_____ all three of the tests. The rules
(5)

here are very different from the rules in Mexico.

Conversation B: The driving teacher, Mr. Brown, is talking to students in Ed's high school driver's education class.

have to wear	can't see	shouldn't worry

Mr. Brown: Today's class is about the tests for your learner's permit.

Does anyone have a question? Karl?

Karl: I'm worried about the vision test. I _____
(1)

very well.

Mr. Brown: You _____. You can take the test with
(2)

your glasses on. But then you _____ your
(3)

glasses in the car too. It's the law.

Lesson 1   107

Grammar
Can, *Should*, and *Have To*
Yes/No Questions
Information Questions
Subject Questions

Context
Using a Car

Car Safety for Children

Before
You Read

1. Where should children sit in a car?

2. Do you have a child in your family?
   What kind of car seat does the child use?

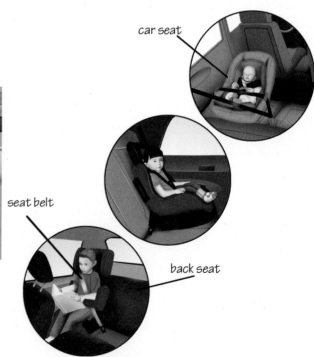

car seat

seat belt

back seat

gas station

gas pump

front of car

back of car

ABC123

🔊 **Read the following conversation. Pay special attention to *yes/no* questions and information questions with *can, should* and *have to.***

CD 2, TR 04

Dorota and Halina are on the way to an outlet mall in another city. Halina asks Dorota about car seats for her daughter, Anna.

Halina: This is my first trip to an outlet mall. **Can I get** a new car seat for Anna there? She's too big for her old infant seat now. And she's still too small for a seat belt.

Dorota: Sure. And things aren't so expensive at the outlet mall.

Halina: **What kind of car seat should I get?**

Dorota: Well, she's two now. Seats for older babies are different. We can look in several stores.

Halina: **How long does Anna have to be** in a car seat, Dorota?

Dorota: In this state, children have to be in a car seat until age eight or 57 inches tall.

Halina: **Where should I put** Anna's seat? **Can I put** it on the front passenger seat?

Dorota: No. Anna shouldn't be in the front seat. The air bag can hurt children. They should sit in the back seat until age 12.

(five minutes later)

Dorota: Halina, I have to stop for gas. Here's a gas station.

Halina: I can pay, Dorota. **Do we have to pay first?**

Dorota: Yes, the sign says "Pay First." But don't worry, Halina. I can put it on my credit card. I can pay right here at the pump.

Halina: **Should I wash** the windows?

Dorota: OK. You can wash the windows. And I can pump the gas.

Halina: **Where can I get** some water? I'm thirsty.

Dorota: Right here. This gas station has a store.

Did You **Know?**

A ticket for not putting a child in a car seat can be between $10 and $200. It depends on the state.

EXERCISE **2** **Fill in the blanks to make *yes/no* questions. Use the phrases from the box below.**

Can I pay	Should I wash	Can I put	Does everyone have to use
Can we go	Should we pay	Does Anna have to sit	

EXAMPLE _____Can I pay_____ with a credit card?

1. _____ for the gas at the pump?

2. _____ to the outlet mall?

3. _____ the car seat in the front?

4. _____ in the back seat?

5. _____ the windows for you?

6. _____ a seat belt?

EXERCISE **3** **Complete the *yes/no* question with *can, should,* or *have to* and the words given.**

EXAMPLE **A:** It's a beautiful day. _____Can we go_____ for a walk in the park?
                                                    (we/go)

B: Yes, we can.

1. **A:** It takes 2 hours to drive to the mall. _____ gas first?
                                                        (we/get)

   B: Yes, we do.

2. **A:** Gas in this station is expensive. _____ another station?
                                                    (we/try)

   B: Yes, we should.

3. **A:** Your car windows are dirty. _____ them for you?
                                              (I/wash)

   B: Yes, you can. Thank you.

4. **A:** I have a new car seat for my son. _____ in the back seat?
                                                      (he/sit)

   B: Yes, he does.

EXERCISE **4** **ABOUT YOU Find a partner. Ask your partner about people and customs in his/her native country. Use the words in parentheses ( ). Your partner can give a short answer.**

EXAMPLE _____Can people buy_____ food and drinks at gas stations? **Yes, they can.**
              (people/can/buy)

1. _____ their own gas at gas stations?
         (people/have to/pump)

2. _____ in a car seat?
              (a young child/have to/sit)

3. _____ on an adult's lap in a car?
              (a child/can/sit)

4. _____ in the front seat?
              (children/can/sit)

5. _____ for their gas at the pump?
         (people/can/pay)

Read the following conversation. Pay special attention to *yes/no* questions and information questions with *can, should* and *have to*.

Dorota and Halina are on the way to an outlet mall in another city. Halina asks Dorota about car seats for her daughter, Anna.

Halina: This is my first trip to an outlet mall. **Can I get** a new car seat for Anna there? She's too big for her old infant seat now. And she's still too small for a seat belt.

Dorota: Sure. And things aren't so expensive at the outlet mall.

Halina: **What kind of car seat should I get?**

Dorota: Well, she's two now. Seats for older babies are different. We can look in several stores.

Halina: **How long does Anna have to be** in a car seat, Dorota?

Dorota: In this state, children have to be in a car seat until age eight or 57 inches tall.

Halina: **Where should I put** Anna's seat? **Can I put** it on the front passenger seat?

Dorota: No. Anna shouldn't be in the front seat. The air bag can hurt children. They should sit in the back seat until age 12.

(five minutes later)

Dorota: Halina, I have to stop for gas. Here's a gas station.

Halina: I can pay, Dorota. **Do we have to pay first?**

Dorota: Yes, the sign says "Pay First." But don't worry, Halina. I can put it on my credit card. I can pay right here at the pump.

Halina: **Should I wash** the windows?

Dorota: OK. You can wash the windows. And I can pump the gas.

Halina: **Where can I get** some water? I'm thirsty.

Dorota: Right here. This gas station has a store.

Vocabulary in Context

on the way	They are in the car. They are **on the way** to the mall.
outlet mall	**Outlet malls** have many stores and good prices. They are usually outside of the city.
trip	We are in the car. We're on a **trip** out of town.
infant	That baby is only three months old. She's an **infant**.
seat belt	Everyone has to wear a **seat belt** in a car. It's the law.
several	We can look in **several** stores. I know three good stores.
until	Children sit in the back seat **until** age 12. Then they can sit in the front.
passenger	A **passenger** sits next to the driver or in the back seat.
air bag	An **air bag** keeps the driver and passengers safe.
hurt	An air bag can **hurt** a small child.
pump (v.) pump (n.)	We have to **pump** our own gas. We can pay at the **pump** with a credit card.

air bag

Listening Activity

CD 2, TR 05

Listen to each statement about the conversation. Circle *true* or *false*.

EXAMPLE Anna needs a new car seat.   (TRUE)   FALSE

1. TRUE   FALSE
2. TRUE   FALSE
3. TRUE   FALSE
4. TRUE   FALSE

5. TRUE   FALSE
6. TRUE   FALSE
7. TRUE   FALSE

5.4 *Can, Should,* and *Have To—Yes/No* Questions

Put *can* or *should* before the subject to make a question.

MODAL VERB	SUBJECT	VERB (BASE FORM)	COMPLEMENT	SHORT ANSWER
Can	I	get	some water?	Yes, you can.
Should	Halina	buy	an infant seat?	No, she shouldn't.
Can	young children	sit	in the front seat?	No, they can't.
Should	Halina	get	a new car seat for Anna?	Yes, she should.

Use *do* or *does* to make questions with *have to*.

DO/DOES	SUBJECT	*HAVE TO*	VERB (BASE FORM)	COMPLEMENT	SHORT ANSWER
Does	Dorota	**have to**	get	gas now?	Yes, she does.
Does	a teenager	**have to**	sit	in the back?	No, he/she doesn't.
Do	I	**have to**	pump	the gas?	Yes, you do.
Do	we	**have to**	pay	inside?	No, we don't.

EXERCISE **1** **Write a short answer for each question. Use the ideas from the conversation on page 109.**

EXAMPLES   Does Dorota have to get gas?

<u>Yes, she does.</u>

Can Anna sit in the front seat?

<u>No, she can't.</u>

lap

1. Should Halina put Anna's car seat in the front passenger seat?

_____

2. Can air bags hurt small children?

_____

3. Does Dorota have to pay in cash for her gas?

_____

4. Can people pump their own gas at the gas station?

_____

5. Do children over age 8 have to use a car seat?

_____

6. Should young children sit in the back seat of the car?

_____

7. Can Anna sit on Halina's lap in the car?

_____

EXERCISE **2** **Fill in the blanks to make *yes/no* questions. Use the phrases from the box below.**

Can I pay	Should I wash	Can I put	Does everyone have to use
Can we go	Should we pay	Does Anna have to sit	

EXAMPLE _____Can I pay_____ with a credit card?

1. _____ for the gas at the pump?

2. _____ to the outlet mall?

3. _____ the car seat in the front?

4. _____ in the back seat?

5. _____ the windows for you?

6. _____ a seat belt?

EXERCISE **3** **Complete the *yes/no* question with *can, should,* or *have to* and the words given.**

EXAMPLE **A:** It's a beautiful day. _____Can we go_____ for a walk in the park?
                                                           (we/go)

B: Yes, we can.

1. **A:** It takes 2 hours to drive to the mall. _____ gas first?
                                                                        (we/get)

   B: Yes, we do.

2. **A:** Gas in this station is expensive. _____ another station?
                                                                   (we/try)

   B: Yes, we should.

3. **A:** Your car windows are dirty, _____ them for you?
                                                              (I/wash)

   B: Yes, you can. Thank you.

4. **A:** I have a new car seat for my son. _____ in the back seat?
                                                                     (he/sit)

   B: Yes, he does.

EXERCISE **4** **ABOUT YOU** **Find a partner. Ask your partner about people and customs in his/her native country. Use the words in parentheses ( ). Your partner can give a short answer.**

EXAMPLE _____Can people buy_____ food and drinks at gas stations? **Yes, they can.**
               (people/can/buy)

1. _____ their own gas at gas stations?
      (people/have to/pump)

2. _____ in a car seat?
           (a young child/have to/sit)

3. _____ on an adult's lap in a car?
         (a child/can/sit)

4. _____ in the front seat?
          (children/can/sit)

5. _____ for their gas at the pump?
      (people/can/pay)

5.5 *Can*, *Should*, and *Have To*—Information Questions

Can/Should

QUESTION WORD(S)	MODAL	SUBJECT	VERB (BASE FORM)	COMPLEMENT	ANSWER
Where	**can**	Halina	get	a car seat?	At the outlet mall.
Why	**should**	we	go	to the outlet mall?	To get a good price.
How	**can**	parents	keep	their children safe in a car?	They can put them in a car seat.
Which car seat	**should**	I	buy	for Anna?	This one is good.

Have To

QUESTION WORD(S)	DO/ DOES	SUBJECT	*HAVE TO*	VERB (BASE FORM)	COMPLEMENT	ANSWER
Where	**does**	Anna	**have to**	sit?		In the back seat.
How much	**do**	we	**have to**	pay	for a car seat?	From $60 to $140.

EXERCISE 5 Answer each question. Use the ideas from the conversation on page 109.

EXAMPLE How can people pay for gas?

<u>They can pay with a credit card or cash.</u>

1. When can a child sit in the front passenger seat?

   _____

2. Why does a small child have to sit in the back seat?

   _____

3. Where can people pay for gas at the gas station?

   _____

4. Why does Halina have to get a new car seat for Anna?

   _____

5. Where can Halina buy water?

   _____

6. What kind of seat should Halina buy?

   _____

7. Why does Dorota have to stop at a gas station?

   _____

EXERCISE **6** **Ask questions about each statement using the question words given.**

EXAMPLE Anna has to sit in the back seat.

Why _does Anna have to sit in the back seat?_

1. They have to stop for gas on their trip.

    How often _____

2. Dorota should drive slowly.

    Why _____

3. An air bag can hurt small children.

    How _____

4. Halina has to buy some things for Anna.

    What _____

5. Anna can't sit in the front seat right now.

    When _____

6. You should get a new car seat for your daughter.

    Why _____

EXERCISE **7** **Complete each short conversation with a question. Use the words given.**

EXAMPLE **A:** Please get in the car.

B: _____ Where should we sit? _____
    (where/we/should sit)

1. **A:** There's child safety information on the Web.

    B: _____
        (which Web site/I/should check)

2. **A:** Halina doesn't have a good car seat for Anna.

    B: _____
        (where/she/can buy a good one)

3. **A:** Anna is two years old.

    B: _____
        (what kind of car seat/Halina/have to buy for her)

4. **A:** Car seats have different prices.

    B: _____
        (how much/she/should spend)

5. **A:** Children have to sit in car seats.

    B: _____
        (why/they/have to sit in car seats)

5.6 Can, Should, and Have To—Subject Questions

Can/Should

QUESTION WORD(S)	MODAL VERB	VERB (BASE FORM)	COMPLEMENT	ANSWER
Who	**should**	pay	for the gas?	Dorota should.
What	**can**	happen	to the baby in the front seat?	The air bag can hurt her.
How many people	**can**	sit	in the back seat?	Three can.

Have To

QUESTION WORD(S)	*HAVE TO*	VERB (BASE FORM)	COMPLEMENT	ANSWER
Who	**has to**	stop	for gas?	Dorota does.
Which children	**have to**	sit	in the back seat?	All small children do.

EXERCISE 8 Ask a question for each answer. Use the following question words as subjects: *who, which, how many,* or *what.* The underlined words are the answer.

EXAMPLE Who has to buy a car seat?

Halina has to buy a car seat.

1. _____

The gas station on my street can give us the best price for gas.

2. _____

Anna should sit in the back seat.

3. _____

Two people have to take a trip today.

4. _____

Air bags can hurt children in a car.

5. _____

Drivers under age 17 have to drive with an adult at night.

6. _____

Halina should buy some water.

Fill in the conversation with a group of words from the box below.

When does he have to take	Can you put	Do you have to use
He should practice	We can stop	I have to take
Ed should learn		

Marta and Simon talk about Ed's driving practice.

CD 2, TR 06

Marta: <u>Do you have to use</u> the car today?
<small>(example)</small>

Simon: Yes.

Marta: _____ some gas in the car for me?
<small>(1)</small>

Simon: Sure. _____ Ed out for driving practice later this
<small>(2)</small>
afternoon. _____ at the gas station.
<small>(3)</small>
_____ how to pump gas too.
<small>(4)</small>

Marta: _____ the driving test?
<small>(5)</small>

Simon: In just three weeks!

Marta: _____ a lot. He doesn't have much time.
<small>(6)</small>

Editing Advice

1. Always use the base form after *can*, *should*, and *have to*.

   She can ~~drives~~ the car. <small>*drive*</small>

2. Don't use *to* after *can* and *should*.

   The child can't ~~to~~ sit in the front seat.

3. Use the correct word order in a question.

   Why you can't drive?

4. Don't forget to use *do* or *does* with *have to* in questions.

   Why ^*do* you have to take a vision test?

5. Don't use *do* or *does* with subject questions.

   Who ~~does have~~ to sit in the back? The baby does. <small>*has*</small>

Editing Quiz

Some of the shaded words and phrases have mistakes. Find the mistakes and correct them. If the shaded words are correct, write *C*.

This is a conversation between Ed and his driving teacher, Mr. Brown, after the first class.

Ed: How many pages ^*do* we have to study in the *Rules of the Road*
(example)

book for tomorrow?

Mr. Brown: You *C* should learn the rules in the first lesson.
(example)

Ed: Tell me about licenses in this state. When I can drive with my
(1)

friends?

Mr. Brown: Let's see. You're only 15. You can to have only one passenger
(2)

in the car under age 20. And your friend have to sit in the
(3)

front passenger seat, not in the back.

Ed: How many hours we have to practice before the driving test?
(4)

Mr. Brown: Fifty hours. But you should to practice more. And you have
(5)

to practice ten hours at night.

Ed: How we can do that? We can't drive at night.
(6) *(7)*

Mr. Brown: You can drive until 11 P.M. and an adult driver has to goes
(8)

with you. Then it's OK.

Ed: Does the adult has to be one of my parents?
(9)

Mr. Brown: No. But he or she has to have a license.
(10)

Ed: Yes, I know. And everybody have to wear a seatbelt too.
(11)

Expansion

❶ Use *can, should,* and *have to* (affirmative and/or negative) to write three sentences about each topic:

- Driver's licenses
- Gas stations
- Children's car seats

❷ Write three questions you still have about driving in the U.S.

Writing Activity

Write one negative and one affirmative sentence about each picture. Use *can, should,* and *have to*. Write about what is wrong with each picture.

EXAMPLE

The baby can't sit on the mother's lap.

The baby has to be in an infant seat.

A.

B.

C.

For more practice using grammar in context, please visit our Web site.

School

1

Grammar
Modal: *Must*—Affirmative and Negative Statements

Must and *Have To*

Must Not and *Don't Have To*

Context
Eating at School

School Lunch Programs

Before
You Read

1. What do children like to eat for lunch?

2. Do elementary schools in your country give free lunches to children?

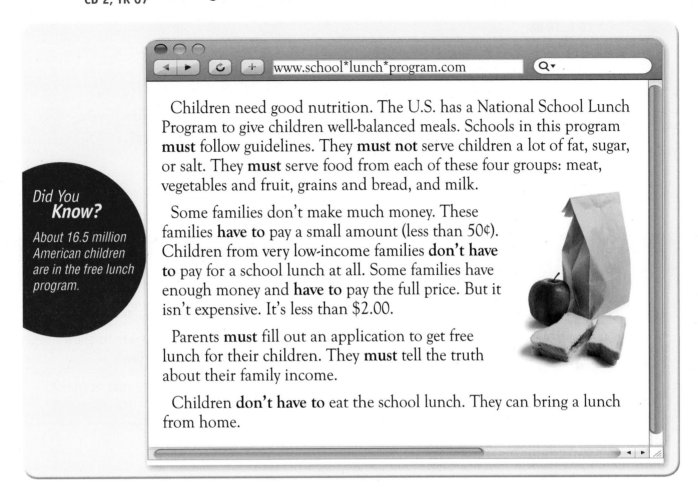

Read the following Web article. Pay special attention to affirmative and negative statements with *must* and *have to*.

CD 2, TR 07

www.school*lunch*program.com

Children need good nutrition. The U.S. has a National School Lunch Program to give children well-balanced meals. Schools in this program **must** follow guidelines. They **must not** serve children a lot of fat, sugar, or salt. They **must** serve food from each of these four groups: meat, vegetables and fruit, grains and bread, and milk.

Some families don't make much money. These families **have to** pay a small amount (less than 50¢). Children from very low-income families **don't have to** pay for a school lunch at all. Some families have enough money and **have to** pay the full price. But it isn't expensive. It's less than $2.00.

Parents **must** fill out an application to get free lunch for their children. They **must** tell the truth about their family income.

Children **don't have to** eat the school lunch. They can bring a lunch from home.

Did You **Know?**

About 16.5 million American children are in the free lunch program.

Vocabulary in Context

 fruits

 vegetables

 grains and bread

 meat

 milk

nutrition	Children need good **nutrition** to be healthy. They need to eat good food.
balanced	A **well-balanced** lunch has items from each food group.
guideline	The National School Lunch Program makes **guidelines.** They tell the schools what to serve.
fat	Potato chips and French fries have a lot of **fat.**
serve	Schools give children lunch. They **serve** lunch every day.
grain	We use **grains** to make bread.
income/ low-income	Their **income** is $30,000 a year. Their children are from a **low-income** family.
amount	Fifty cents is a small **amount** of money.
less than	The lunch costs $1.75. It's **less than** $2.00.
tell the truth	**Tell the truth** on the application. Don't give false information.

EXAMPLE School lunches have vegetables.   (TRUE)   FALSE

1. TRUE	FALSE	**5.** TRUE	FALSE
2. TRUE	FALSE	**6.** TRUE	FALSE
3. TRUE	FALSE	**7.** TRUE	FALSE
4. TRUE	FALSE		

6.1 Modal: *Must*—Affirmative and Negative Statements

EXAMPLES	EXPLANATION
Schools **must** serve milk to children. Parents **must** fill out an application for the free lunch program.	We use *must* to show rules or laws.
School lunches **must not** have a lot of sugar. School lunches **must not** have a lot of fat.	When the rule is "don't do this," use *must not*.

EXERCISE 1   Fill in the blanks with one of the verbs from the box below.

be	fill out	tell	sign	pay	serve

EXAMPLE The lunch is not free for everyone. Some families must _____pay_____.

1. The school must _____ a nutritious lunch.

2. Parents must _____ an application for the school lunch program.

3. Parents must _____ the application.

4. Parents must _____ the truth about their family income.

5. School lunches must _____ well-balanced.

6. Schools must _____ meat, vegetables, fruit, grains, and milk with every lunch.

Bayside Public Schools
Application for Free and Reduced Price Meals

To apply for free and reduced price meals for your child(ren), you must fill out this form and sign it. Use a pen.

Part 1 List the names of children at school.

Name(s) of Child(ren) Last Name, First Name	Age	School	Grade	Class
1.				
2.				
3.				

Part 2 List the names of all adult household members and their monthly incomes.

Last Name, First Name	Monthly Income
1.	
2.	
3.	

Part 3 Signature and Social Security Number. I certify that all the above information is true.

Signature of Parent or Guardian	Mailing Address
Social Security Number	Phone Number

Social Security Number boxes: ☐ ☐ ☐ – ☐ ☐ – ☐ ☐ ☐ ☐   Phone Number: (   )

For school use only

Date received _____ Date approved _____

EXERCISE 2   Look at the application for the school lunch program above. Change the sentences below from imperative statements to statements with *must* or *must not.*

EXAMPLES   Print your answers. You **must print your answers.**

Don't use a pencil. You **must not use a pencil.**

1. Fill out the application. You _____

2. Sign your name. You _____

3. Don't write in the last box. You _____

4. Write your monthly income. You _____

5. Use a pen. You _____

6. Don't use a pencil. You _____

7. Don't give false information. You _____

6.2 Must and Have To

Must and *have to* have very similar meanings.

EXAMPLES	EXPLANATION
You **must** write your family income. You **have to** write your family income. Schools **must** serve children milk. Schools **have to** serve children milk.	*Must* is very formal. We use *must* for rules and laws. We can also use *have to* for rules and laws. *Must* is stronger than *have to*.
Marta **has to** make lunch for her daughter. We **have to** buy more bread.	Use *have to* for personal necessity. Don't use *must* for personal necessity.

Language Note: In a question, *have to* is more common than *must*.
    Do I **have to** sign the application?
    Do schools **have to** serve children milk?	

EXERCISE 3   Fill in the blanks with *must* + a verb to talk about rules. Answers will vary.

EXAMPLE   Students _____ *must apply* _____ for the school lunch program.

1. Schools _____ guidelines from the National School Lunch Program.

2. On an application, parents _____ their names.

3. On the school lunch application, parents _____ their family income.

4. School lunches _____ food from each of the four groups.

5. Schools _____ children milk with every lunch.

EXERCISE 4   Fill in the blanks to talk about personal necessities. Use *have to/ has to* + a verb. Answers will vary.

EXAMPLE   I _____ *have to call my mom* _____ every day.

1. In class, we _____.

2. The teacher _____.

3. A mother _____.

4. Children _____.

5. College students _____.

6. I _____ every day.

6.3 Must Not and Don't Have To

Have to and *must* have very similar meanings. *Don't have to* and *must not* have very different meanings.

EXAMPLES	EXPLANATION
School lunches **must not** have a lot of fat. You must tell the truth. You **must not** give false information.	*Must not* gives a rule.
Children **don't have to** eat the school lunch. They can bring a lunch from home. Children of low-income families **don't have to** pay for lunch. They can get a free lunch.	*Don't have to* shows that something is not necessary.

EXERCISE 5 **ABOUT YOU** Work with a partner. Name three things you *don't have to* do.

EXAMPLE I don't have to work on Saturdays.

EXERCISE 6 **ABOUT YOU** Work with a partner. Name three things students *must not do* at this school or in this class.

EXAMPLE Students must not talk in the library.

EXERCISE 7 Fill in the blanks with the negative of *must* or *have to*. Remember, they do NOT have the same meaning.

EXAMPLES Schools in the lunch program _____must not_____ serve a lot of sugar.

Children ____don't have to____ be in the school lunch program.

1. Many families in the school lunch program _____ pay. Their children get free lunch.

2. Maya _____ eat at school. She can eat at home.

3. Parents _____ give false information on the application.

4. You _____ drink the milk. You can drink water.

5. Ed _____ study at home. He can study in the library.

6. You _____ talk loudly in the school library. It's a rule.

7. Children _____ come late to school.

Grammar

Count and Noncount Nouns

Quantity Expressions with Noncount Nouns

***Much/A Lot Of/A Little* with Noncount Nouns**

***Some/Any* with Noncount Nouns**

Context

Lunch Food

Maya's School Lunch

Before
    You Read

1. What foods are good for children?

2. What are some things children don't like to eat?

🔊 **Read the following conversation. Pay special attention to quantity expressions with count and noncount nouns.**

Victor: How are the lunches at your school? Do you like them?

Maya: Sometimes I do. Sometimes I don't. My favorite lunches are pizza, grilled cheese sandwiches, macaroni and cheese, and tacos. Sometimes we get a **piece of fish,** but I don't like fish.

Victor: What do you drink?

Maya: We always get a small **carton of milk.**

Victor: Do you get **any fruit?**

Maya: Yes. We always get a **piece of fruit**—an apple, an orange, a banana, or a small **bunch of grapes.** But some kids don't like the fruit. Sometimes they throw away the fruit.

Victor: That's terrible! Fruit is so good for you. Do the kids get **any soda?**

Maya: No. The teacher says that we shouldn't have **much sugar.** Sugar isn't good for us. But I love soda.

Victor: Your teacher's right. Do all children get school lunches?

Maya: No. Some kids bring a lunch from home. My friend Wanda always brings her lunch to school in a lunch box. Her mother usually gives her a sandwich and a **candy bar** or a **bag of potato chips.** She always brings a small **bottle of juice.** Juice is good for you, isn't it? It doesn't have **much sugar.**

Victor: Juice has **a lot of sugar.** It's better to eat a **piece of fruit.** Please eat your fruit. Don't throw it away!

Maya: Dad, why do you always have a **can of soda** with you? It's better to drink a **bottle of water.**

Victor: You're right. But this soda doesn't have **any sugar.**

Vocabulary in Context

favorite	Maya loves pizza. Pizza is her **favorite** lunch.
bunch of	The kids sometimes get a small **bunch of** grapes with lunch.
throw away	Don't **throw away** the fruit. It's good for you.
terrible	It isn't good to throw away fruit. It's **terrible!**
lunch box	Some kids take their lunches to school in a **lunch box.**
better	Juice is okay, but water is **better.**

Listening Activity

CD 2, TR 10

Listen to the sentences about the conversation. Circle *true* or *false*.

EXAMPLE   Maya always likes her school lunch.   TRUE   (FALSE)

1. TRUE   FALSE   4. TRUE   FALSE
2. TRUE   FALSE   5. TRUE   FALSE
3. TRUE   FALSE   6. TRUE   FALSE

6.4 Count and Noncount Nouns

Some nouns are count nouns. We can count them. Some nouns are noncount nouns. We don't count them.

EXAMPLES	EXPLANATION
One **sandwich** has jelly. Two **sandwiches** have cheese. One **child** has a lunch box from home. Twenty **children** get free lunch.	A count noun has a singular and a plural form. We can use a number with a count noun.
You need **bread** for a sandwich. Victor drinks **coffee** every day. The school always serves **milk.**	A noncount noun has no plural form. We don't use a number with a noncount noun.

Common noncount nouns are:

milk	bread	pizza	meat	soup
butter	food*	coffee	tea	juice
water	chicken	soda	fruit*	cheese
cream	candy	corn	butter	sugar
salt	pork	fat	macaroni	fish
oil	rice	popcorn		

*You sometimes see the plural of *fruit* and *food*. **Fruits** means different kinds of fruit. **Foods** means different kinds of food.

EXERCISE 1 **ABOUT YOU** Tell how often you eat or drink each item. Practice noncount nouns (no plural form) and the frequency words from the box below.

always	every day	often	sometimes	rarely	never

EXAMPLES fruit
I eat fruit every day.

popcorn
I never eat popcorn.

coffee
I rarely drink coffee.

1. milk
2. tea
3. coffee
4. water
5. soda
6. juice
7. bread
8. rice

9. pizza
10. meat
11. chicken
12. fish
13. fruit
14. popcorn
15. candy
16. cheese

EXERCISE 2 **ABOUT YOU** Tell how often you eat or drink each item. Practice count nouns and frequency words.

EXAMPLES potato(es)
I eat potatoes at least once a week.

banana(s)
I eat one banana a day.

avocado(es)
I never eat avocadoes.

1. banana(s)

2. apple(s)

3. potato chip(s)

4. cookie(s)

5. grape(s)

6. egg(s)

7. cracker(s)

8. orange(s)

9. hamburger(s)

10. hot dog(s)

6.5 Quantity Expressions with Noncount Nouns

EXAMPLES	EXPLANATION
I eat **three pieces of fruit** a day. I drink **two cups of tea** a day. Children get **one carton of milk** with lunch.	To talk about quantity with a noncount noun, use a unit of measurement that you can count: *cup of, bowl of, carton of, teaspoon of, piece of,* etc.

QUANTITY EXPRESSIONS WITH NONCOUNT NOUNS

a slice of pizza	a leaf of lettuce
a loaf of bread	a piece of fish
a slice of bread	a piece of meat
a piece of bread	a can of tuna
a slice of cheese	a piece of chicken
a carton of milk	a jar of jelly
a gallon of milk	a jar of peanut butter
a glass of milk	a piece of candy
a can of soda	a piece of fruit
a cup of coffee	an ear of corn
a pound of coffee	a teaspoon of salt
a cup of tea	a stick of butter
a glass of juice	a bowl of rice
a bottle of juice	a bowl of popcorn
a bottle of oil	a teaspoon of sugar
a bowl of soup	a jar of mayonnaise
a can of soup	a tablespoon of mayonnaise

EXERCISE 3 **Complete this conversation with one of the words from the box below.**

can	jar	candy	fruit	milk

Amy: Mom. I'm hungry. Can I have a piece of ___candy___?
(example)

CD 2, TR 11 **Marta:** You know it isn't good for you. Have a piece of _____.
(1)

Amy: Can I have a peanut butter and jelly sandwich too? Where's the peanut butter?

Marta: You can find a _____ of peanut butter in the cabinet
(2)
next to the refrigerator.

Amy: I see a _____ of soda in the refrigerator. Can I have it too?
(3)

Marta: No. Soda has a lot of sugar. Drink a glass of _____.
(4)

EXERCISE 4 **Victor is teaching Maya to make a tuna sandwich. Fill in the blanks with a quantity expression. Answers may vary.**

Victor: You can find a _____loaf_____ of bread on the table. Take
(example)
two _____ of bread and put them on a plate. Open a
(1)
_____ of tuna and put the tuna in a bowl. You can find
(2)
a _____ of mayonnaise in the refrigerator. Add two
(3)
_____ of mayonnaise.
(4)
Mix the tuna and mayonnaise. Put the
tuna on the bread. Now you have a
healthy lunch.

Maya: Dad, can I have a _____
(5)
of soda with my sandwich?

Victor: Sorry. But you can have a
_____ of water with it.
(6)
And you can have a _____
(7)
of fruit after lunch.

EXERCISE 5   **ABOUT YOU** Add a quantity if you eat or drink these items. If not, say, "I don't eat/drink _____."

EXAMPLE   I eat _____<u>two slices</u>_____ of bread a day. OR **I don't eat bread.**

1. I drink _____ of water a day.

2. I eat _____ of fruit a day.

3. I drink _____ of coffee a day.

4. I drink _____ of milk a day.

5. I drink _____ of tea a day.

6. I drink _____ of juice a week.

6.6 *Much/A Lot Of/A Little* with Noncount Nouns

EXAMPLES	EXPLANATION
I eat **a lot of** cheese. I don't drink **a lot of** milk. I don't use **much** sugar.	Use *a lot of* with large quantities. In negatives, you can also use *much*.
He uses **a little** sugar. He drinks **a little** tea.	Use *a little* with small quantities.

Language Note: We say *use*, not *eat*, with **sugar, salt,** and **butter.** We add these things to food.

EXERCISE 6   **ABOUT YOU** Tell if you eat, drink, or use these items. Use *a lot of* or *much*.

EXAMPLES   milk
I don't drink a lot of milk.

meat
I eat a lot of meat.

salt
I don't use much salt.

1. cheese   6. coffee

2. popcorn   7. salt

3. rice   8. sugar

4. candy   9. butter

5. milk   10. soup

Fill in the blanks with *a little* and one of the words from the box below. Answers may vary.

meat	butter	milk	salt	sugar	oil

EXAMPLE Use _____ a little oil _____ to cook.

1. Put _____ and _____ in the coffee.

2. The pizza has _____ and a lot of cheese.

3. Put _____ on the bread.

4. Put _____ in the soup.

6.7 *Some/Any* with Noncount Nouns

EXAMPLES	EXPLANATION
A: Does the pizza have **any** meat? B: Yes. The pizza has **some** meat. A: Do kids get **any** soda with their lunches? B: No. They don't get **any** soda. A: Do you want **some** coffee? B: No. I don't want **any** coffee.	We use *any* or *some* in questions. We use *some* in affirmatives. We use *any* in negatives.

EXERCISE 8 **Fill in the blanks with *some* or *any*. In some cases, both answers are possible.**

EXAMPLE The pizza has _____ some _____ meat.

1. I don't want _____ soda.

2. The school lunch doesn't have _____ candy.

3. Do you want _____ milk?

4. I want _____ juice.

5. The sandwich has _____ mayonnaise.

6. Does the soup have _____ salt?

7. She's a vegetarian. She doesn't eat _____ meat.

8. I can't buy my lunch today. I don't have _____ money.

9. You should eat _____ fruit every day.

Grammar

Count and Noncount Nouns
Some vs. *Any*
A Lot Of and *Much* vs. *Many*
A Few vs. *A Little*
How much vs. *How many*

Context

School in the U.S.

School Supplies

Before
    You Read

1. What do children need for school?

2. Should small children have a lot of homework?

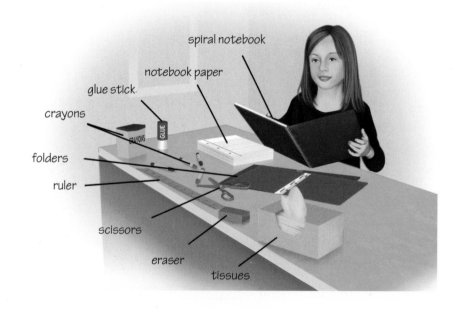

Read the following conversation. Pay special attention to quantity expressions with count and noncount nouns.

It's Maya's first day of school. She has a note for Victor.

Victor: What's this?

Maya: It's a note from school. It has **a lot of information** about the school. And this is my list of school supplies. I need **a lot of supplies** for school.

Victor: **How many things** do you need?

Maya: I need **two erasers, one ruler, two spiral notebooks, ten pencils, one glue stick, one pair of scissors, one large package of notebook paper, four folders, one box of tissues,** and **one box of crayons.**

Victor: **How many crayons** are in one box?

Maya: I don't know, but we need at least 24.

Victor calls Simon for help.

Victor: I have **a few questions** about my daughter's school. I need **some advice.** Do you have **any time** now?

Simon: Yes, Victor. I have **a little free time** now.

Victor: My daughter has a list of school supplies. Where do I buy them?

Simon: **Many stores** sell school supplies, but the office supply store near my house has a sale on school supplies now. I have **a few coupons.** We can go together.

Victor: Do I have to buy **any books? How much money** do I need for books?

Simon: You don't have to buy **any books** for public school. The school gives books to the students. Students return them at the end of the school year.

Victor: That's good. The note from school has **a lot of information** about homework. Do American kids get **a lot of homework?**

Simon: Yes, they do.

Victor: One more question. Do I have to buy a uniform for my daughter?

Simon: I don't know. Children in some schools need uniforms. Read me the information from your daughter's school.

Victor: OK.

Did You **Know?**

Most children start school at the age of 5.

Vocabulary in Context

coupons

school supplies	Children need **school supplies.** They need pencils, paper, rulers, and more.
note	The teacher sometimes writes a **note** to parents.
advice	Victor needs Simon's **advice** about school.
coupon	I can save money. I can get 50¢ off with this **coupon.**
public school	Every child can go to **public school.** Public school is free.
return	Students don't keep books. They **return** them to the school.
uniform	In some schools, all the children wear the same **uniform.**

Listening Activity

CD 2, TR 14

Listen to the sentences about the conversation. Circle *true* or *false*.

EXAMPLE Victor has a note from Maya's teacher. (TRUE)   FALSE

1. TRUE   FALSE   4. TRUE   FALSE
2. TRUE   FALSE   5. TRUE   FALSE
3. TRUE   FALSE   6. TRUE   FALSE

6.8 Count and Noncount Nouns: *Some* vs. *Any*

EXAMPLES	EXPLANATION
Maya has **some** information from her teacher. Victor has **some** questions for Simon.	Use *some* with noncount nouns and plural count nouns.
Does she need **any/some** glue? Does she need **any/some** pencils?	Use *any* or *some* with both noncount nouns and plural count nouns in questions.
Maya doesn't have **any** homework today. Victor doesn't have **any** coupons.	Use *any* with both noncount nouns and plural count nouns in negatives.

Language Note: *Homework, information,* and *advice* are noncount nouns. They have no plural form. To add a specific quantity, we can say a *homework assignment; a piece of information; a piece of advice.*

EXERCISE 1 **Fill in the blanks with *some* or *any*.**

EXAMPLE I need ___*some*___ paper for school.

1. Do you have _____ homework today?

2. We have _____ math homework.

3. I don't have _____ problems with my homework.

4. Maya needs _____ notebooks.

5. I don't need _____ paper for my gym class.

6. Do you need _____ erasers for school?

7. We need _____ crayons for school.

8. Victor needs _____ advice from Simon.

EXERCISE **2** **ABOUT YOU** Answer the questions. Use *some* or *any* in your answers.

EXAMPLE Do you have any time to watch TV?
Yes. I have some time to watch TV after school.

1. Do you have any homework today?

2. Do you need any books for this course?

3. Does this class have any students from Korea?

4. Do you need any paper to do this exercise?

5. Do you have any information about universities in the U.S.?

6. Do you have any advice for new students?

6.9 Count and Noncount Nouns: *A Lot Of* and *Much* vs. *Many*

EXAMPLES	EXPLANATION
Maya needs **a lot of/many** school supplies. Does she need **a lot of/many** pencils? She doesn't need **a lot of/many** notebooks.	Use *a lot of* or *many* with count nouns.
Does Victor have **a lot of/much** information about the school? He doesn't have **a lot of/much** money. Maya needs **a lot of** paper.	Use *a lot of* or *much* with noncount nouns in questions and negatives. In affirmative statements, use *a lot of*. Don't use *much*.

EXERCISE **3** Circle the correct answer. In some cases, both answers are possible.

EXAMPLE I have (*much* / (*a lot of*)) paper, but I don't have ((*many*)/(*a lot of*)) pencils.

1. Some children drink (*much* / *a lot of*) juice, but they don't drink (*many* / *much*) water.

2. Maya eats (*a lot of* / *many*) fruit, but she doesn't eat (*much* / *many*) bananas.

3. (*Many* / *Much*) stores have school supply sales in August.

4. I need (*a lot of* / *much*) information about schools in the U.S.

(continued)

5. Children need (*a lot of* / *much*) school supplies.

6. I have (*much* / *a lot of*) homework, but I don't have (*much* / *many*) time to do it.

7. (*Many* / *A lot of*) children get a free lunch in the U.S.

6.10 Count and Noncount Nouns: *A Few* vs. *A Little*

EXAMPLES	EXPLANATION
Maya needs **a few** erasers. She needs **a few** pencils.	Use *a few* with count nouns.
Victor spends **a little** time with Maya every day. School lunches cost **a little** money.	Use *a little* with noncount nouns.

EXERCISE 4 **Fill in the blanks with *a few* or *a little*.**

EXAMPLE Maya drinks __a little__ juice every day.

1. Victor has _____ time to help Maya with her homework.

2. Maya has _____ good friends at school.

3. Maya watches _____ TV programs on the weekend.

4. Victor needs _____ advice from Simon.

5. Maya needs _____ pencils for school.

EXERCISE 5 **ABOUT YOU** **Fill in the blanks.**

EXAMPLE I have a few _____*good friends*_____.

1. I need a little _____.

2. I know a few _____.

3. I eat a little _____ every day.

4. I eat a few _____ every week.

5. I use a little _____.

6.11 Count and Noncount Nouns: *How Much* vs. *How Many*

EXAMPLES	EXPLANATION
How many coupons do you have? **How many** pencils does Maya need for school?	Use *how many* with count nouns.
How much paper does she need? **How much** money do I need for books?	Use *how much* with noncount nouns.
How much does this book cost? **How much** is the school lunch?	Use *how much* to ask about cost.

EXERCISE 6 **ABOUT YOU** Find a partner. Ask these questions about an elementary school in your partner's country.

EXAMPLE How many days a week do kids go to school?
They go to school five days a week.

1. How many months a year do kids go to school?
2. How many kids are in an average class?
3. How much time do kids spend on homework?
4. How many hours a day are kids in school?
5. How much time do kids have for vacation?
6. How much money do kids spend on books?
7. Do kids get school lunch? How much does it cost?
8. Do kids wear a uniform? How much does a uniform cost?

EXERCISE 7 **ABOUT YOU** Fill in the blanks with *much* or *many*. Then answer the question.

EXAMPLE How ___many___ lessons do we do a day?
We do one lesson a day.

1. How _____ classes do you have now?
2. How _____ money do you need to take one class?
3. How _____ paper do you need for your homework?
4. How _____ students in this class speak Spanish?
5. How _____ books do we need for this course?
6. How _____ time do you spend on your homework?
7. How _____ homework do you have today?
8. How _____ dictionaries do you have?

EXERCISE 8 Circle the correct word(s) in parentheses ( ) to complete this conversation between Victor and his neighbor, Maria. In some cases, both answers are possible.

CD 2, TR 15

Maria: I have (*a little* / *a few*) questions. I need (*a little* / *a few*) information. Do you have (*any* / *some*) time to answer my questions?

Victor: Yes. I have (*a little* / *a few*) time right now.

Maria: Can my kids get into the free lunch program?

Victor: Maybe. If you don't make (*many* / *much*) money, they can probably get into the free lunch program.

Maria: I don't make (*many* / *a lot of*) money. What should I do?

Victor: You have to fill out a form. The form has (*many* / *much*) questions.

Maria: How (*much* / *many*) does a school lunch cost?

Victor: The full price is $1.75. That's not (*much* / *any*) money.

Maria: I have (*a lot of* / *much*) kids in school, so for me it's (*much* / *a lot of*) money.

Victor: How (*much* / *many*) kids do you have?

Maria: Six. Four are in school, so I really need to learn about the free lunch program.

Editing Advice

1. Don't use *to* after *must*.

   Schools must ~~to~~ serve a good lunch. *OR*

   Schools have to serve a good lunch.

2. Don't put *a* or *an* before a noncount noun.

   I like to eat ~~a~~ rice.

3. Use *of* with a unit of measure.

   I want a cup ^of^ coffee.

4. Don't forget *of* with *a lot of*.

   I don't have a lot ^of^ homework today.

5. Don't confuse *much* and *many*, *a little* and *a few*.

   He doesn't have ~~much~~ ^{many} friends.

   Maya doesn't have ~~many~~ ^{much} homework today.

   I eat a ~~little~~ ^{few} grapes every day.

   Put a ~~few~~ ^{little} salt in the soup.

6. Don't use *much* in affirmative statements.

   He drinks ~~much~~ ^{a lot of} tea.

7. Don't use *no* after a negative verb.

   I don't have ~~no~~ ^{any} money.

8. Don't use the plural form with noncount nouns.

   Victor gets a lot of ~~informations~~ ^{information} from Simon.

Editing Quiz

Some of the shaded words and phrases have mistakes. Find the mistakes and correct them. If the shaded words are correct, write *C*.

Maya is home with Victor after school.

Maya: Daddy, can I have a ~~little~~ grapes? And can I have some milk too?
                      few   *C*
             (example)   *(example)*

Victor: I'm sorry. We don't have no milk today. Do you want a glass water?
                                  (1)   *(2)*

Maya: I don't like to drink a water. Do we have any juice?
                           (3)   *(4)*

Victor: Yes, but you can have just a little. Juice contains much sugar.
                               (5)   *(6)*

Maya: But you drink soda, Daddy. Soda contains a lot sugar.
                                         (7)

Victor: My soda doesn't have any sugar.
                             (8)

Maya: Oh. Can I watch TV now?

Victor: Do you have any homework today?
                       (9)

Maya: I just have a homework for math.
                    (10)

Victor: Do your homework first. Then you can watch TV.

Maya: OK. I have a paper for a school trip. You must to sign it. Sign here.
                                                (11)

Victor: I have to read it first. Hmmm. I don't understand something here.
              (12)

I can call Simon for some advices.
                                 (13)

Expansion

Learner's Log

1 **What did you learn in this unit? Write three sentences about each of these topics:**

- Rules for school lunch programs
- Foods in school lunch programs
- Healthy foods
- School supplies

2 **Write three questions you still have about American elementary schools.**

Writing Activities

1 **Use information from Exercise 6 on page 139 to write a short paragraph of five or six sentences about schools in your partner's country.**

2 **Rewrite the following paragraph. Add a quantity word or expression before the underlined words.**

I buy <u>healthy food</u> for my family. And I try to be a good example for my family. For example, I drink <u>water</u> before each meal. Then I'm not so hungry. I don't drink <u>soda</u>. I drink <u>tea</u> after a meal. I have <u>cereal</u> for breakfast. I have salad with <u>soup</u> for lunch. I eat <u>fruit</u> every day too. I don't eat <u>red meat</u>. I try to eat <u>fish or chicken</u> every week. I always eat <u>vegetables</u> with dinner. <u>Friends</u> ask me about food for their kids. I always give them <u>advice</u>: "A parent has to be a good example."

EXAMPLE

> I buy a lot of healthy food for my family. And I try to be a good example for my family....

For more practice using grammar in context, please visit our Web site.

Shopping

Grammar
Time Expressions with Prepositions

Time Expressions without Prepositions

Prepositions of Place

Prepositions in Common Expressions

Context
Buying Necessary Things

Twenty-Four/Seven

Before
You Read

1. Do you shop late at night? Why or why not?
2. What stores do you like? Why?

Read the following conversation between Sue and Rick, an American couple. Pay special attention to prepositions.

CD 2, TR 16

Sue: Look. We're **out of** coffee. We need coffee for tomorrow morning. Can you go out and buy some?

Rick: Now? It's late. It's **after** 9:30. We can get it **in** the morning. I always wake up early.

Sue: Tomorrow is Saturday. The stores are crowded **on** Saturday. I don't like to shop **on** the weekend. Anyway, we like to drink coffee **in** the morning.

Rick: But the supermarket is closed **at** night.

Sue: You're right. But the convenience store is open. It's open 24/7.

Rick: My news program is **on** TV **at** 10 P.M. I don't have time **before** the news program. It starts **in** 20 minutes.

Sue: You can go **after** the news.

(*Rick is now **at** the convenience store. Sue calls him **on** his cell phone.*)

Rick: Hello?

Sue: Hi. Are you **at** the convenience store now?

Rick: I'm still **in** the car. I'm **in** the parking lot.

Sue: Can you go **to** the pharmacy too and get some aspirin? I have a headache.

Rick: Can I get the aspirin **at** the convenience store?

Sue: You can, but aspirin is **on** sale this week **at** the pharmacy—two bottles **for** $5.00.

Rick: Which pharmacy?

Sue: The pharmacy **near** the convenience store. It's **on** the corner. It's **next to** the gas station.

Rick: Is the pharmacy open late too?

Sue: Yes, it's open 24/7.

Did You Know?

Prices at a convenience store are sometimes high. You are paying for the convenience of 24/7.

Vocabulary in Context

24/7	**24/7** means a place is open 24 hours a day, seven days a week.
wake up	Rick **wakes up** early for work.
shop/ go shopping	I like to **shop** in the morning. I like to **go shopping** early.
convenience store	A **convenience store** is a small supermarket. It's open late, often 24/7.
program(s)	TV has many **programs.** Every hour you can see a different **program.**
news	The **news** tells us about city, country, and world happenings.
still	Rick's not at the store. He's **still** in the car.
aspirin/ headache	Take an **aspirin** for your **headache.**
pharmacy	You can buy aspirin and other medicine in a **pharmacy.**
corner	The store is on the **corner** of Main Street and Willow Street.

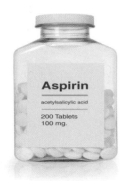

Listening Activity

CD 2, TR 17

Listen to the sentences about the conversation. Circle *true* or *false*.

EXAMPLE   Sue and Rick like to drink coffee in the morning.

(TRUE)   FALSE

1. TRUE   FALSE   **5.** TRUE   FALSE

2. TRUE   FALSE   **6.** TRUE   FALSE

3. TRUE   FALSE   **7.** TRUE   FALSE

4. TRUE   FALSE

7.1 Time Expressions with Prepositions

Prepositions are connecting words. We can use prepositions with time expressions.

The store is open	**in** the morning.
	in the daytime.
	in the afternoon.
	in the evening.
	at night.
The news program starts	**at** 10 P.M.
	in 20 minutes.
You can go out	**after** 9:30.
	after the news program.
	after work.
Sue goes to sleep	**before** 10:30.
The stores are crowded	**on** Saturdays.
	on the weekend.

Language Note: A sentence can have two time expressions.
Rick goes to work **at** 7 A.M. **in** the morning.
He wakes up **at** 8 A.M. **on** the weekend.

EXERCISE 1 **Fill in the blanks with the correct preposition of time: *in, on, after, before,* or *at.***

EXAMPLE Sue and Rick don't work ____**at**____ night.

1. They work _____ Monday.

2. They don't work _____ the evening.

3. They don't work _____ the weekend.

4. They can buy coffee _____ the morning.

5. Many stores open _____ 9 A.M.

6. The convenience store is open _____ night.

7. It's 9:37 now. It's _____ 9:30.

8. We go shopping _____ the afternoon.

9. The supermarket closes at 10 P.M. Go there _____ 10.

ABOUT YOU **Ask a question with *When do you* . . . and the words given. Another student will answer.**

EXAMPLE   watch TV

A: When do you watch TV?

B: I watch TV at night.

1. drink coffee
2. relax
3. go to sleep
4. wake up
5. go shopping
6. listen to OR watch the news

7. wash your clothes
8. eat lunch
9. read the newspaper
10. see your friends
11. do your homework
12. take an aspirin

7.2 Time Expressions without Prepositions

In some cases, we don't use a preposition with time.

The store is open	24 hours a day.
The store is open	seven days a week.
We shop	three times a month.
They buy milk	once a week.
We cook	every day.
The convenience store is open	24/7.
The convenience store is open	all day and all night.

EXERCISE **3**   **ABOUT YOU** **Fill in the blanks.**

EXAMPLE   I ____visit my parents____ once a month.

1. I _____ 7 days a week.

2. I _____ once a day.

3. I _____ twice a week.

4. I _____ all night.

5. I _____ all day.

EXERCISE 4 **ABOUT YOU** Fill in the blanks with a time expression. Tell about your country.

EXAMPLE   People usually listen to the news _____*every day.*_____

1. Pharmacies are usually open _____

2. Supermarkets in big cities are open _____

3. Most banks are open _____

4. Most people shop for food _____

EXERCISE 5 **ABOUT YOU** Ask a question with *how many* and the words given. Use a time expression. Another student will answer.

EXAMPLE   days a week / work

A: How many days a week do you work?

B: I work five days a week.

1. times a day / check your e-mail
2. hours a day / talk on the phone
3. times a month / go to the library

4. hours a night / sleep
5. times a day / cook
6. times a week / shop for food

7.3 Prepositions of Place

We can use prepositions with a place.

PREPOSITION	EXAMPLES
in	Rick is **in** the car. He is **in** the parking lot.
near	The pharmacy is **near** the convenience store.
next to	The pharmacy is **next to** the gas station.
on	The convenience store is **on** the corner.
at	Rick is **at** the convenience store now. Sue and Rick are **at** home in the evening. They are **at** work in the daytime.
to	Go **to** the pharmacy.

Language Note: Compare:
    I'm **in** the store. (I'm not outside the store.)
    I'm **at** the store. (I may be inside or in the parking lot, ready to go in.)	

This is a phone conversation between Victor and Lisa. Lisa is at home. Victor is on his cell phone in his car. Fill in the blanks with the correct preposition: *in, on, at, near, to,* or *next to.*

CD 2, TR 18

Victor: Hello?

Lisa: Hi. It's Lisa. Where are you now?

Victor: I'm ___**at**___ school. Where are you?
(example)

Lisa: I'm _____ home. Are you _____ class?
(1)   (2)

Victor: No, I'm _____ the parking lot. My class starts in ten
(3)

minutes.

Lisa: Can you go _____ the
(4)

store on your way home?

We need milk. There's a sale

on milk _____ Tom's Market.
(5)

Victor: Where's Tom's Market?

Lisa: It's _____ the school. It's _____ the corner.
(6)   (7)

It's _____ the laundromat.
(8)

7.4 Prepositions in Common Expressions

We can use prepositions in many common expressions.

PREPOSITION	EXAMPLE
on	Rick is **on the phone**.
	The news program is **on TV.** You can hear the news **on the radio**.
	Aspirin is **on sale**.
	Buy milk **on your way** home.
for	Aspirin is on sale this week, two bottles **for $5.00**.
out of	We don't have any coffee. We're **out of** coffee.

EXERCISE **7** **Fill in the blanks in this conversation with *on, in, next to, of, after, out of* or *for*.**

CD 2, TR 19

Simon: I'm going to the store ___**after**___ work. Eggs are on
                                     (example)

sale—two dozen _____ $1.89.
                        (1)

Marta: Buy bananas too. They're _____ sale—one pound
                                           (2)

_____ 39 cents.
    (3)

Simon: Anything else[1]?

Marta: Oh, yes. Buy coffee too.

Simon: Are we _____ coffee? So soon?
                        (4)

Marta: Yes. We drink a lot of coffee.

dozen = 12

(*Simon is _____ the store now. He's _____ the phone with Marta*)
                (5)   (6)

Simon: I'm at Tom's Market now. Do we need anything else?

Marta: Yes. Buy some tea. The tea is _____ the coffee.
                                              (7)

Then come home right away. Your favorite show is _____
                                                        (8)

TV at 7 P.M.

---

[1]*Anything else* means anything more.

Fill in the blanks in this conversation with the correct preposition: *in, on, at, to,* or *after.*

CD 2, TR 20

Sue: Hi. I'm ____on____ my cell phone.
(example)

Rick: Are you _____ the car?
(1)

Sue: No, I'm still _____ work. I can't come home right now.
(2)

_____ work, I have to make a few stops. I can be home
(3)

_____ about² an hour and a half.
(4)

Rick: Where do you need to go?

Sue: I need to buy gas. Then I have to go _____ the supermarket.
(5)

Rick: Then can you come home?

Sue: No. Then I have to go to the post office. The post office closes

_____ 6 P.M.
(6)

Rick: Why do you have to do all of this now? I'm preparing dinner

now. And it's almost ready.

Sue: Oh, thanks, Rick. I can go to the supermarket _____
(7)

dinner. And you can get gas _____ your way to work.
(8)

Rick: Good. Then just stop _____ the post office.
(9)

And don't be too late.

²*About* an hour and a half can be 90 minutes, 95 minutes, 85 minutes, etc.

Grammar

There Is and *There Are*—Affirmative Statements

There Is and *There Are*—Negative Statements

Quantity Words

Context

Large Stores and Small Stores

Good Prices or Good Service

Before You Read

1. Are clerks in stores usually helpful?
2. Do you like to shop in big stores or small stores? Why?

home supply store   hardware store

Read the following conversations. Pay special attention to affirmative and negative forms of *there is* and *there are*.

Conversation 1: At a big home supply store

Sue: You know I don't like to shop on Saturday. **There are** a lot of shoppers, and **there's** no place to park.

Rick: Look. **There's** a space over there.

Sue: (*In the store*) **There are** no shopping carts.

Rick: Let's take a basket. We only need lightbulbs.

Sue: **There are** so many things in this store. It's hard to find things.

Rick: **There's** a clerk over there. Let's ask him. Excuse me, sir. I need to find lightbulbs.

Clerk: Lightbulbs are in aisle 3. **There's** a clerk there. He can help you.

(*After visiting aisle 3*)

Sue: **There's** no one in aisle 3 to help. Can you please help us?

Clerk: Sorry. I don't work in aisle 3. That's not my department.

Sue: (*To Rick*) The service here is terrible. **There aren't** enough clerks in this store. No one is interested in helping us.

Rick: But the prices are good here. And **there are** always coupons for this store in the newspaper. I have a coupon for a package of six lightbulbs for $10.

Conversation 2: In a small store

Clerk: Can I help you?

Peter: Yes. I need lightbulbs.

Clerk: Lightbulbs are downstairs, but **there's** no elevator in this store. I can get the lightbulbs for you. Do you want some coffee? **There's** a coffee machine over there. It's free for customers.

Peter: Thanks for your help. (*Thinking*) I prefer this store. **There's** good service here. **There are** helpful clerks here. And **there's** free coffee.

Did You
Know?

Big home supply stores often teach free classes in home repair.

Package of
6 for **$10.00**
Expires Dec. 31, 2012

EG
lightbulbs

Vocabulary in Context

home supply store/hardware store	A **home supply store** and a **hardware store** have many things for the home: tools, lightbulbs, paint, etc.
shopping cart	We use a **shopping cart** for our items in a store.
basket	We can use a **basket** for a few items in a store.
lightbulb/lamp	Rick needs a **lightbulb** for his **lamp**.
aisle	Lightbulbs are in **aisle**[3] 3.
clerk	A **clerk** works to help people in a store.
interested	The clerk isn't **interested** in helping Rick.
service	Peter likes good **service**. He likes help in a store.
enough	There are a lot of shoppers, but there aren't **enough** clerks.
40% off	The coupon says 40**% (percent) off**. The package of lightbulbs is $5. It's $3.00 with the coupon.
downstairs	We're on the first floor. Lightbulbs are **downstairs**.
elevator	Peter needs an **elevator** to go downstairs.
prefer	Peter doesn't like the big store. He **prefers** the small store.

Listening Activity

🔊 CD 2, TR 22

Listen to the sentences about the conversation. Circle *true* or *false*.

EXAMPLE   There's a coupon in the newspaper for lightbulbs.

         (TRUE)   FALSE

1. TRUE   FALSE   **4.** TRUE   FALSE

2. TRUE   FALSE   **5.** TRUE   FALSE

3. TRUE   FALSE   **6.** TRUE   FALSE

---

[3]The pronunciation of *aisle* is /'ail/. Don't pronounce the *s*.

7.5 *There Is* and *There Are*—Affirmative Statements

Sometimes we use *there is* or *there are* to introduce the subject.

Singular Nouns

THERE	IS	A/AN/ONE	SINGULAR NOUN	PREPOSITIONAL PHRASE
There	is	a	parking lot	at the store.
There	is	an	elevator	in the hardware store.
There	is	one	clerk	in aisle 4.

Noncount Nouns

THERE	IS	(QUANTITY WORD)	NONCOUNT NOUN	PREPOSITIONAL PHRASE
There	is		free coffee	for the customers.
There	is	some	milk	near the coffee machine.
There	is	a lot of	sugar	in your coffee.

Language Note: The contraction for *there is: there's.*

Plural Nouns

THERE	ARE	(QUANTITY WORD)	PLURAL NOUN	PREPOSITIONAL PHRASE
There	are		coupons	in the newspaper.
There	are	two	clerks	in aisle 6.
There	are	a lot of	cars	in the parking lot.

Language Note: *There are* has no contraction.

EXERCISE **1** **Fill in the blanks with *there is* or *there are*. Make a contraction whenever possible.**

EXAMPLE _____*There are*_____ a lot of items in the big store.

1. _____ a sale on lightbulbs this week.

2. _____ a lot of lightbulbs in aisle 3.

3. _____ two elevators in the big store.

4. _____ many shoppers in the big store.

5. _____ a sign near the lightbulbs.

6. _____ coffee for the customers in the small store.

7. _____ good service in the small store.

EXERCISE 2 This is a cell phone conversation between Simon and Victor. Fill in the blanks with *there is* or *there are*. Make a contraction whenever possible.

CD 2, TR 23

Simon: Hello?

Victor: Hi, Simon. It's Victor.

Simon: Are you at home?

Victor: No, I'm not. I'm at the department store[4] with my wife.

__There's__ a big sale at this store—50% off all winter
(example)

items. Lisa loves sales. She wants to buy a winter coat.

_____ a lot of women in the coat department,
(1)

but _____ only one clerk.
(2)

Where are you?

Simon: I'm at home. _____ a football game on TV.
(3)

Victor: I know. I think all the men are at home in front of the TV.

_____ only one man in the department—me.
(4)

Simon: That's too bad. It's a great game.

Victor: I know. _____ a TV in the store, and
(5)

_____ some nice chairs in front of the TV.
(6)

So I can watch the game too.

Simon: _____ two games today. Maybe you can watch
(7)

the next game with me.

Victor: That's great!

---

[4]A *department store* sells many different things: clothes for men and women, toys, furniture, and more.

7.6 *There Is* and *There Are*—Negative Statements

We can use *there is* and *there are* in negative statements.

Singular Count Nouns

THERE	IS	NO	SINGULAR COUNT NOUN	PREPOSITIONAL PHRASE
There	is	no	coffee machine	in the big store.
There	is	no	elevator	in the big store.
There	is	no	clerk	in aisle 3.

Noncount Nouns

THERE	ISN'T	ANY	NONCOUNT NOUN	PREPOSITIONAL PHRASE
There	isn't	any	space	in the parking lot.
There	isn't	any	coffee	in the big store.
There	isn't	any	time	for shopping now.

THERE	IS	NO	NONCOUNT NOUN	PREPOSITIONAL PHRASE
There	is	no	space	in the parking lot.
There	is	no	coffee	in the big store.
There	is	no	time	for shopping now.

Plural Nouns

THERE	AREN'T	ANY	PLURAL NOUN	PREPOSITIONAL PHRASE
There	aren't	any	lightbulbs	in this aisle.
There	aren't	any	shopping carts	in the small store.

THERE	ARE	NO	PLURAL NOUN	PREPOSITIONAL PHRASE
There	are	no	lightbulbs	in this aisle.
There	are	no	shopping carts	in the small store.

EXERCISE **3** **Change to a negative statement.**

EXAMPLE There's a small hardware store near my house. _____There are no_____ big stores near my house.

1. There are coupons for the big store. _____ coupons for the small store.

2. There are lightbulbs in aisle 3. _____ lightbulbs in aisle 5.

3. There's usually a clerk in aisle 3. _____ clerk in aisle 3 now.

4. There's an elevator in the big store. _____ elevator in the small store.

5. There's free coffee in the small store. _____ free coffee in the big store.

7.7 Quantity Words

QUANTITY	EXAMPLES
xxxxxx	There are **many/a lot of** cars in the parking lot.
xxx	There are **some** lamps in aisle 3.
xx (You need xxxx.)	There aren't **enough** clerks in the big store.
x	There is **one/an** elevator in the big store.
0	There aren't **any** lightbulbs in aisle 3. There are **no** lightbulbs in aisle 3.

EXERCISE **4** **ABOUT YOU** Use *there is* or *there are* and the words given to tell about your class and your school. Use quantity words from the chart above. You may have to change the noun to the plural form.

EXAMPLES copy machine
There's a copy machine in the library.

Korean student
There are some Korean students in this class.

1. desk for all students
2. elevator
3. computer

4. young student
5. telephone
6. African student

EXERCISE 5 **ABOUT YOU** Fill in the blanks to tell about the place where you live.

EXAMPLE There are no _____ children _____ in my building.

1. There's no _____ in my building.

2. There aren't many _____ in my building.

3. There are a lot of _____ in my building.

4. There are some _____ in my apartment.

5. There aren't enough _____ in my apartment.

6. There's a(n) _____ in my kitchen.

7. There aren't any _____ in my bedroom.

EXERCISE 6 Fill in the blanks with *any, some, many, a lot of, enough, one,* or *no* to complete this conversation. In some cases, more than one answer is possible.

CD 2, TR 24

Sue: Where are the batteries? I need _____ some _____ batteries
(example)

for the flashlight.

Rick: Look in the closet.

Sue: There aren't _____ batteries in the closet.
(1)

Rick: Look in the kitchen. There are _____ batteries
(2)

there, I think.

Sue: There's only _____ battery here. This flashlight
(3)

needs two batteries. We need to go to the hardware store and get

more batteries.

Rick: Let's go to the home supply store.

Sue: I prefer the small store. In the big store, there aren't

_____ clerks to help you. Sometimes I have
(4)

questions, but there are _____ clerks to answer
(5)

them. Or I find a clerk and he says, "That's not my department."

Rick: I don't have _____ questions about batteries.
(6)

A battery is a battery. Look at this section of the newspaper.

There are _____ things on sale at the big
(7)

store—hundreds of things.

Sue: We don't need hundreds of things. We just[5] need batteries.

[5]*Just* means only.

EXERCISE 7 Fill in the blanks with the missing words from the box below. You can combine two words to fill in some blanks. Make a contraction wherever possible.

there	they	is	are
it	not	isn't	

Rick: Let's go to the hardware store today. _____There's_____ a
(example)

sale on tools. _____ really cheap today.
(1)

Sue: Let's go to the department store. _____ a sale
(2)

on all shoes. _____ 50 percent off. Let's go to
(3)

the department store first and then to the hardware store.

Rick: _____ enough time. It's almost 4:00. The hardware
(4)

store closes at 5:30. _____ Saturday today, and the
(5)

hardware store _____ open late on Saturday.
(6)

Sue: The small hardware store _____ open late, but
(7)

the home supply store is open 24/7. You know, I don't really want

to go to the hardware store with you. I'm not interested in tools.

I have an idea. You can go to the hardware store, and I can go to

the department store. I need shoes.

Rick: Need or want? You have 20 pairs of shoes.

Sue: _____ all old. I need new shoes.
(8)

Rick: And I need new tools.

Lesson 3

Grammar
There Is and *There Are—Yes/No* Questions

There Is and *There Are—Information Questions*

Context
Smart Shopping

Choices

Before
You Read

1. Is it easy to make choices in a store? Why or why not?

2. Do you compare prices when you shop?

Read the following conversation. Pay special attention to *yes/no* **questions and information questions using** *there is* **and** *there are.*

Halina and Peter are in the supermarket.

Peter: There are many brands of shampoo. **Why are there** so many brands? Do people need so many choices?

Halina: I don't think so. **Is there** a difference between this shampoo for $2.99 and that shampoo for $7.99?

Peter: I don't know. Let's buy the cheap one.

Halina: OK. There's probably no difference.

Peter: **Are there** any other items on the shopping list?

Halina: Just two. We need sugar. The sugar is in aisle 6.

bread, sugar
rice, cheese
fruit, milk
shampoo
aspirin
dog food

(in aisle 6)

Halina: This sign says 25 ounces for 89¢. That one says five pounds for $2.18. Which one is a better buy?

Peter: I don't know. What's an ounce?

Halina: It's part of a pound.

Peter: **How many ounces are there** in a pound?

Halina: Sixteen.

Peter: We need a calculator.

Halina: No, we don't. Look. There's a small sign under the sugar. The five-pound bag is about 2.7¢ an ounce. The 25-ounce bag is about 3.5¢ an ounce. The big bag is a better buy.

Peter: You're a smart shopper. Are we finished? **Is there** anything else on the list?

Halina: Yes. There's one more thing—dog food.

Peter: Wow! Look. There are over 20 kinds of dog food.

Halina: Dogs have choices too.

Did You **Know?**

One pound = .45 kilograms. One ounce = 28.35 grams.

Vocabulary in Context

choice	There are 20 kinds of dog food. There are a lot of **choices**.
shampoo	I need to wash my hair. I need **shampoo**.
brand	Many companies make shampoo. There are a lot of **brands** of shampoo.
difference between	What's the **difference between** the cheap shampoo and the expensive one?
better buy	The large bag of sugar is a **better buy**. We can save money.
ounce	One pound = sixteen **ounces**.
calculator	I need a **calculator** to do math.

Listening Activity

CD 2, TR 27

Listen to the sentences about the conversation. Circle *true* or *false*.

EXAMPLE   There are many different brands of shampoo in the store.

(TRUE)   FALSE

1. TRUE   FALSE   4. TRUE   FALSE
2. TRUE   FALSE   5. TRUE   FALSE
3. TRUE   FALSE   6. TRUE   FALSE

7.8 *There Is* and *There Are*—*Yes/No* Questions

Compare statements and questions with *there is* and *there are*.

STATEMENT	QUESTION	SHORT ANSWER
There's a shampoo aisle.	**Is there** a tool aisle in this store?	No, there isn't.
There are large bags of sugar.	**Are there** any small bags of sugar?	Yes, there are.
There's dog food in this aisle.	**Is there** any cat food in this aisle?	Yes, there is.
Language Notes: 1. We often use *any* in questions with noncount and plural count nouns. 2. Don't make a contraction in an affirmative short answer.		

EXERCISE 1 Finish the short answers.

EXAMPLE Are there any clerks in the store? Yes, _____there are._____

1. Is there a price on the shampoo bottles? No, _____
2. Are there a lot of shoppers in the store? Yes, _____
3. Is there any dog food on sale this week? No, _____
4. Are there a lot of choices of dog food? Yes, _____
5. Is there a coupon for sugar? Yes, _____
6. Are there any shopping carts in this store? No, _____

EXERCISE 2 Complete the questions.

EXAMPLE _____Is there_____ good service in a small store? Yes, there is.

1. _____ any shoppers in the dog food aisle?
Yes, there are.
2. _____ a clerk in the dog food aisle? No, there isn't.
3. _____ any space in the parking lot? No, there isn't.
4. _____ any coupons for shampoo in the newspaper?
Yes, there are.
5. _____ an elevator in the supermarket? No, there isn't.
6. _____ a lot of shoppers today? Yes, there are.

EXERCISE 3 Ask a question with *is there* or *are there any* and the words given. Another student will answer.

EXAMPLE an elevator / in this building

A: Is there an elevator in this building?
B: No, there isn't.

1. Mexican students / in this class
2. hard exercises / in this lesson
3. new words / in this lesson
4. pictures / on this page
5. a verb chart / in your dictionary
6. a computer lab / at this school
7. public telephones / on this floor
8. a gym / at this school

7.9 *There Is* and *There Are*—Information Questions

How much/how many and *why* are common question words with *is there* and *are there*. Notice question word order.

QUESTION WORD(S)	IS/ARE	THERE	PHRASE	ANSWER
How much sugar	**is**	**there**	in the bag?	One pound.
How many ounces	**are**	**there**	in a pound?	Sixteen.
Why	**are**	**there**	20 different kinds of shampoo?	I don't know.

Compare *yes/no* questions and information questions.

YES/NO QUESTIONS	INFORMATION QUESTIONS
Are there ten items on the list?	How many items **are there** on the list?
Are there different kinds of shampoo?	Why **are there** different kinds of shampoo?
Are there many kinds of dog food?	How many kinds of dog food **are there**?
Is there a difference between this shampoo and that shampoo?	Why **is there** a difference in price?

EXERCISE 4 Read the statements. Write an information question with the words in parentheses ( ).

EXAMPLE   There are ten kinds of dog food. (how many / shampoo)

<u>How many kinds of shampoo are there?</u>

1. There are a few items on the list. (how many)

   _____

2. There are 16 ounces in a pound. (how many / in two pounds)

   _____

3. There are some people in this line. (how many)

   _____

4. There are many kinds of dog food. (why)

   _____

5. There is a pharmacy in the store. (why)

   _____

6. There's a difference in price between these two shampoos. (how much)

   _____

EXERCISE 5 Use the following words to ask and answer questions about your class or school. Use *how much* or *how many* in your questions.

EXAMPLE desks / in this class

A: How many desks are there in this class?
B: There are 20 desks in this class.

1. students / in this class
2. windows / in this room
3. paper / on the floor
4. telephones / in this room

5. men's washrooms / on this floor
6. floors / in this building
7. pages / in this book
8. grammar information / on this page

EXERCISE 6 Write questions and answers for the items in the box below.

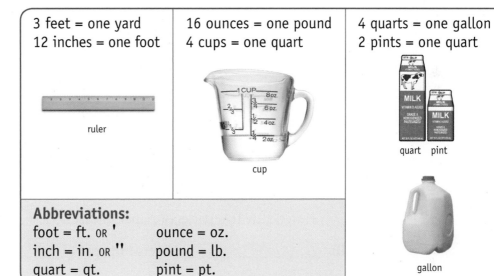

3 feet = one yard 12 inches = one foot	16 ounces = one pound 4 cups = one quart	4 quarts = one gallon 2 pints = one quart
ruler	cup	quart pint gallon

Abbreviations:
foot = ft. OR '   ounce = oz.
inch = in. OR "   pound = lb.
quart = qt.   pint = pt.

EXAMPLE How many feet are there in a yard? There are 3 feet in a yard.

1. _____

2. _____

3. _____

4. _____

5. _____

EXERCISE 7 · Fill in the blanks with the missing words from the box below.

there's	there is	there are
is there	are there	how many

CD 2, TR 28

Ali: I'm going for a walk.

Shafia: Wait. I need a few things at the supermarket. Let me look at my shopping list.

Ali: How many items _____are there_____ ?

(example)

Shafia: About ten. Also go to the office supply store. We need CDs.

Ali: Where's the office supply store?

Shafia: _____ a few office supply stores near

(1)

here. _____ one next to the

(2)

supermarket on Elm Street.

Ali: _____ CDs _____ in a package?

(3)   (4)

Shafia: You can buy a package of 50.

Ali: _____ anything else on your list?

(5)

Shafia: Yes, _____. We need computer paper for the

(6)

printer. Buy five packs of paper, please.

Ali: _____ sheets of paper _____

(7)   (8)

in a pack?

Shafia: Five hundred, I think.

Ali: I need the car. _____ enough gas in it?

(9)

Shafia: I don't think so. Please get some gas too.

EXERCISE 8 Fill in the blanks to complete the conversation. Use *there is, there are, is there,* or *are there.* Make a contraction whenever possible.

sweater

Marta: The kids need new coats. Let's go shopping today. _____**There's**_____ a 12-hour sale at Baker's
(example)
Department Store—today only.

Simon: _____ a sale on men's coats too?
(1)

Marta: Yes, _____. _____
(2)   (3)
a lot of great things on sale: winter coats, sweaters,
boots, gloves, and more.

Simon: How do you always know about all the sales in town?

Marta: _____ an ad in the store window. It says,
(4)
"End of winter[6] sale. All winter things 50% off."

Simon: Why _____ a sale on winter things? It's still winter.
(5)

Marta: Spring is almost[7] here.

Simon: It's only January. It's so cold. _____ two or
(6)
three more months of winter.

Marta: We think it's winter. But stores need
space for new things.

boots

gloves

[6]The four seasons are: *summer, fall, winter,* and *spring.*
[7]*Almost* means very close in time.

Editing Advice

1. Use the correct preposition.

   at
   Sue likes to shop ~~in the~~ night.

   in
   Your favorite program begins ~~after~~ 20 minutes.

2. Don't use prepositions with certain time expressions.

   Simon works five days ~~in~~ a week.

3. Don't use *to* after *near*.

   There's a convenience store near ~~to~~ my house.

4. Don't write a contraction for *there are*.

   There are
   ~~There're~~ 20 students in the class.

5. Don't use *a* after *there are*.

   There are ~~a~~ good sales this week.

6. Don't use a double negative.

   any
   There aren't ~~no~~ lightbulbs in this aisle.

7. Use correct word order.

   are there
   How many batteries ~~there are~~ in the flashlight?

Editing Quiz

Some of the shaded words and phrases have mistakes. Find the mistakes and correct them. If the shaded words are correct, write _C_.

Ali: I need a lightbulb for this lamp. ~~Are there~~ *C* any extra lightbulbs?
(example)

Shafia: No, there ~~isn't~~ *aren't*. We need to buy more.
(example)

Ali: Let's go ~~in~~ the hardware store. Is it open now?
(1)

Shafia: No. It's late. The hardware store isn't open ~~in the~~ night. It closes
(2)

~~in~~ 6:00 P.M. But the big store ~~near to~~ the bank is open very late.
(3)   *(4)*

Ali: ~~There are~~ a lot of things ~~in~~ sale ~~at~~ that store. Let's make a list.
(5)   *(6)*   *(7)*

Shafia: We don't need a lot of things. We only need lightbulbs.

Ali: What about batteries? ~~Are there~~ ~~a~~ batteries in the house?
(8)   *(9)*

Shafia: ~~There're~~ some AA batteries.
(10)

Ali: But we need C batteries for the radio.

Shafia: There ~~aren't no~~ C batteries in the house.
(11)

Ali: Do you want to go ~~to~~ the store with me?
(12)

Shafia: My favorite program starts ~~after~~ five minutes. Can you go alone?
(13)

Ali: OK.

Shafia: There's ~~no~~ rice in the house. Can you get some rice too?
(14)

Ali: There isn't ~~any~~ rice at the hardware store.
(15)

Shafia: Of course not. But the hardware store is ~~next~~ the supermarket.
(16)

In fact, you don't need the hardware store at all. ~~There are~~ ~~a~~ lightbulbs
(17)   *(18)*

and batteries at the supermarket too.

Ali: ~~There's no~~ need to go to two stores. Is this supermarket open ~~at night~~?
(19)   *(20)*

Shafia: Yes. It's open seven days ~~in a~~ week. And it's open ~~all night~~.
(21)   *(22)*

Expansion

Log

❶ What did you learn in this unit? Write three sentences about each of these topics:

- Shopping in the United States
- Different types of stores
- Getting a good price

❷ Write three questions you still have about shopping in the U.S.

Writing

Activity

Write five or six sentences to describe each picture. You can write affirmative or negative statements. Or you can write questions.

Picture A

Picture B

EXAMPLE

> In picture A, there are two customers in the aisle. They're Simon and Victor. Why are they in the pharmacy?

 For more practice using grammar in context, please visit our Web site.

Errands

Grammar

The Present Continuous
Tense—Affirmative Statements

Spelling of the *-ing* Form

Uses of the Present Continuous Tense

The Present Continuous
Tense—Negative Statements

Context

Mail in the U.S.

At the Post Office

Before
You Read

1. What services does the U.S. post office have? What does it sell?

2. Do you send packages to your country? Why or why not?

CD 3, TR 01 **Victor's wife, Lisa, is at the post office today. She's writing in her journal. She's learning some new words. Read the following journal entry. Pay special attention to the present continuous tense.**

November 8

It's Friday morning. People **are doing** errands. I'm at the post office. Many things **are happening** at the post office. The clerks are very busy. Many people **are waiting** in line. They**'re not getting** fast service today. But they **aren't complaining.** Halina and Dorota are first in line. Halina's daughter, Anna, is with her.

A customer at the counter has two packages. A clerk is behind the counter. The clerk **is weighing** one package. He**'s using** a scale. The customer **is holding** the second package. He **isn't paying** for the postage in cash. He**'s using** his credit card.

Marta **is picking up** a package. Amy is with her. Amy **is holding** Marta's hand. Marta **is giving** her identification (ID) to the clerk.

A customer **is using** the automated postal center. He **isn't waiting** in line. He**'s mailing** a package, and he**'s weighing** the package on the scale. He**'s paying** by credit card. The machine **is printing** the postage label. Self-service is fast.

A customer **is buying** stamps from a stamp machine. He**'s paying** in cash. He**'s not using** coins. He**'s putting** a ten-dollar bill in the stamp machine. Stamp machines in the post office give coins for change. This man **is getting** some one-dollar coins in change. Nobody **is buying** mailing supplies today.

Did You Know?

The U.S. made its first stamps in 1847. They cost 5 cents. Today people send more than 202 billion pieces of mail each year.

Vocabulary in Context

do errands	Marta's **doing errands** today. She's going to the post office and the bank.
line/wait in line	The **line** is long. The customers have to **wait in line**.
counter	The clerks work behind the **counter** at the post office.
weigh	The clerk is **weighing** a customer's package. The package **weighs** two pounds.
scale	We use a **scale** to weigh things.
postage/stamp	When we mail a package, we have to pay **postage.** When we mail a letter, we put a **stamp** on it.
customer	One **customer** is buying stamps.
pick up/package	Marta is **picking up** her **package.** She is getting it from the clerk.
hold/ hold hands	A customer is **holding** a package. He has the package in his hands. Marta is **holding** Amy's **hand.**
automated postal center	We can weigh our packages and pay for postage at the **automated postal center.** We don't need a clerk.
print	In the automated postal center, a machine weighs a package. It also **prints** the postage.
self-service	You don't need a clerk to buy stamps. You can use a machine. It's **self-service.**
mailing supplies	**Mailing supplies** are boxes and envelopes.

Listening Activity

CD 3, TR 02

Listen to the sentences about the activities in the post office. Circle *true* or *false*.

EXAMPLE   People are waiting in line at the post office.   (TRUE)   FALSE

1. TRUE	FALSE		**5.** TRUE	FALSE
2. TRUE	FALSE		**6.** TRUE	FALSE
3. TRUE	FALSE		**7.** TRUE	FALSE
4. TRUE	FALSE		**8.** TRUE	FALSE

8.1 The Present Continuous Tense—Affirmative Statements

We form the present continuous tense with a form of *be* + verb *-ing*.

SUBJECT	BE	VERB *-ING*	COMPLEMENT
I	am	mailing	a letter.
Dorota	is	waiting	in line.
Nobody	is	buying	mailing supplies.
We	are	using	the stamp machine.
You	are	picking up	a package.
The clerks	are	standing	behind the counter.

Language Notes:
1. We can make contractions with a pronoun + *be*.
    I'm mailing a letter.
    She's waiting in line.
    We're using the stamp machine.
2. We can make contractions with a singular noun + *is*.
    Lisa's writing in her journal.
3. There is no contraction for a plural noun + *are*.

EXERCISE 1 Fill in the blanks with the present continuous tense. Use contractions where possible. Use the ideas from the reading and the verbs in the box below. Answers may vary.

wear	give	weigh	help	pay	stand	buy	wait	do

EXAMPLE One customer ___'s buying___ some stamps.

1. Dorota _____ next to Halina and Anna.

2. Dorota, Halina, and Anna _____ in line.

3. Marta _____ her ID to the postal clerk.

4. Nobody _____ boxes or envelopes.

5. The clerks _____ the customers.

scale

6. A customer _____ a package at the automated postal center.

7. A lot of people _____ errands today.

8. Some customers _____ in cash.

8.2 Spelling of the -ing Form

VERB	-ING FORM	RULE
go eat look	go**ing** eat**ing** look**ing**	In most cases, add -ing to the base form.
sit plan	si**tting** plan**ning**	If a one-syllable verb ends in consonant + vowel + consonant, double the last consonant. Then add -ing.
give write	giv**ing** writ**ing**	If the verb ends in a consonant + e, drop the e. Then add -ing. Do not double the last consonant after you drop the e. WRONG: writting
show pay fix	show**ing** pay**ing** fix**ing**	Do not double final w, x, or y. Just add -ing.

EXERCISE 2 Fill in the blanks with the present continuous tense of the verb in parentheses ( ). Spell the -ing form correctly. Use contractions where possible.

EXAMPLE Marta **'s picking** _____ up a package.
(pick)

1. A man _____ some stamps from a machine.
   (get)

2. Halina _____ with Dorota.
   (wait)

3. The clerk _____ a customer's credit card.
   (take)

4. Halina and Dorota _____.
   (talk)

5. They _____ the people in the post office.
   (look at)

6. Two customers _____ machines.
   (use)

7. A man _____ money in the stamp machine.
   (put)

8. One customer _____ a package.
   (weigh)

9. Nobody _____ to buy mailing supplies.
   (plan)

10. Marta _____ her ID to a clerk.
    (give)

11. Lisa _____ in her journal now.
    (write)

8.3 Uses of the Present Continuous Tense

EXAMPLES	EXPLANATION
People **are buying** stamps now.	The action is happening now, at this time.
Halina**'s standing** near the counter. Marta and Amy **are holding** hands. Nobody**'s buying** envelopes.	The verbs *stand, sleep, sit, wear, hold,* and *wait* have no action. We use the present continuous tense to describe a present situation.
I**'m working** overtime this week. Lisa**'s learning** some new words today.	The action is happening during a specific present time period.

Language Note: Some common time expressions with the present continuous tense are: *now, right now, at the moment, at this time, today, all day, this week,* and *this month.*

EXERCISE **3** **Write two sentences about each picture with verbs from the box.**

stand	wait	wear	play	hold	give	take	write	use
leave	work	pick up	go	buy	put	mail	get	sit

EXAMPLE

This man is going into the post office. He's holding some envelopes.

1. _____
_____
_____

2. _____
_____
_____

(continued)

3. _____
_____
_____

4. _____
_____
_____

5. _____
_____
_____

6. _____
_____
_____

8.4 The Present Continuous Tense—Negative Statements

SUBJECT	BE	NOT	VERB -ING	COMPLEMENT
I	am	not	getting	mailing supplies.
Marta	is	not	buying	stamps.
You	are	not	going	to the bank.
Halina and Dorota	are	not	talking	to the clerk.

Language Note: We can make negative contractions with *be*.
Marta**'s not** using the stamp machine.   She **isn't** mailing a letter.
We**'re not** buying supplies.   We **aren't** mailing a package.
I**'m not** waiting in line. (There's only one contraction for *I am not*.)

EXERCISE 4 **Rewrite each sentence below. Make a negative sentence with the words given.**

EXAMPLE   Marta is picking up a package. (talk to Amy now)

She's not talking to Amy now.   OR   _She isn't talking to Amy now._

1. A customer is buying stamps. (use his credit card)

   _____

2. Many people are waiting in line. (complain about the service)

   _____

3. Halina and Dorota are waiting for service. (use self-service)

   _____

4. Lisa's writing in her journal. (mail a package)

   _____

5. Halina is doing errands today. (shop with Peter)

   _____

EXERCISE 5 **ABOUT YOU** **Use the words below to write true sentences about your activities at the present time. Make an affirmative or negative statement. If you write a negative statement, write a true affirmative statement also.**

EXAMPLES   I / do errands now

I'm not doing errands now. I'm doing an exercise in English.

We / use pencils now

We're using pencils now.

1. I / write in a journal

   _____

2. The teacher / wear sneakers

   _____

3. We / use a dictionary

   _____

4. The teacher / look at my ID

   _____

5. We / talk about the supermarket

   _____

(continued)

6. The students / complain about this exercise

_____

7. I / try to learn all the new words

_____

8. The teacher / help me now

_____

EXERCISE 6   **Marta has her package now. She's leaving the post office. She sees Dorota and Halina. Read their conversation. Then make two sentences about the conversation with the words given. Use the present continuous tense, affirmative and/or negative. Answers will vary.**

Marta: Hi, Dorota. It's nice to see you, Halina. How are you?

Halina: I'm fine. It's good to see you, Marta.

Dorota: Hi, Marta. I'm mailing this package to my son. He's in college now. He's living in Canada this year. As usual, this line isn't moving very fast.

Marta: The post office has services online now. The Web site has prices for all packages. You can print the postage. You can pay for it online with your credit card. Then you can give the package to your mail carrier the next day. The cost is the same. And it's fast!

Dorota: I know. But I can't weigh the package at home. I don't have a scale. I need to send this package today. My son's waiting for his winter clothes.

Marta: This post office has a new automated postal center. You can weigh the package and pay for postage from a machine now. It's over there. And nobody's waiting.

Dorota: That's OK. It's my turn now.

Marta: Amy and I are going to lunch now. Do you both want to come with us?

Halina: I'm sorry. We can't. Peter's waiting for us outside in the car.

EXAMPLE   Halina / listen

<u>Halina is listening to Marta and Dorota..</u>

<u>She isn't talking much.</u>

1. Dorota's son / live

_____

_____

2. Dorota / mail

_____

_____

3. Dorota's son / expect

_____

_____

4. Dorota / complain

_____

_____

5. Marta / talk about

_____

_____

6. Peter / wait

_____

_____

7. Marta and Amy / leave

_____

_____

Lesson 1   185

EXERCISE **7** **Complete the short conversations with an affirmative or negative verb in the present continuous tense. Use contractions where possible.**

EXAMPLE **A:** Can I use your computer?

B: Sorry, I __'m using_____ it at the moment. Can you wait?
$\qquad\qquad$ _(use)_

1. **A:** Can you mail this letter for me?

   B: Sorry, I _____ home all day today.
   $\qquad\qquad$ _(stay)_

   I _____ to the post office.
   $\qquad$ _(go)_

   I _____ my homework.
   $\qquad$ _(do)_

2. **A:** Dorota can't do these errands with you now.

   B: Why not?

   A: Her friend _____ her today.
   $\qquad\qquad$ _(visit)_

3. **A:** I need help at the post office.

   B: Victor _____ today. He can help you.
   $\qquad\qquad$ _(work)_

4. **A:** Please don't use the phone right now.

   B: Why not?

   A: Because I _____ to make an important call.
   $\qquad\qquad$ _(plan)_

5. **A:** What's wrong[1] with this stamp machine?

   B: I don't know. But it _____ right today. Let's wait in
   $\qquad\qquad$ _(work)_

   line for a clerk.

6. **A:** This post office is very busy right now.

   B: Yes. A lot of people _____ in line.
   $\qquad\qquad$ _(wait)_

7. **A:** Look at the line at the counter. It's too long.

   B: But nobody _____ the automated postal center.
   $\qquad\qquad$ _(use)_

   A: Then let's go there.

8. **A:** My credit card is in the machine. But it _____
   $\qquad\qquad$ _(print)_

   the postage label. What's wrong?

   B: I don't know. Let's ask the clerk.

[1]*"What's wrong?"* asks about a problem.

Grammar
The Present Continuous Tense
Yes/No Questions
Information Questions
Subject Questions

Context
Easy Banking

The Drive-Through

Before
You Read

1. Are there any drive-throughs in your neighborhood?

2. Which drive-throughs do you use?

Read the following conversation. Pay special attention to *yes/no* **questions and information questions using the present continuous tense.**

Americans do a lot of errands from their cars. They use drive-throughs. Marta and Amy are at their bank drive-through now.

Amy: **Are we going** home now, Mommy?

Marta: Not yet. I still have a few errands.

Amy: **Where are we going** now?

Marta: To the bank. I need some quarters for the washing machine. I can get a roll of quarters at the bank.

Amy: **Why are you turning** here, Mommy? The bank's over there.

Marta: I'm using the drive-through, and it's right here.

Amy: There's someone ahead of us. **What's she doing? Is she getting** quarters too?

Marta: I don't know. She's probably getting money. Maybe she's cashing a check.

Amy: **Who's talking?** I hear someone.

Marta: That's the teller. She's behind the window. She's using a microphone.

Amy: **What's that man doing** over there?

Marta: He's sending a deposit to the teller at the window. There's money or checks in that envelope.

Amy: **What's he holding?**

Marta: It's a tube. It's a place for his deposit. He can put checks or cash in the tube, and a machine takes the tube to the teller.

Amy: **Is the teller helping** both customers at the same time?

Marta: Yes.

Did You
Know?

Many businesses have drive-throughs: banks, restaurants, and pharmacies.

Vocabulary in Context

drive-through	Marta and Amy are using a **drive-through.** They don't have to get out of the car for service.
roll	You can get a **roll** of quarters at a bank.
turn	They are **turning** into the drive-through.
ahead of	Three people are **ahead of** us in line. We have to wait.
probably/ maybe	That customer is giving money to the teller. He's **probably** making a deposit. But **maybe** he needs money. I'm not sure.
cash a check	The woman has a check. She needs cash. She's **cashing** her **check** at the bank.
deposit (v.) deposit (n.)	We put money in the bank. We **deposit** money. The man is making a **deposit** in the bank.
teller	A **teller** is helping a customer at the bank.
microphone	The teller is using a **microphone** to talk to people.
tube	A customer is using a **tube** to send a deposit to the teller.

Listening Activity

CD 3, TR 04

Listen to the following questions about the conversation. Circle *true* **or** *false.*

EXAMPLE   Amy is asking a lot of questions.   (TRUE)   FALSE

1. TRUE   FALSE   5. TRUE   FALSE
2. TRUE   FALSE   6. TRUE   FALSE
3. TRUE   FALSE   7. TRUE   FALSE
4. TRUE   FALSE   8. TRUE   FALSE

8.5 The Present Continuous Tense—*Yes/No* Questions

BE	SUBJECT	VERB -*ING*	COMPLEMENT	SHORT ANSWER
Am	I	**using**	the right envelope?	Yes, you are.
Are	you	**talking**	to the teller?	Yes, I am.
Is	Halina	**going**	into the bank?	No, she isn't.
Are	we	**turning**	here?	No, we're not.
Are	they	**waiting**	in their cars?	Yes, they are.

EXERCISE **1** **Make a *yes/no* question with the words given. Answer the question with a short answer. Use the ideas from the conversation on page 188.**

EXAMPLE   Amy / talk to her mother
<u>Is Amy talking to her mother? Yes, she is.</u>

1. Marta and Amy / use the drive-through

   _____

2. Marta / cash a check

   _____

3. Marta and Amy / wait in the car

   _____

4. Marta / answer Amy's questions

   _____

5. the teller / help Marta now

   _____

6. the man / hold the tube

   _____

7. the man / ask for a roll of quarters

   _____

8. two customers / get service at the same time

   _____

EXERCISE **2** **ABOUT YOU** **Use the words given to ask a partner questions about his or her activities right now. Your partner will answer with a short answer first and then add information. Write the questions and answers for practice.**

EXAMPLE   (you / speak English)
A: <u>Are you speaking English now?</u>
B: <u>Yes, I am. I'm using the present continuous tense.</u>

1. you / ask for help

   _____

   _____

2. someone / help you

   _____

   _____

3. your teacher / complain about your work

_____

_____

4. you / write in your book

_____

_____

5. your teacher / stand in front of the class

_____

_____

6. you / learn a lot of new words today

_____

_____

7. you / wait for something

_____

_____

8.6 The Present Continuous Tense—Information Questions

QUESTION WORD(S)	BE	SUBJECT	VERB -ING + COMPLEMENT	SHORT ANSWER
What	**are**	you	**doing**?	Waiting for service.
Where	**is**	he	**going**?	To the drive-through.
How many people	**is**	the teller	**helping**?	Two.
Who	**is**	the teller	**helping**?	A man and a woman.
Why	**are**	we	**waiting**?	Because the teller is busy.
How	**are**	some customers	**making** a deposit?	In a tube.
Why	**are**	people	**using** the drive-through?	Because it's easy and fast.
What	**is**	Amy	**asking** about?	The drive-through.

Language Notes:
1. Sometimes a preposition (*about, to,* etc.) comes at the end of a question.
2. Remember, we can make a contraction with some question words and *is*.
   What's Amy asking about?

EXERCISE 3   **Write questions for the answers given. Use the question words:** *who, what, where, why, how many,* **and** *how.* **The underlined phrase is the answer.**

EXAMPLE   <u>What is Amy asking Marta?</u>

Amy's asking Marta <u>about the drive-through</u>.

1. _____

The teller is talking to <u>a customer</u>.

2. _____

Marta is waiting for <u>some quarters</u> at the bank.

3. _____

Marta is expecting to get <u>one</u> roll of quarters.

4. _____

The customer is putting a deposit <u>in a tube</u>.

5. _____

The teller is talking to customers <u>with a microphone</u>.

6. _____

The teller is helping <u>two</u> customers at the moment.

7. _____

Marta and Amy are talking about <u>the customers</u>.

8. _____

<u>Because it's easy and convenient to use the drive-through.</u>

EXERCISE 4   **Complete the conversation between Marta and Amy at the drive-through of a fast-food restaurant. Use the words and expressions in the box.**

are waiting	He's asking	is putting
What are you ordering	Why are we going	is it doing

🔊
CD 3, TR 05

Amy: Mommy, the sign is talking. How _____**is it doing**_____ that?
                                                    (example)

Marta: It's not the sign. It's the clerk. Look. He's over there behind the

window. _____ for our order².
                        (1)

Amy: _____, Mommy?
                    (2)

Marta: A chicken sandwich and a salad. Milk too. What about you, Amy?

²An *order* is a list of food people want from a restaurant.

Amy: Ummmmmm.

Marta: Hurry, Amy, the clerk's waiting. And customers _____ behind us.
(3)

Amy: Ummmm. I want a chicken sandwich too.

Marta: (*speaking to the clerk*) Two chicken sandwiches, two salads, and two cartons of milk, please.

Clerk: That's $7.79.

Amy: _____ to the next window?
(4)

Marta: To pick up our food. Look. The clerk _____
(5)
our lunch in a bag.

Clerk: Two dollars and 21 cents is your change. Thank you. Have a good day.

8.7 The Present Continuous Tense—Subject Questions

QUESTION WORD(S)	BE	VERB PHRASE	ANSWER
Who	**is**	**talking**?	Amy and Marta are.
What	**is**	**happening** at the bank?	Customers are doing business.
Which customer	**is**	**waiting** in line?	Marta is.
How many customers	**are**	**getting** quarters now?	One customer is.

Language Notes:
1. Use a plural verb (*are*) after *how many*, even if the answer is singular.
2. Use a singular verb (*is*) after *who*, even if the answer is plural.

EXERCISE 5 Make questions for each answer given. The underlined word or phrase is the answer. Use the question words *who, which, what,* and *how many* as subjects.

EXAMPLE Which customer is using the tube? OR Who is using the tube?

A man is using the tube.

1. _____

   The teller is using a microphone.

2. _____

   One customer is making a deposit.

3. _____

   A man and a woman are getting help now.

4. _____

   Something is happening at the bank.

5. _____

   Three customers are using the drive-through.

6. _____

   A tube is taking the man's deposit to the teller.

Editing Advice

1. Always use a form of *be* with the present continuous tense.

   is

   He working at that store.
   ^

2. Don't forget to use the *-ing* form with present continuous verbs.

   are waiting

   Marta and Amy ~~are wait~~ at the drive-through.

3. Use the correct word order in a question.

   is he

   What ~~he is~~ doing there?

4. Don't use the present continuous tense for usual or customary actions.

   works

   Sometimes Simon ~~is working~~ on Saturdays.

5. Follow the spelling rules for the *-ing* form.

   taking

   A clerk is ~~takeing~~ a customer's order.

Editing Quiz

Some of the shaded words and phrases have mistakes. Find the mistakes and correct them. If the shaded words are correct, write C.

Amy and Marta continue their conversation in the car.

Amy: Why ~~you are~~ *are you* turning here?
(example)

Marta: I need to stop at the pharmacy. A lot of cars are waiting *C* at the
(example)

drive-through. Let's go inside.

Amy: But usually you're using the drive-through. Why are we go inside now?
(1) *(2)*

Marta: The drive-through is very busy and I want to talk to a pharmacy clerk.

(inside, at the pharmacy counter)

Amy: That woman's wearing a white coat. Is she a doctor?
(3)

Marta: No. She's a pharmacy clerk. She's busy. She talking to a customer. We
(4)

have to wait.

Amy: What are they talking about?
(5)

Marta: That customer's buying aspirin. Maybe he asking about the brands of
(6) *(7)*

aspirin. Or maybe the clerk's giveing the customer advice. Now it's our turn.
(8)

(in the car again)

Marta: What are you doing, Amy?
(9)

Amy: I'm hungry. I'm eat my sandwich now.
(10)

Learner's

Log ❶ **What did you learn in this unit? Write three sentences about each topic.**

- U.S. post office services
- Drive-throughs

❷ **Write three questions you still have about the post office, banks, or drive-throughs in the U.S.**

Writing

Activity **Write a paragraph of five or six sentences about what is or isn't happening in the picture.**

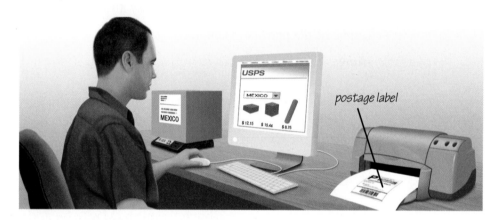

postage label

EXAMPLE

Simon is working on his computer. He isn't

going to the post office today.

 For more practice using grammar in context, please visit our Web site.

Unit

9

Making Changes

Grammar

The Future Tense with *Be Going To*
Affirmative Statements
Negative Statements
Uses
Time Expressions

Context
Baby Needs

Getting Ready for a New Baby

Before
You Read

1. What do parents have to buy for a new baby?
2. What changes in family life are necessary for a new baby?

Resale Shop
Clothing and Furniture 4 Kids

stroller   high chair   crib

🔊 **Read the following conversation. Pay special attention to affirmative and negative statements with *be going to*.**

*Shafia and her husband, Ali, **are going to have** a baby in August. Dorota and Halina are visiting Shafia. Ali is at work.*

Shafia: My baby**'s going to arrive** in two months. I'm not ready.

Dorota: Let's see. You**'re going to need** a crib, a high chair, and a car seat.

Halina: You can use my daughter's crib. She's two now, and she has a bigger bed. She**'s not going to need** the crib anymore.

Shafia: That's wonderful, Halina. Thank you. **I'm not going to need** a car seat for a while. We don't have a car right now.

Dorota: Then you**'re going to need** a stroller to take the baby outside. There's a resale shop for kids in my neighborhood. You can get a high chair and a stroller there. Resale shops are not expensive.

Shafia: What's a resale shop, Dorota?

Dorota: It's a store with used items. People take their used clothing and furniture there. The shop sells them at a low price. The money often goes to a charity. Resale shops are very popular.

Shafia: That's a great idea. We can go on Thursday.

Dorota: That's fine. But don't buy too many clothes for the baby. People **are going to give** you gifts.

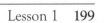

Shafia: You're right. We have a lot of relatives. We**'re not going to buy** too much.

Halina: You're also **going to need** some help for the first weeks. New babies are a lot of work. And you**'re not going to get** much sleep.

Shafia: I know. My mother**'s going to help**. She**'s going to stay** with us for the first month. She's so excited. She**'s going to be** a grandmother for the first time.

Vocabulary in Context

arrive	Ali isn't home now. He's going to **arrive** at 6 P.M.
crib	Babies sleep in **cribs**.
high chair	Babies sit in a **high chair** to eat.
wonderful	I'm so happy for your help. Your help is **wonderful**.
for a while	She's going to stay here **for a while**. I don't know how long.
stroller	You can take a baby outside in a **stroller**.
used	This furniture is not new. It's **used**.
resale shop	You don't need to buy new items. You can buy good used items at a **resale shop**.[1]
furniture	She needs baby **furniture:** a crib and a high chair.
charity	The resale shop gives money to a **charity**. The charity helps sick children.
relative	She is my husband's sister. She is a **relative** of our family.
gift	Relatives and friends are going to buy **gifts** for the baby.
get some sleep/ not get much sleep	I'm tired. I need to **get some sleep**. I **don't get much sleep** these days. I have a new baby.
excited	My family is **excited** about the baby. They're very happy.

Listening Activity

CD 3, TR 07

Listen to the sentences about the conversation. Circle *true* or *false*.

EXAMPLE Resale shops sell only new things. TRUE (FALSE)

1. TRUE	FALSE		**5.** TRUE	FALSE
2. TRUE	FALSE		**6.** TRUE	FALSE
3. TRUE	FALSE		**7.** TRUE	FALSE
4. TRUE	FALSE		**8.** TRUE	FALSE

[1]*Resale shops* are sometimes called "thrift stores."

9.1 The Future Tense—Affirmative Statements

Be Going To—Forms

SUBJECT	BE	GOING TO	VERB (BASE FORM)	COMPLEMENT
I	am	going to	need	some help.
My mother	is	going to	help	me.
We	are	going to	have	a baby.
You	are	going to	give	us a crib.
Shafia and Ali	are	going to	buy	a used high chair.
Their relatives	are	going to	help	them.
There	is	going to	be	a change in Shafia's life.

Language Note: In informal speech, we pronounce *going to* /gənə/. Listen to your teacher pronounce the sentences in the chart above.

EXERCISE **1** Fill in the blanks with the affirmative of the verb in parentheses ( ). Use the future tense with *be going to*. Make a contraction wherever possible.

EXAMPLE Shafia <u>'s going to get</u> some things for the baby.
(get)

1. Halina and Dorota _____ Shafia again on Thursday.
(see)

2. Shafia's mother _____ her with the new baby.
(help)

3. The new baby _____ soon.
(arrive)

4. Shafia's relatives _____ a lot of gifts for the baby.
(bring)

5. Halina and Dorota _____ Shafia to the resale shop.
(take)

6. Shafia _____ a stroller for the baby.
(need)

7. Shafia and Ali _____ parents for the first time.
(be)

8. With the help of her friends, Shafia _____ ready for the baby.
(be)

9. Shafia's mother _____ her daughter for a month.
(visit)

10. Shafia and Ali _____ their new baby.
(enjoy)

9.2 The Future Tense—Negative Statements

SUBJECT	FORM OF *BE* + *NOT*	*GOING TO*	VERB (BASE FORM)	COMPLEMENT
I	**am not**	**going to**	**need**	a new car seat.
Shafia's father	**is not**	**going to**	**visit**	her in August.
We	**are not**	**going to**	**buy**	a lot of things.
You	**are not**	**going to**	**give**	us a stroller.
Shafia's relatives	**are not**	**going to**	**come**	to the resale shop on Thursday.
There	**are not**	**going to**	**be**	many people at the resale shop.

EXERCISE **2** **Fill in the blanks with the negative form of *be going to*. Use the verbs in parentheses ( ). Use contractions where possible.**

EXAMPLE Shafia ___*isn't going to buy*___ a lot of baby clothes.
(buy)

1. With a new baby, Shafia and Ali _____ a lot of sleep.
(get)

2. Shafia's mother _____ for a year.
(stay)

3. Shafia _____ a car seat for a while.
(need)

4. Dorota, Halina, and Shafia _____ at the resale store today.
(shop)

5. There _____ enough space in Dorota's car for the baby
(be)
furniture.

6. Relatives _____ Shafia a crib.
(give)

7. The resale shop _____ open next Sunday.
(be)

8. Dorota and Halina _____ any baby clothes at the
(buy)
resale shop.

9. Ali _____ Shafia to the resale shop.
(take)

202   Unit 9

9.3 The Future Tense—Uses

EXAMPLES	EXPLANATION
Shafia**'s going to buy** some things for the baby.	We use *be going to* with future plans.
You**'re not going to get** much sleep.	We use *be going to* with predictions for the future.

Language Note: We often shorten *going to go* to *going*.
We're **going to go** to the resale shop next week. = We're **going** to the resale shop next week.

EXERCISE 3 **Fill in the blanks with the affirmative or negative form of *be going to* and the verb in parentheses ( ). Use the information from the conversation on page 199. Make a contraction wherever possible.**

EXAMPLES Halina and Dorota ___are going to help___ Shafia.
(help)

Shafia and Ali ___aren't going to buy___ a lot of clothes for the baby.
(buy)

1. Shafia _____ a crib.
(buy)

2. Shafia's mother _____ a grandmother.
(be)

3. Halina _____ Shafia Anna's crib.
(give)

4. Shafia _____ a high chair for the baby.
(need)

5. Shafia, Halina, and Dorota _____ to the resale shop
(go)
this afternoon.

6. Shafia's baby _____ next month.
(arrive)

7. There _____ a new baby in Shafia's house soon.
(be)

8. Shafia and Ali _____ a lot of gifts for the baby.
(get)

9. There _____ many changes in Shafia and Ali's life.
(be)

10. Shafia's mother _____ her the first month.
(help)

11. The resale shop isn't expensive. Shafia _____ a lot
(spend)
of money there.

9.4 Time Expressions

Time expressions can go at the beginning or end of the sentence. Learn the prepositions with each time expression.

EXAMPLES	EXPLANATION
She's going to visit me **in two weeks.** **In January,** he's going to visit me. They're going to visit me **in 2015.**	We use *in* with numbers of days, weeks, months, or years in the future. It means *after*. We use *in* with years or names of months.
I'm going to visit you **on January 12.**	We use *on* with dates.
On Thursday, I'm going shopping. I'm going shopping **this Thursday.**	We use *on* or *this* with names of days. *This* means a future day in a present week.
This week, I'm going to get some new clothes. My parents are going to visit **next week.**	We use *this* with future time in the same week, month, or year. Use *next* with future time after the present week.
Tomorrow I'm going to help you. I'm not going to help you **tonight.**	We use *tomorrow* for the day after today. *Tonight* means this night.
She's going to stay with us **for a while.**	*For a while* means for an indefinite amount of time.
She's going to live here **for a year.**	We use *for* with a time period.
We're going to see our relatives **soon.**	We use *soon* for a near future time that is not specific.
Ali's going to come home from work **at 6:00.**	We use *at* for a specific time in the future.

EXERCISE 4 Fill in the blanks with the correct preposition for each time expression. Use *in, on, at,* and *for.*

EXAMPLE   Shafia's going to have her baby _____in_____ two months.

1. Shafia's going to visit the resale shop _____ Thursday.

2. Shafia and Ali are going to stay in their apartment _____ a while.

3. Ali's going to be home _____ 6:00 P.M. today.

4. Ali's life is going to change a lot _____ August.

5. Shafia's mother is going to stay with her _____ a month.

6. Shafia's mother is going to arrive _____ August 10.

7. Shafia and Ali's child is going to be in school _____ 2015.

EXERCISE 5 **ABOUT YOU** Make predictions about your future. Think about your life in ten years. Use the verbs given in the affirmative or negative with *be going to*. Add more information where possible.

EXAMPLE   live in an apartment

In ten years, I'm not going to live in an apartment.

I'm going to have a house.

1. live in this city

_____

_____

2. be a student

_____

_____

3. work in an office

_____

_____

4. have a big family

_____

_____

5. be a U.S. citizen

_____

_____

6. forget my language

_____

_____

7. return to my country to live

_____

_____

8. have a car OR have a different car

_____

_____

EXERCISE **6** Look at part of Shafia's calendar for June. Write about her activities. Make affirmative and/or negative statements with *be going to* and the words given. Add a time expression in the future. Then rewrite the sentence with a different time expression. Use the expressions on page 204.

EXAMPLE Shafia / be busy

Shafia's going to be busy this month.

She isn't going to go shopping tomorrow.

TUE	WED	THUR	FRI
2 TODAY	3	4 Resale shop 1 P.M.	5
9 Doctor's appointment 3 P.M.	10	11	12 Visit Ali's parents
16	17 Exercise class 9 A.M. to 11 A.M.	18	19 Dinner with Halina and Peter 7 P.M.
23 Doctor's appointment 3 P.M.	24	25 Get ready for the trip to New York-Ali	26 Movie at home with Dorota—Ali out of town

1. Ali / be out of town

_____

_____

2. Shafia / take an exercise class

_____

_____

3. Dorota / come to Shafia's house

_____

_____

4. Shafia / see the doctor

_____

_____

5. Ali / get ready for a trip to New York

_____

_____

6. Shafia, Halina, and Dorota / go to the resale shop

_____

_____

7. Shafia and Ali / have dinner with Halina and Peter

_____

_____

8. Shafia and Ali / visit Ali's parents

_____

_____

9. Shafia / have free time

_____

_____

EXERCISE **7** **Complete the conversations. Use the verbs given in the affirmative or negative with _be going to_. Make contractions where possible.**

🔊 _Conversation A:_

CD 3, TR 08

Halina and Shafia are talking about the new baby's room.

Halina: Where's the baby's room?

Shafia: We have an extra room. It's small. But there **_'s going to be_** _____
(example: be)

enough space for a crib.

Halina: What's in the room now?

Shafia: There's a desk and a computer. But we _____
(1 leave)

them there. Ali _____ them to the living room
(2 move)

next month. His brother _____ him. The desk
(3 help)

is very heavy.

Halina: What about the color of the walls?

Shafia: We _____ them pink. But not now. There
(4 paint)

_____ enough time.
(5 be)

paint

Conversation B:

Halina, Dorota, and Shafia are talking about the baby's name.

Halina: Shafia, do you have a name for the baby?

Shafia: No. Ali and I _____ a name right now.
(1 choose)
After the baby's birth, we _____ some of our
(2 ask)
relatives for ideas. It's very important to choose the right name.

Dorota: There are long lists of names on the Web. Just search for[2] "baby
names." You can even find the meaning of each name.

Shafia: That's interesting. But the baby _____ an
(3 have)
American name. We _____ the baby a name
(4 give)
from our country.

Dorota: There are names from other countries on the Web too. There
are thousands of names for boys and girls.

Shafia: Thanks, Dorota. But we _____ to see the baby
(5 wait)
first.

> "Dorota" means gift
> from God.
> "Halina" means light.

[2]*Search for* means look for.

Grammar

The Future Tense with *Be Going To*
** *Yes/No* Questions**
** Information Questions**
** Questions with *How Long***
** Subject Questions**

Context

A Change of Address

Moving to a New Apartment

Before
You Read

1. Is it hard to move? Why or why not?

2. How do people prepare to move?

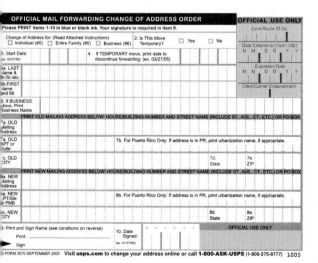

CD 3, TR 09

Read the following conversation. Pay special attention to *yes/no* **questions and information questions with** *be going to.*

Victor:	I'm going to move in two weeks. There's so much to do!
Simon:	You're right. **Are you going to hire** a mover?
Victor:	No, I'm not. I'm going to rent a truck. We don't have a lot of things. But I'm going to need some help. **Are you going to be** available on the 25th of this month?
Simon:	Sure. I can help you.
Victor:	Thanks, Simon. What should I do about my mail?
Simon:	You can fill out a change-of-address card at the post office. Or you can fill it out online. It's easy to do. The post office sends your mail to your new address for one year.
Victor:	**What's going to happen** with my phone?
Simon:	You have to call the phone company. **Is your new apartment going to be** in the same neighborhood?
Victor:	Yes, it is. Why?
Simon:	Then you can probably keep the same phone number.
Victor:	That's good. **How long is it going to take** for the new service?
Simon:	You can usually get it on the same day. There's a fee to change phone service from one place to another. But it's not usually more than $50.
Simon:	**When are you going to pack? Are you going to need** boxes?
Victor:	I'm starting to pack now. I have some boxes, but not enough.
Simon:	Go to some stores in your neighborhood. You can ask them for their old boxes.
Victor:	That's a good idea. I also have a lot of old things. **What am I going to do** with them? I don't want to move them.
Simon:	You can give them to charity. There's a resale shop in this neighborhood.

Did You **Know?**

Many Americans move every year. But the number is going down. Only 11.9 percent of Americans moved in 2008. It was the lowest number since 1948.

move (v.) mover (n.)	We're going to **move** to a new apartment in two weeks. We need a **mover** to help us with the furniture.
hire	Victor isn't going to **hire** movers. His friends are going to help him.
address	Victor's **address** is 1245 Madison Street.
truck	The car isn't big enough. You're going to need a **truck**.
rent	I can **rent** a truck for one day. It's not expensive.
neighborhood	Victor is moving close to his old apartment. His new apartment is in the same **neighborhood**.
fee	He's going to pay a **fee** to change his phone service.
pack	I'm going to **pack** my things. I'm going to put them in boxes.

Listening
Activity ◀)))

CD 3, TR 10

**Listen to the sentences about the conversation.
Circle *true* or *false*.**

EXAMPLE   Victor is going to rent a truck.   (TRUE)   FALSE

1. TRUE   FALSE   4. TRUE   FALSE
2. TRUE   FALSE   5. TRUE   FALSE
3. TRUE   FALSE   6. TRUE   FALSE

9.5 The Future Tense—*Yes/No* Questions

BE	SUBJECT	*GOING TO*	VERB (BASE FORM)	COMPLEMENT	SHORT ANSWER
Am	I	**going to**	**need**	a change-of-address card?	Yes, you are.
Is	Victor	**going to**	**move**	to another city?	No, he isn't.
Are	we	**going to**	**get**	a new phone number?	No, you aren't.
Are	Victor and Lisa	**going to**	**hire**	a mover?	No, they aren't.
Are	there	**going to**	**be**	any problems?	No, there aren't.

Language Note: Compare word order in statements and questions:
You are going to move. **Are you** going to move to a new neighborhood?
I am going to need a truck. **Am I** going to need boxes?

EXERCISE 1 **Write *yes/no* questions about Victor and Simon's conversation on page 210. Use *be going to* and the words given. Give a short answer.**

EXAMPLE   Victor / move soon

Is Victor going to move soon? Yes, he is.
_____

1. Victor / hire a mover

_____

2. he / buy some boxes

_____

3. his new apartment / be in the same neighborhood

_____

4. he / change his phone number

_____

5. it / take a long time to get new phone service

_____

6. the post office / send Victor's mail to his new address

_____

7. there / be a fee to change phone service

_____

8. Victor / move all his things to his new apartment

_____

EXERCISE 2 **Complete the short conversations. Write a *yes/no* question with *be going to*. Use the words in parentheses ( ).**

EXAMPLE   **A:** We're going to move.

   B: Are you going to move this week?
   _____
                     (this week)

1. **A:** I'm going to change my address.

   B: _____
                     (your phone number too)

2. **A:** He's going to pay for that service.

   B: _____
                     (more than $50)

3. **A:** They're going to move.

   B: _____
                     (to a house)

4. A: Simon's going to help.

B: _____
(Marta too)

5. A: Victor's not going to move all his things.

B: _____
(give some things to charity)

6. A: Victor's going to rent a new apartment.

B: _____
(in a different city)

7. A: Victor's going to get a change-of-address card.

B: _____
(online)

9.6 The Future Tense—Information Questions

QUESTION WORD(S)	*BE*	SUBJECT	*GOING TO*	VERB (BASE FORM) + COMPLEMENT	SHORT ANSWER
Why	**are**	you	**going to**	**move?**	Because my apartment is too small.
Where	**is**	Victor	**going to**	**live?**	In the same neighborhood.
What	**is**	he	**going to**	**give** to charity?	His old things.
When	**are**	they	**going to**	**get** boxes?	Next week.
How many boxes	**are**	they	**going to**	**get?**	About 50.
What kind of fee	**is**	there	**going to**	**be?**	A service fee of $50.

Language Notes:
1. Compare word order in statements and questions.
   You are going to move. When **are you** going to move?
   I am going to need boxes. How many boxes **am I** going to need?
2. Remember, some question words can contract with *is*.
   Where's Victor going to live?
   Why's he going to move?

EXERCISE 3 Ask an information question about each statement. Use the question words in parentheses ( ).

EXAMPLE A: Victor's going to get a change-of-address card. (Where)

B: _Where's he going to get it?_

1. A: I'm going to rent a truck. (When)

   B: _____

2. A: Victor's going to change his phone service. (Why)

   B: _____

3. A: There are going to be some problems. (What kind of)

   B: _____

4. A: Victor's friends are going to help him. (How)

   B: _____

5. A: You're going to need boxes. (How many)

   B: _____

6. A: The truck is going to cost money. (How much)

   B: _____

7. A: I'm going to give some items to charity. (Which)

   B: _____

8. A: We're going to get some boxes. (Where)

   B: _____

EXERCISE **4** **Look at the short answer to each question below. Then ask a question with the words given. Use the correct question word with *be going to*.**

EXAMPLE **A:** <u>When's Victor going to move?</u>
(Victor / move)

B: In about two weeks.

1. **A:** _____
(Victor and Lisa / rent)
   B: A truck.

2. **A:** _____
(the fee / be for new phone service)
   B: Less than $50.

3. **A:** _____
(they / move)
   B: Because their apartment is too small.

4. **A:** _____
(Simon / help Victor)
   B: On the 25th of this month.

5. **A:** _____
(Victor / get boxes)
   B: From a store in the neighborhood.

6. **A:** _____
(Victor and Lisa / rent)
   B: A large, three-bedroom apartment.

7. **A:** _____
(Victor and Lisa / pack)
   B: 50 boxes.

8. **A:** _____
(Victor / do)
   B: Give them to charity.

9. **A:** _____
(the phone company / change your service)
   B: On moving day.

10. **A:** _____
(you / have the same phone number)
    B: Because I'm going to live in the same neighborhood.

9.7 The Future Tense—Questions with *How Long*

EXAMPLES	EXPLANATION
A: **How long** are you going to stay? B: **Until** next week.	We use *how long* to ask about specific amounts of time. We can use *until* in answers to **how long** questions. Use *until* when the action ends at a specific time.
A: **How long** are they going to wait? B: **For** 15 minutes.	We can use *for* in answers to **how long** questions. Use *for* when the action takes an amount of time.

EXERCISE 5　**ABOUT YOU**　**Find a partner. Ask and answer questions with *How long* and *be going to* for each statement. Your partner can give an answer with *for* or *until*. Write the questions and answers.**

EXAMPLE　you / be in this class

A: How long are you going to be in this class?

B: I'm going to be in this class until the end of the semester.

1. our class / work on this exercise

A: _____

B: _____

2. we / use this book

A: _____

B: _____

3. you / stay at school today

A: _____

B: _____

4. this school / be open today

A: _____

B: _____

5. you / be a student

A: _____

B: _____

6. you / stay in the U.S.

A: _____

B: _____

9.8 The Future Tense—Subject Questions

QUESTION WORD(S)	BE	GOING TO	VERB (BASE FORM)	COMPLEMENT	ANSWER
What	is	going to	happen?		I'm going to move.
Who	is	going to	help	you?	My friends are.
How many friends	are	going to	help	you?	Two.
Which services	are	going to	change?		Only the phone service.

EXERCISE 6 Write a subject question for each statement. Use the question word(s) in parentheses ( ). Make a contraction where possible.

EXAMPLE Somebody's going to visit me. (Who)

Who's going to visit you?

1. Something's going to change. (What)

   _____

2. Many people are going to move this year. (How many)

   _____

3. Some services are going to be expensive. (Which)

   _____

4. Somebody's going to give me some boxes. (Who)

   _____

5. Something's going to happen on Thursday. (What)

   _____

6. A mover's going to help me. (Which)

   _____

7. Some apartments are going to be available. (How many)

   _____

EXERCISE **7** **Victor is calling a truck rental company. He wants to rent a truck for his move. Complete Victor's conversation using yes/no questions and information questions with be going to. Use the words in parentheses ( ).**

CD 3, TR 11

Clerk: Avery Truck Rental. How can I help you?

Victor: I need to rent a truck. I'm going to move, and I need some information about prices.

Clerk: Sure. _____Are you going to return_____ the truck here or in another city?
(example: you/return)

Victor: I'm going to return it here.

Clerk: O.K. _____?
(1 what kind of truck/you/need)

Victor: Uh . . . I don't know.

Clerk: Well, _____?
(2 how many rooms/you/move)

Victor: It's a two-bedroom apartment.

Clerk: A 15-foot truck is enough.

Victor: _____?
(3 it/have/room for my sofa)

Clerk: Oh, yes. It's going to be fine. _____?
(4 when/you/move)

Victor: In two weeks.

Clerk: _____ on the weekend or during the week?
(5 it/be)

Victor: I'm not sure. Why is that important?

Clerk: It's $20 a day more on the weekend. And we don't have many trucks available on the weekends.

Victor: _____ any trucks available two weeks from today?
(6 there/be)

Clerk: (checking computer) Sorry. Saturday's our busiest day. All of our trucks are going to be out that day.

Victor: OK, then. I can move on a weekday.

Clerk: _____ enough?
(7 one day/be)

Victor: Yes. I need it for just one day.

Clerk: OK. It's going to be $39.99 a day and 99 cents a mile.
_____, cash or credit?
(8 How/you/pay)

Victor: I'm not ready to pay now. I'm only calling about prices. Thank you.

EXERCISE 8 Complete the conversation between Victor and Simon. Use the phrases from the box below.

are going to help	I'm going to get	I'm going to invite
are you going to pack	aren't going to move	Are you going to be
We're going to meet		

Simon: When __are you going to pack__ the rest of your things?
(example)

Victor: This week. _____ more boxes today.
(1)

Simon: Ed and I can help you move on Saturday, the 25th. We're available all day.

Victor: Thanks, but the people in my new apartment _____
(2)
until Saturday. _____ available on Sunday?
(3)

Simon: I think so. How many people _____ you?
(4)

Victor: Just two of my friends. _____ at my house
(5)
at 1:00. Then later, _____ you all for pizza.
(6)

Editing Advice

1. Use a form of *be* with *going to*.

   're
   We ∧ going to shop at a resale shop.

2. Use the correct word order in questions.

   are they
   Where ~~they are~~ going to work?

3. Use the correct preposition with time expressions.

   in
   We are going to move ~~after~~ two weeks.

4. Don't forget *to* after *going*.

   to
   Victor's going ∧ rent a truck.

5. Don't forget the *-ing* on *going to*.

   going
   I'm ~~go~~ to move next week.

Editing Quiz

Some of the shaded words and phrases have mistakes. Find the mistakes and correct them. If the shaded words are correct, write C.

Dorota:
   're
   We ∧ going to have a party for Shafia. It's going to be at my house.
   (example)   C *(example)*

   Can you help me?

Halina: Sure. What kind of party are you go to have?
   (1)

Dorota: A baby shower.

Halina: Baby shower? What's that?

Dorota: At a baby shower, people have lunch together. And everyone brings a gift for the baby.

Halina: When it's going to be?
   (2)

Dorota: The party going to be next weekend, on Saturday, the 12th.
(3)   (4)

Halina: Who's going be there?
(5)

Dorota: Shafia's relatives and good friends.

Halina: Are we going to cook?
(6)

Dorota: We're going to cook some things. But we're go to buy food
(7)   (8)

at the deli too.

Halina: What time the party going to start?
(9)

Dorota: On 2 P.M.
(10)

Halina: But Peter has to work until 4 P.M. on Saturday.
(11)

Dorota: Don't worry. This shower's for women only.

Expansion

Learner's Log

❶ What did you learn in this unit? Write three sentences about each topic.

- Resale shops
- Preparing for a new baby
- Preparing to move
- Renting a truck

❷ Write two questions you still have about each topic above.

Write a paragraph of six to eight sentences about the picture. Write about what is happening now and what is going to happen.

EXAMPLE

Victor is coming out of his apartment building. He is moving today. He is going to put some boxes on the truck.

 For more practice using grammar in context, please visit our Web site.

Choices

Grammar

Comparative Forms of Adjectives

Spelling of the *–er* Form

Comparisons with Nouns and Verbs

Context

Higher Education

Community Colleges and Universities

Before
You Read

1. Where is the state university in this state?

2. What community colleges do you know about in this area?

Read the following magazine article. Pay special attention to comparative forms.

Did You Know?

There are different levels of college degrees: associate's degree, bachelor's degree, master's degree, and PhD (or doctorate)

In the U.S., many students choose to go to a community college. Students can get a two-year certificate or degree. Some students start their education at a community college. Then they go to a four-year college or university to get a bachelor's degree.

A four-year university is **more expensive than** a community college. The average tuition at a community college is $2,360 a year. At a four-year state university, it's $6,185 a year.[1] A community college is often **closer** to home **than** a four-year college. Community colleges in big cities often have several campuses.

There are other differences too. A community college often has **smaller classes than** a university. Some university classes can have **more than** 100 students. Also, students at a community college are usually **older than** students at a four-year college. The average age of students at a community college is 29. At a university, most students are between the ages of 18 and 24.

Community college students are often **busier** too. Many students have full- or part-time jobs and families. Community colleges are **more convenient than** universities for students with small children. Many community colleges offer child-care services. There are more night and weekend classes too.

Which is **better** for you: a community college or a four-year college?

Vocabulary in Context

education	We go to school to get an **education**.
certificate	My cousin has a **certificate** from a community college to work with children.
bachelor's degree	My brother has a **degree** from a four-year college. He has a **bachelor's degree** in French.
tuition	College is not free. Students have to pay **tuition** to go to college.
campus	My college has several **campuses.** There is a **campus** near my house. There is another **campus** downtown.
between	The number 20 is **between** 18 and 24.
child care	People with small children need **child care** when they work or go to school. (**Child care** is sometimes called "day care.")
offer	The college **offers** good services for students. It has child-care services and weekend classes.

[1]These statistics are from 2007-2008.

EXAMPLE You can get a two-year certificate from a community college.

(TRUE)   FALSE

1. TRUE	FALSE		**4.** TRUE	FALSE
2. TRUE	FALSE		**5.** TRUE	FALSE
3. TRUE	FALSE		**6.** TRUE	FALSE

10.1 Comparative Forms of Adjectives

We can compare two people or things.

SIMPLE FORM	COMPARATIVE FORM	EXAMPLES	EXPLANATION
old tall	old**er** tall**er**	Community college students are **older than** university students.	After a one-syllable adjective, add **-er**.
busy happy	bus**ier** happ**ier**	Community college students are often **busier than** university students.	After a two-syllable adjective that ends in *y*, change *y* to *i* and add **-er**.
simple quiet	simpl**er** **more** simple quiet**er** **more** quiet	Math 1 is **simpler than** Math 2. Math 1 is **more simple than** Math 2.	Some two-syllable adjectives have two forms: *simple, quiet, friendly, common*.
helpful crowded expensive	**more** helpful **more** crowded **more** expensive	University tuition is **more expensive than** community college tuition.	With most other two-syllable adjectives and all three-syllable adjectives, add *more* before the adjective.
good bad	**better** **worse**	A C grade is **better than** a D grade. An F grade is **worse than** a D grade.	Some comparative forms are irregular. We change the word completely.

Language Notes:
1. We use *than* to complete the comparison. We omit *than* if we do not mention the second item of comparison.
   The university is **bigger than** the college, but the college is **more convenient.**
2. We can put *much* before a comparative form.
   Those students are **much younger** than we are.
3. It is very formal to use the subject pronoun after *than*. Most Americans use the object pronoun.
   FORMAL: You are busier than **I** am.
   INFORMAL: You are busier than **me.**

10.2 Spelling of the *-er* Form

SIMPLE ADJECTIVE	COMPARATIVE ADJECTIVE	EXPLANATION
old cheap	old**er** cheap**er**	Add **-er** to most adjectives.
big hot	big**ger** hot**ter**	If a one-syllable adjective ends with consonant + vowel + consonant, double the final consonant before adding **-er**.
nice late	nic**er** lat**er**	If the adjective ends in *e*, add **-r** only.
busy easy	bus**ier** eas**ier**	If a two-syllable adjective ends in *y*, change *y* to *i* and add **-er**.

EXERCISE **1** **Write the comparative forms of the adjectives. Use correct spelling with *-er* endings. In some cases, there are two answers.**

EXAMPLES busy _____ *busier* _____

excited _____ *more excited* _____

common _____ *commoner OR more common* _____

1. convenient _____
2. big _____
3. fine _____
4. lazy _____
5. hard _____
6. funny _____
7. expensive _____
8. friendly _____
9. interesting _____
10. quiet _____

11. hot _____
12. good _____
13. kind _____
14. mad _____
15. late _____
16. bad _____
17. cheap _____
18. simple _____
19. long _____
20. beautiful _____

EXERCISE 2 Use the information in the table below to do the exercise. Fill in the blanks with the comparative form of one of the adjectives in the box. Add *than* where necessary. The numbers in the table go with the numbers in the exercise.

WILSON COMMUNITY COLLEGE	JACKSON UNIVERSITY
EXAMPLE: has night and weekend classes	doesn't have night or weekend classes
1. $90 per credit hour^2	$450 per credit hour
2. average class size = 16 students	average class size = 30 students
3. 80 percent of students have jobs	10 percent of students have jobs
4. has a child-care center	doesn't have a child-care center
5. All classes are in one building.	The campus has more than 60 buildings.
6. College opened in 1985.	University opened in 1910.
7. good for me	good for my brother

busy	good	big	convenient
old	small	expensive	

EXAMPLE Wilson is __more convenient than__ Jackson for people with day jobs.

1. Jackson is _____ Wilson.

2. Classes at Wilson are _____ classes at Jackson.

3. Most students at Wilson work full-time. Students at Wilson are _____ students at Jackson.

4. Wilson is _____ Jackson for parents with small children.

5. Jackson is _____ Wilson.

6. Jackson is _____ Wilson.

7. Wilson is good for me, but Jackson is _____ for my brother because he's finishing his bachelor's degree.

^{2}College students get credits for their classes. The number of credits usually depends on the number of hours in class per week. For a three-hour course, a student gets three credits.

EXERCISE 3 Use the comparative form of the words in the boxes to fill in the blanks. Add *than* where necessary.

convenient	cheap	busy
close	old	young

🔊 **Conversation 1**

CD 3, TR 14

A: I don't plan to go to Cassidy University. I prefer Newtown Community College.

B: Why?

A: The tuition's only $1,200 a semester. It's _____cheaper_____ than a
(example)
four-year college. Also it's _____ to my home, so I can
(1)
walk there. And the students are _____. I'm 32. A lot
(2)
of the students are in their 30s and 40s.

B: You're right. Most of the students at Cassidy University are
_____ the students at Newtown Community
(3)
College. They're under 22 years old.

Conversation 2

A: A lot of the community college students have small children. Newtown
has a child-care center. So it's _____ for people with
(1)
small children.

B: You don't have kids.

A: No. But my sister does. We're planning to take classes together. She's
got a full-time job. Her kids are 3 and 5 years old. So she's much
_____ I am. The child-care center is really good
(2)
for her.

(continued)

expensive	bad	convenient	cheap
slow	hard	interesting	good

Conversation 3

A: I prefer Cassidy University.

B: Why? The tuition is high. Cassidy is _____ Newtown.

(1)

A: I know. But I want to be a nurse, and Cassidy's nursing program is
_____ Newtown's nursing program. I can

(2)
save money with my textbooks. I can buy them online. They're
_____ online than at the bookstore.

(3)

B: But it's _____ to get your books online. Sometimes

(4)
it takes a week.

A: Yes, but it's _____. The books come right to my

(5)
house.

Conversation 4

A: I'm having a problem with my grades. My classes this semester are
_____ my classes last semester. And my grades are not

(1)
so good. My grades this semester are _____ my grades

(2)
last semester.

B: You should go to your teachers for help.

A: You're right. How are your classes this semester?

B: I love my history class, but my math class is just numbers. My history
class is _____ my math class.

(3)

EXERCISE 4 **ABOUT YOU** Compare yourself to another person.

EXAMPLE   tall _I am taller than my best friend. OR My brother is taller than me._

1. responsible _____
2. helpful _____
3. busy _____
4. funny _____
5. friendly _____
6. polite _____
7. strong _____
8. quiet _____

10.3 Comparisons with Nouns and Verbs

EXAMPLES	EXPLANATION
Part-time students need **more time** to finish college **than** full-time students do.	We can use *more* before nouns to make a comparison statement. Use *than* before the second item of comparison.
You spend **less money** at a community college. My math class has **fewer students than** my biology class.	We can use *less* or *fewer* with nouns to make a comparison. • Use *less* with noncount nouns. • Use *fewer* with count nouns.
I prefer the city college because it costs **less**. You pay much **more** at a university. I study **harder** on the weekends.	We can use a comparative form after verbs.

EXERCISE 5 **ABOUT YOU** Find a partner. Ask your partner questions about the items below. Write sentences about you and your partner with the words given. Read your sentences to the class.

EXAMPLE   have books _I have more books than Max._

1. work hard _____
2. take classes _____
3. walk _____
4. have time to relax _____
5. study _____
6. have brothers and sisters _____

EXERCISE 6 Compare Newtown Community College and Cassidy University using the information below. Add *than* where necessary. The numbers in the table go with the numbers in the exercise.

	Newtown Community College	Cassidy University
EXAMPLE: students	2,000	10,000
1. cost per credit hour	$80	$200
2. night classes	150	50
3. books in library	8,000	50,000
4. campuses	5	2
5. average number of students in a class	16	30
6. students over the age of 40	215	77
7. married students	800	200

EXAMPLE Cassidy has _____more students_____ than Newtown.

1. Newtown costs _____ per credit hour.

2. Newtown has _____ Cassidy.

3. Newtown has _____ in its library.

4. Newtown has _____ Cassidy.

5. Newtown has _____ in a class.

6. Newtown has _____ over the age of 40.

7. Cassidy has _____ Newtown.

EXERCISE 7 Shafia is in college. In her journal, she is comparing herself to Simon's daughter Tina. Tina is in high school. Fill in the blanks to complete this story. Make comparisons with adjectives, nouns, or verbs. Answers will vary.

Tina is in high school, and I'm in college. I have _____more_____ (example)

responsibilities than she does. Tina doesn't have to work, but I do.

I have a part-time job, and I'm taking 12 credit hours. I have

_____ work but _____ time to study.
    (1)   (2)

College classes are _____ high school classes. Tina
                 (3)

studies only two hours a day. I study four hours a day. I have

much _____ homework than she does.
      (4)

The class size is different too. My classes are

_____ Tina's classes. Her classes have 25 students.
   (5)

Some of my classes at college have 200 students.

Students at my college are all ages. Many students in my class are

much _____ I am. Some of them are my parents' age.
      (6)

In high school, all the students are about the same age.

Lesson 2

Grammar

Superlative Forms of Adjectives

Spelling of the *-est* Form

Superlatives with Nouns and Verbs

Context

Buying a Car

Choosing a Used Car

Before
  You Read

1. Do you have a car? Is it a new car or a used car? What kind of car is it?

2. What's your favorite car? Why?

Read the following conversation. Pay special attention to superlative forms.

Victor: I want to buy a used car. My coworker, Sam, wants to sell me his 2001 car. He wants $6,000. Is that a good price?

Simon: I don't know. **The best** way to get information about used car prices is in the "blue book."

Victor: What's the "blue book"?

Simon: The "blue book" shows prices and other information about new and used cars. It can help you. We can look at it online. Then you can make a decision.

(after Simon goes online)

Simon: Look. Here's your coworker's car.

Victor: There are three prices for the same car. Why?

Simon: The price depends on several things: condition of the car, mileage, and extras, like air-conditioning and power windows. Cars in **the best** condition with **the lowest** mileage and **the most** extras are **the most expensive.** Cars with **the highest** mileage and **the most** problems are **the cheapest.**

Victor: Sam says his car is in good condition.

Simon: **The best** way to know for sure is to take it to a mechanic. You need a good car. Repairs are very expensive.

Victor: But it costs money to go to a mechanic.

Simon: It's better to lose $200 than $6,000. But the price of the car is not the only thing to consider. Also consider fuel economy. There's a Web site that compares fuel economy. Here it is. Look. Your coworker's car gets only 19 miles per gallon (mpg). Look at these other two cars. This car gets 30 miles per gallon. This one gets 35 miles per gallon. Your coworker's car is **the cheapest** to buy but it isn't **the most economical** to use.

Victor: There's a lot to know about buying a used car!

Did You
Know?

When you buy a new or used car, you do not have to pay the asking price. The buyer can try to get a lower price from the seller.

Vocabulary in Context

coworker	Victor works with Sam. Sam is Victor's **coworker**.
make a decision	There are many choices. Victor has to **make a decision**.
condition	My car is in good **condition**. I have no problems with it.
depend on	The price of the car **depends on** miles, condition, etc.
mileage	How many miles does the car have? What is its **mileage**?
air-conditioning	**Air-conditioning** makes the car cool.
extras	This car has a lot of **extras**: air-conditioning, a CD player, etc.
like	My car has extras, **like** air-conditioning.
mechanic	A **mechanic** fixes cars.
repair	An old car needs a lot of **repairs**.
consider	You have to **consider** a lot of things before you buy a car.
fuel economy/ economical	This car doesn't use a lot of gas. This car has good **fuel economy**. It is very **economical**.

Listening Activity

CD 3, TR 16

Listen to the sentences about the conversation. Circle *true* or *false*.

EXAMPLE Victor's coworker wants to sell his car for $2,000.   TRUE   (FALSE)

1. TRUE   FALSE
2. TRUE   FALSE
3. TRUE   FALSE
4. TRUE   FALSE

5. TRUE   FALSE
6. TRUE   FALSE
7. TRUE   FALSE

10.4 Superlative Forms of Adjectives

We use the superlative form to point out the number-one item in a group of three or more. Add *the* before the superlative form.

SIMPLE FORM	SUPERLATIVE FORM	EXAMPLES	EXPLANATION
low tall	**the** low**est** **the** tall**est**	Car A has **the lowest** mileage.	After a one-syllable adjective, add **-est.**
easy happy	**the** eas**iest** **the** happ**iest**	**The easiest** way to compare prices is with the blue book.	After a two-syllable adjective that ends in *y*, change *y* to *i* and add **-est.**
simple quiet	**the** simpl**est** **the most** simple **the** quiet**est** **the most** quiet	Car A is **the most quiet.** Car A is **the quietest.**	Some two-syllable adjectives have two forms: *simple, quiet, friendly, common.*
helpful expensive	**the most** helpful **the most** expensive	Car A is **the most expensive** car.	With most other two-syllable adjectives and all three-syllable adjectives, add **the most** before the adjective.
good bad	**the best** **the worst**	Which car is in **the best** condition? Car C is in **the worst** condition.	Some superlative forms are irregular. We change the word completely.

Language Notes:
1. We often add a prepositional phrase after a superlative phrase.
   Your car is the oldest car **in the parking lot.**
2. You can use *one of the* before a superlative form. The noun after it is plural.
   The blue car **is one of the** worst car<u>s</u> in the parking lot.
3. Omit *the* after a possessive form.
   My best friend has a new car.

Car A
28,000 miles
$11,000

Car B
75,000 miles
$5,500

Car C
150,000 miles
$800

10.5 Spelling of the -est Form

SIMPLE ADJECTIVE	SUPERLATIVE ADJECTIVE	EXPLANATION
old cheap	old**est** cheap**est**	Add **-est** to most adjectives.
big hot	big**gest** hot**test**	If the adjective ends with consonant + vowel + consonant, double the final consonant before adding **-est**.
nice late	nic**est** lat**est**	If the adjective ends in e, add **-st** only.
busy easy	bus**iest** eas**iest**	If a two-syllable adjective ends in y, change y to **i** and add **-est**.

EXERCISE 1 Write the superlative form of the adjectives below. Use correct spelling with -est endings. In some cases, there are two answers.

EXAMPLES interesting _the most interesting_ early _the earliest_

1. convenient _____
2. big _____
3. fine _____
4. lazy _____
5. funny _____
6. expensive _____
7. friendly _____
8. quiet _____
9. hot _____
10. good _____
11. kind _____
12. mad _____
13. late _____
14. helpful _____
15. busy _____
16. common _____

EXERCISE 2 Victor is comparing three cars. Write superlative sentences about these three cars, using the information in the table and the words in the box on the following page.

	CAR A	CAR B	CAR C
mileage	28 mpg	25 mpg	20 mpg
size	big enough for four passengers	big enough for five passengers	big enough for six passengers
year	2002	2008	2006
cost	$4,000	$12,000	$10,000
condition	needs work	in very good condition	in average condition

expensive	big	economical	old
good	cheap	bad	new

EXAMPLE   Car A gets 28 miles per gallon. It's __the most economical__ .

1. Car C is _____ inside.
2. Car A is from 2002. It's _____.
3. Car B is from 2008. It's _____.
4. Car B costs $12,000. It's _____.
5. Car A costs $4,000. It's _____.
6. Car B is in very good condition. It's _____.
7. Car A is in very bad condition. It's _____.

EXERCISE 3   **Fill in the blanks with the superlative form of one of the words from the boxes. Answers may vary.**

big	hard	close	good	convenient

Part A:

1. *On the phone:*

Shafia: I need your help. I want to buy a car. This is one of

_____the biggest_____ decisions of my life. What's
        (example)

_____ car?
        (1)

Dorota: I can't answer that question. It depends on your needs.

2. *At home:*

Marta: This is your last year of high school. Let's talk about college

for you. I prefer Lake College for you because it's

_____ to our home. It's _____
        (2)   (3)

because you can walk there.

Tina: But Lake College isn't very good. I want to go to

_____ college in the U.S. I want to be a doctor.
        (4)

Marta: It takes many years to be a doctor. You are choosing one of

_____ professions[3].
        (5)

Tina: I know, but I really want to be a doctor. I'm

_____ student in my biology class.
        (6)

[3]A *profession* is a job for a person with a college degree.

hard	slow	early	economical
easy	fast	good	expensive

Part B:

3. *At the college:*

Halina: Which English class should we take?

Shafia: How about⁴ this one? It starts at 8:00 A.M. It's

_____ class in the day.

(1)

Halina: I don't like morning classes. How about this one?

Shafia: No, no. Not that one! That teacher is _____

(2)

at the school.

4. *At the electronics store:*

Halina: I need to buy a new computer. My old computer is slow. I want

to buy _____ one. How about this one?

(3)

Peter: Yes, it's fast. But look at the price! It's _____

(4)

computer in the store!

5. *At the post office:*

Halina: What's _____ way to send this package? I need

(5)

to save money.

Clerk: You can send it by third-class mail.

But it's _____ way. It can take a week.

(6)

EXERCISE 4   **ABOUT YOU** **Write about the number-one person in your family for each of these items.**

EXAMPLE   tall _My brother Tim is the tallest person in our family._

1. helpful _____

2. beautiful _____

3. interesting _____

4. serious _____

5. funny _____

6. old _____

7. good at sports _____

8. bad at sports _____

⁴We use *how about* to offer a helpful idea.

10.6 Superlatives with Nouns and Verbs

EXAMPLES	EXPLANATION
Which car uses **the most gas**?	We can use *the most* before nouns to make superlative statements.
I want to spend **the least money** possible. This car has **the fewest extras.**	We can use *the least* and *the fewest* before nouns. • Use *the least* with noncount nouns. • Use *the fewest* with count nouns.
Which car costs **the least**? Who drives **the best** in your family?	We can use a superlative form after verbs.

EXERCISE 5 Victor and Simon are looking at car prices online. Fill in the blanks with the superlative forms of the words from the box. Answers may vary.

repairs	cheap	good
economical	extras	expensive

CD 3, TR 17

Victor: Look at these ten cars. Should I get ___the cheapest___ car?
(example)

Simon: _____(1)_____ is sometimes _____(2)_____.

Victor: How is that possible?

Simon: The cheapest car sometimes needs _____(3)_____. You should also consider fuel economy. This car gets 35 miles per gallon. It's _____(4)_____.

Victor: But I like this one _____(5)_____.

Simon: That one gets only 22 miles per gallon.

sunroof

Victor: But it has _____(6)_____: air-conditioning, power windows, sunroof, and more.

Simon: You want my advice, right? This is my _____(7)_____ advice.

EXERCISE **6** **ABOUT YOU** **Form a group with three or more classmates. Find the answers to these questions. Report your answers to the class.**

1. Who speaks the most languages?
2. Who's the youngest?
3. Who's the best student?
4. Who has the longest last name?
5. Who's the newest immigrant?
6. Who's the shortest?
7. Who has the largest family?
8. Who lives the closest to the school?
9. Who's taking the most classes?
10. Who talks the most in class?

EXERCISE **7** **Fill in the blanks with the comparative or superlative form of the word in parentheses ( ). Add *than* or *the* where necessary.**

1. Gas in Europe is _____ gas in the U.S.
   (expensive)

2. There are three kinds of gas. Premium gas is _____.
   (expensive)

3. Can you help me buy a used car? You have _____
   (information)
   I do.

4. I have many choices. I'm thinking of buying _____
   (economical)
   car.

5. Is a Japanese car _____ an American car?
   (good)

6. This car is _____ that car.
   (cheap)

7. I'm looking at three cars. This car is _____ of all
   (pretty)
   of them. And it is in _____ condition. It probably
   (good)
   needs _____ repairs.
   (few)

8. My new car is _____ my old car.
   (beautiful)

9. A car is _____ a bicycle.
   (convenient)

Editing Advice

1. Don't use *-er* and *more* together.

   My new car is ~~more~~ better than my old car.

2. Don't use *-est* and *most* together.

   I want to buy the ~~most~~ cheapest car.

3. Use *than* before the second item of comparison.

   This car is more expensive ᵗʰᵃⁿ that car.

4. Don't confuse *then* and *than*.

   My English class is easier ~~then~~ ᵗʰᵃⁿ my math class.

5. Use *the* before a superlative form.

   Which is ᵗʰᵉ best college in this city?

6. Don't use *more* in superlative statements.

   My brother is the ~~more~~ ᵐᵒˢᵗ interesting person in my family.

7. Use correct spelling with the comparative and superlative forms.

   My brother is the ~~lazyest~~ ˡᵃᶻⁱᵉˢᵗ student in his class.

   My English class is ~~biger~~ ᵇⁱᵍᵍᵉʳ than my art class.

8. Don't use *the* with a possessive form.

   Math is my ~~the~~ worst subject in school.

Editing Quiz

Some of the shaded words and phrases have mistakes. Find the mistakes and correct them. If the shaded words are correct, write C.

Halina wants to get a new job soon. She needs child care for Anna during the day.

Halina: I have to find good child care for Anna. Can you help me find ˄ best *(the) (example)*

one for my family? You know more about this than I do.
(C) (example) (1)

Marta: Let's look for information on the Internet. That's the easyest way
(2)

to get information. Here's a list of ten child-care centers in this city.

Halina: Play-Time is the more expensive. It's too expensive for me.
(3)

What about these two, Kiddy-Place and Tiny Tot?

Marta: I think Kiddy Place is more better for you then Tiny-Tot. It's very close
(4) (5)

to your home. So it's more convenient for you. How old is Anna now?
(6)

Halina: She's two and a half.

Marta: Kiddy-Place only takes children three years old and older. We have
(7)

to find a place that takes more younger children.
(8)

Halina: What about this one, Baby Bear? It's cheaper Kiddy-Place and
(9)

closer to my house.
(10)

Marta: That's a good choice. My sister has three boys, and

her the youngest son goes to that child-care center. Her son loves it,
(11)

and she's very happy with it too.

Halina: You always give me best advice. Thanks for your help.
(12)

Expansion

Learner's Log

1 What did you learn in this unit? Write three sentences about each topic.

- Community colleges and four-year universities
- Comparing used cars

2 Write three questions you still have about each topic above.

Writing Activities

1 Write a paragraph. Compare three classes you are taking (for example: math, grammar, and reading). Write six or seven superlative sentences about your classes. Write about hours of class each week, price of books, how easy the classes are, your grades in the classes, the amount of homework, how many students are in the classes, and how important each class is for you.

EXAMPLE   My chemistry class has the most credit hours.

2 Write six or seven sentences about the pictures. Compare Shafia's and Halina's English classes. Compare the room, the desks, the teachers, the time of class, and the homework.

Shafia's English class

Halina's English class

EXAMPLE

Shafia's class has fewer students than Halina's class.

 For more practice using grammar in context, please visit our Web site.

Getting a Job

Lesson 1

Grammar

The Past Tense of *Be*
Affirmative and Negative Statements
Time Expressions in the Past
Yes/No Questions
Information Questions
Subject Questions

Context

Job Applications

Applying for a Job in a Store

Before
You Read

1. What jobs can people get in stores?

2. How do people look for jobs?

CD 3, TR 18 **Read the following conversation. Pay special attention to the past tense of the verb *be*.**

Halina is talking to Dorota on the phone.

Dorota: Hi, Halina. I **was** at your house several hours ago, but you **weren't** home.

Halina: I **was** at Baker's Department Store today.

Dorota: **Were** there any good sales?

Halina: I **wasn't** there for the sales. I **was** there to apply for a job as a clerk. Positions are available now for the holidays. A lot of people **were** there, but they **weren't** happy. There **was** a long line to apply for jobs.

Dorota: **Were** there interviews today too?

Halina: There **were** no interviews. I **was** surprised. The application **was** on a computer.

Dorota: Many big stores have job applications on the computer now. Employers usually interview people later. How **were** the questions on the application? **Were** they hard to answer?

Halina: They **weren't** hard at all. They **were** easy. The first questions **were** about my job history and education. There **were** questions about references. You **were** one of my references, Dorota.

Dorota: You can use me as a reference anytime. What **were** some other questions?

Halina: There **were** some funny questions. One **was:** "Your job starts at 8:00. Where should you be at 8:00? A) in the parking lot, B) in the employees' room, or C) in your department."

Dorota: That's interesting. What **was** your answer?

Halina: It **wasn't** A or B. Time is important here. It **was** C, of course.

Vocabulary in Context

apply for	I want to **apply for** a new job. I have to fill out an application.
position	There are jobs available at Baker's. What **position** do you want to apply for?
the holidays	Store employers often hire extra clerks in November and December before the Christmas and New Year **holidays**.
interview (v.) interview (n.)	People from the store are going to talk to me. They are going to **interview** me. The **interview** is tomorrow.
employer/ employee	My **employer** has a big business. He hires new people each year. These people are his **employees**.
reference	Dorota is a **reference** for Halina. Employers are going to call her. They're going to ask her questions about Halina.
as	He uses his past employers **as** references. She works **as** a cashier. He wants a job **as** a clerk.

Listening Activity

CD 3, TR 19

Listen to the sentences about the conversation. Circle *true* or *false*.

EXAMPLE   Halina wants a job in a department store.   (TRUE)   FALSE

1. TRUE	FALSE		**5.** TRUE	FALSE	
2. TRUE	FALSE		**6.** TRUE	FALSE	
3. TRUE	FALSE		**7.** TRUE	FALSE	
4. TRUE	FALSE				

11.1 The Past Tense of *Be*—Affirmative Statements

Affirmative Statements with *Was*

SUBJECT	BE	COMPLEMENT
I		at the store this morning.
It		crowded.
Dorota		at home.
She	**was**	busy.
Peter		at home.
He		with Anna.
There		a long line at the store.

Affirmative Statements with *Were*

SUBJECT	BE	COMPLEMENT
You		at home.
We		in line.
The questions	**were**	easy.
They		sometimes funny.
There		a lot of questions.

EXERCISE **1** **Fill in the blanks with *was* or *were*. Use the information from the conversation on page 249.**

EXAMPLE Halina ___was___ at Baker's Department Store today.

1. Halina's job application _____ online.
2. Some of the questions _____ funny.
3. The application _____ easy to fill out.
4. There _____ questions about Halina's job history on the application.
5. People _____ in line for jobs at Baker's today.
6. Dorota _____ at Halina's house today.
7. Positions _____ available today for the holidays.
8. There _____ a question about time.

11.2 The Past Tense of *Be*—Negative Statements

Negative Statements

SUBJECT	BE	COMPLEMENT
I	**was not**	late.
The store	**wasn't**	open until 8:00 A.M.
We	**were not**	happy in line.
The questions	**weren't**	hard.

Language Notes:

1. Use *not* to form the negative. The contractions are *wasn't* and *weren't*.
2. After *there,* you can use *wasn't/weren't any* or *was/were no*.

There **weren't any** interviews today.   There **wasn't any** time for questions.

OR   OR

There **were no** interviews today.   There **was no** time for questions.

EXERCISE **2** **Fill in the blanks with the affirmative or negative form of the verb *be* in the past tense. Use the ideas from the conversation on page 249.**

EXAMPLES Halina ____was____ at the store to apply for a job.

She __wasn't__ there to shop.

1. The questions on the application _____ hard.

2. The question about time _____ funny for Halina.

3. Anna _____ with Halina today. Anna _____ at home with Peter.

4. Some people _____ happy because the lines were long.

5. There _____ questions about references.

6. Simon _____ one of Halina's references.

7. There _____ some positions available for the holidays.

8. There _____ any interviews today.

9. Halina _____ surprised by the funny questions.

11.3 Time Expressions in the Past

EXAMPLES	EXPLANATION
I was at Baker's two days **ago**.	We use *ago* with numbers of minutes, hours, days, weeks, months, or years. It means *before now*.
Dorota wasn't at work **yesterday**.	*Yesterday* is the day before today.
We were at the store **last week**. They weren't with us **last night**.	We use *last* with the words *night*, *week*, *month*, and *year*. It means the night, week, month, or year before the present one.

EXERCISE 3   **ABOUT YOU** Make statements about you. Use the words given. Use the affirmative or negative form of *be* in the past tense.

EXAMPLE   in a department store two hours ago

     <u>I wasn't in a department store two hours ago.</u>

1. late for work (or class) last week

   _____

2. at a job interview yesterday

   _____

3. an employee of a store last year

   _____

4. an employer in my country

   _____

5. in my country last year

   _____

6. surprised by the questions on Halina's application

   _____

7. with my family last weekend

   _____

8. at a different school a few months ago

   _____

9. in college in my country

   _____

11.4 The Past Tense of *Be*—*Yes/No* Questions

BE	SUBJECT	COMPLEMENT	SHORT ANSWER
Was	I	on time today?	Yes, you were.
Was	Halina	at home this morning?	No, she wasn't.
Were	you	surprised by the questions?	Yes, I was.
Were	Anna and Peter	with you?	No, they weren't.
Was	there	a line at the store?	Yes, there was.
Were	there	any interviews today?	No, there weren't.

Language Note: Compare statements and *yes/no* questions:
    You were at Baker's. **Were you** on time?
    There was an application online. **Was there** a paper application?

EXERCISE **4**   **Write a *yes/no* question about each statement. Use the words in parentheses ( ). Answer with a short answer. Use the ideas from the conversation on page 249.**

EXAMPLE   Halina was at Baker's Department Store today. (at a job interview)

Was she at a job interview? No, she wasn't.
_____

1. Many people were at Baker's today. (to apply for jobs)
_____

2. There were questions on Halina's application. (about her family)
_____

3. The job application was online. (easy to fill out)
_____

4. Halina was surprised. (by some of the questions)
_____

5. Many people were in line. (for interviews)
_____

6. Halina wasn't home this morning. (with Dorota)
_____

11.5 The Past Tense of *Be*—Information Questions

QUESTION WORD(S)	BE	SUBJECT	COMPLEMENT	ANSWER
When	**was**	Baker's	open?	Early this morning.
How long	**was**	Halina	at Baker's?	For about an hour.
Who	**was**	your last employer?		Community Bank.
How	**was**	your job	at Community Bank?	It was great!
Where	**were**	the job applications?		Online.
Why	**were**	there	a lot of people at Baker's?	Because there were jobs available.

Language Note: Compare statements and information questions:
The line **was** long. How long **was the line**?

EXERCISE 5 **Complete the short conversations. Ask an information question about each statement. The underlined words are the answers.**

EXAMPLE   **A:** I wasn't at work today.

B: <u>Where were you?</u>

A: I was <u>at a job interview</u>.

1. **A:** My employer was surprised.

   B: _____

   A: <u>Because I was an hour late for work</u>.

2. **A:** There were a lot of questions on the application.

   B: _____

   A: They were <u>easy</u>.

3. **A:** They were out of town for the holidays.

   B: _____

   A: <u>In Florida</u>.

4. **A:** I was at Baker's several days ago.

   B: _____

   A: <u>On December 23</u>.

5. **A:** We were in your country last year.

   B: _____

   A: <u>For about 3 months</u>.

11.6 The Past Tense of *Be*—Subject Questions

QUESTION WORD(S)	BE	COMPLEMENT	ANSWER
What kinds of questions	**were**	on the application?	Questions about education and job history.
How many employees	**were**	late today?	Only one.
Which employee	**was**	late?	The new employee.
Who	**was**	at Baker's?	Halina was.
What	**was**	on the Web site?	The job application was.

EXERCISE **6** Complete the short conversations with information questions as subjects. Use *be* in the past tense.

EXAMPLE   **A:** Some employees were at the office yesterday.

B: Who *was there?* _____

1. **A:** Many questions were on the application.

B: What kinds of _____

2. **A:** Some people were surprised.

B: Who _____

3. **A:** Positions were available in that company last month.

B: How many _____

4. **A:** Something was wrong with your application.

B: What _____

5. **A:** Some of the questions were funny.

B: Which _____

EXERCISE **7** Shafia is interested in Halina's job application. She is asking a lot of questions. Fill in their conversation with items from the box below. You can use some items more than once.

there were	were	was	what was
were there	weren't	wasn't	were you

🔊
CD 3, TR 20

Shafia: So, your application was on a computer. *Were you* OK with that?
(example)

Halina: Sure. I know a lot about computers. The computer was an

important part of my job in Poland.

Shafia: _____ your job in Poland?
(1)

Halina: I was a department manager in the shoe department of a big store. Part of my job was to write reports.

Shafia: _____ a lot of questions about your job
(2)
history? American employers are very interested in that.

Halina: Yes, but I have a very short job history.

Shafia: _____ it difficult to find references? I worry
(3)
about that. I don't know many people here.

Halina: I can always use Dorota as a reference. And two references
_____ my college teachers. It
(4)
_____ difficult to find references. People are
(5)
happy to be a reference for you.

Shafia: _____ any questions about American work
(6)
customs? Those are difficult. I don't know much about work
customs here.

Halina: _____ some questions. But they
(7)
_____ difficult to answer. There were three
(8)
possible answers. It _____ easy to choose
(9)
the correct answer most of the time.

Grammar

The Simple Past Tense—Affirmative
Regular Forms
Spelling of the *-ed* Form
Irregular Forms

The Simple Past Tense—Negative

Context

Job Interviews

Applying for a Job in an Office

Before You Read

1. Do you want a job in an office? Why or why not?

2. Where do you want to work? Why?

My old job was difficult.

Read the following conversation. Pay special attention to simple past tense verbs, affirmative and negative.

Halina: I **had** a job interview today.

Dorota: Great! Was it at Baker's Department Store?

Halina: No. I **applied** for a job in an office. I **saw** an ad online for a sales position a few weeks ago. I **sent** my résumé. And they **called** me yesterday. I **went** for the interview this morning.

Dorota: That was fast. How was the interview?

Halina: Well, I **didn't get** there on time. I **didn't find** parking close to the office building. I **had to park** three blocks away.

Dorota: How late were you?

Halina: Only 15 minutes.

Dorota: Next time, go to the place the day before the interview. You can check travel time and parking then.

Halina: I **didn't like** the interview, Dorota. It **took** an hour. There were two people behind a desk. They **asked** me a lot of questions. And I was nervous.

Dorota: What were some of the questions?

Halina: Well, one question was, "Why do you want this job?" I **told** them the truth. My last job was difficult. I **worked** a lot of hours. I **didn't make** enough money.

Dorota: You shouldn't complain about your past jobs. Instead, say positive things about this new company.

Halina: I **did**. I **told** them some good things. Their company isn't too far from my neighborhood. It's easy to get there. I **didn't complain** about the parking.

Dorota: But you **didn't say** anything about the company. Find some information on the company's Web site. What does the company do? What do you like about it? It's important to know something about the company.

Halina: I **made** a lot of mistakes in this interview. I **said** the wrong things.

Dorota: Don't worry. It was good practice. The next time is going to be easier. You're going to be more prepared.

Did You Know?

Sometimes companies hire people for 90-day trial periods. If the employee does good work, he or she can be a regular employee.

Vocabulary in Context

sales position	Halina wants a **sales position**. She wants to sell things in a store.
résumé	Your **résumé** is very important. It shows your job history and your education history.
get (to a place)/ get there	The company is near my house. It's easy to **get to** the office. I can **get there** by bus.
block	Halina parked three **blocks** from the office.
difficult	My last job was **difficult.** It was hard for me.
instead	Don't drive. Take the bus **instead**.
positive	Don't complain. Say something **positive** instead.
make mistakes	Some of her answers on the test were wrong. She **made mistakes**.
prepared	It's important to be **prepared** for a job interview.
nervous	I answered some questions wrong. I was **nervous.**

Listening Activity

CD 3, TR 22

Listen to the sentences about the conversation. Circle *true* or *false*.

EXAMPLE   Halina made mistakes in her job interview.   (TRUE)   FALSE

1. TRUE   FALSE   5. TRUE   FALSE

2. TRUE   FALSE   6. TRUE   FALSE

3. TRUE   FALSE   7. TRUE   FALSE

4. TRUE   FALSE

11.7 The Simple Past Tense of Regular Verbs—Affirmative Statements

We add -ed to the base form of the verb to form the simple past tense of regular verbs.

SUBJECT	VERB + -ED	COMPLEMENT
I	**complained**	about my last job.
Halina	**filled out**	the application.
She	**needed**	a reference.
We	**talked**	about my job history.
You	**wanted**	a better job.
The employers	**asked**	me a lot of questions.

Language Note: The simple past tense of regular verbs is the same for all persons:
 I **worked** hard.   She **worked** hard.   They **worked** hard.

Pronunciation Note: The -ed ending has three sounds: /d/, /t/, and /ɪd/. We pronounce the /ɪd/ sound if the verb ends in a t or d sound. Listen to your teacher pronounce the following sentences:

/d/ Peter **stayed** home.   /t/ She **parked** three blocks away.
     Halina **used** the car.   I **talked** about my last job.

     /ɪd/ You **expected** to get the job.
          I **decided** to try again.

EXERCISE 1 Fill in the blanks with the simple past tense of the verb in parentheses ( ).

EXAMPLE   Halina _____ parked _____ three blocks from the office building.
                      (park)

1. Halina _____ an application for a sales position.
                (fill out)

2. A company _____ Halina for an interview.
                    (call)

3. Two people _____ Halina.
                   (interview)

4. The people _____ Halina about her job history.
                    (ask)

5. Halina _____ about her old job.
                (complain)

6. Dorota and Halina _____ about the interview.
                          (talk)

7. Halina _____ references for this position.
                (need)

8. She _____ Dorota as a reference.
             (use)

11.8 Spelling of the -ed Form

BASE FORM	PAST FORM	EXPLANATION
work	work**ed**	For most verbs, add **-ed** to the base form.
live	live**d**	If the verb ends in e, add **-d** only.
study	stud**ied**	If the verb ends in consonant + y, change y to *i* and add **-ed**.
stay	stay**ed**	If the verb ends in a vowel + y, do not change the y to *i*.
shop	sho**pped**	Double the final consonant if a single syllable word ends in consonant + vowel + consonant.

EXERCISE 2 Fill in the blanks with the simple past tense of the verb in parentheses ( ). Use the spelling rules from chart 11.8 above.

EXAMPLE   I _____liked_____ my job in that company.
                  (like)

1. Halina _____ for the sales position.
                  (apply)
2. Employees in that company _____ business in college.
                                        (study)
3. You _____ the car in front of the office building.
         (stop)
4. Several employees _____ to work on Saturday.
                          (plan)
5. We _____ at the interview for half an hour.
         (stay)
6. Baker's _____ new workers for the holidays.
              (hire)

11.9 The Simple Past Tense of Irregular Verbs—Affirmative Statements

Some verbs do not use -ed to form the past tense. We call these irregular verbs. Here are some common irregular verbs.

BASE FORM	PAST FORM	BASE FORM	PAST FORM	BASE FORM	PAST FORM
take	**took**	say	**said**	send	**sent**
have	**had**	tell	**told**	go	**went**
get	**got**	make	**made**	see	**saw**
know	**knew**	give	**gave**	do	**did**

Language Notes:
1. We use irregular forms in the affirmative statements and in subject questions.
2. For a list of irregular past tense forms, see Appendix D.

EXERCISE **3** Fill in the blanks with the simple past tense of a verb from the box below. Use chart 11.9 to check for irregular forms of the simple past tense.

see	have	send	give
go	get	tell	take

EXAMPLE Halina _____ saw _____ two people at her interview.

1. Halina _____ a job interview last week.
2. She _____ her résumé to a company.
3. She _____ to the office building for an interview.
4. The interview _____ an hour.
5. Halina _____ information about the job online.
6. Halina _____ Dorota about her interview.
7. Dorota _____ Halina some good advice.

11.10 The Simple Past Tense—Negative Statements

We use *didn't* + the base form for the negative of both regular and irregular verbs in the past. *Didn't* is the contraction for *did not*.

SUBJECT	*DIDN'T*	VERB (BASE FORM)	COMPLEMENT
I	**didn't**	work	at Baker's last year.
Halina	**didn't**	arrive	on time.
My employer	**didn't**	hire	any new employees.
You	**didn't**	apply	for the job.
We	**didn't**	know	all the answers.
They	**didn't**	give	the right answer.

Language Note: Compare the affirmative and the negative.
She **worked** on Saturday. She **didn't work** on Sunday.
They **went** by car. They **didn't go** by bus.

EXERCISE 4   Use the words in parentheses ( ) to make a negative statement about the sentence given.

EXAMPLE   Halina said many things. (positive things about the company)

But *she didn't say positive things about the company.*

1. Halina parked her car. (close to the office building)

   But _____

2. Halina had an interview for an office job. (at Baker's)

   But _____

3. Dorota went with Halina to the supermarket. (to her job interview)

   But _____

4. The new employees worked during the week. (on the weekends)

   But _____

5. Halina used Dorota as a reference on her application. (Simon)

   But _____

EXERCISE 5   Complete the short conversations with the affirmative or negative of the verb in parentheses ( ). Use the simple past tense.

EXAMPLES   A: I used you and Dorota as references on a job application.

   B: Yes, I know. The company _____*called*_____ Dorota yesterday.
   (call)

   But they _____*didn't call*_____ me.
   (call)

1. A: Halina applied for a job at Baker's last month.

   B: Yes, but she _____ the job. She's still looking
   (get)
   for a job.

2. A: You look nervous. What's wrong?

   B: I _____ a big mistake at work today.
   (make)

3. A: You didn't apply for the sales position. Why?

   B: I _____ time. I'm going to apply next week.
   (have)

4. A: I was surprised by the news.

   B: We were all surprised. We _____ this news.
   (expect)

5. A: Why did you leave your last job?

   B: The company _____ me out of town on business
                       (send)

       too often. I _____ my family enough.
                    (see)

6. A: You have a new job now.

   B: I know. Your friend Jesse _____ me.
                           (tell)

EXERCISE 6 **ABOUT YOU** **Use the words given to talk about your past activities. Make an affirmative or negative past tense sentence.**

EXAMPLE work on weekends in my country
I worked on weekends in my country. OR I didn't work on weekends.

1. apply to come to this school

_____

2. use the computer to fill out the application

_____

3. go to high school in my country

_____

4. take a test to enter this class

_____

5. study English in my country

_____

6. get a job my first month in the U.S.

_____

7. take classes at a different school last year

_____

8. see my friends last night

_____

9. need to buy a book for this class

_____

10. make a lot of mistakes in this exercise

_____

EXERCISE **7** **Complete the conversation between Dorota and Halina about another job interview three weeks later. Use the affirmative or negative of the verb in parentheses ( ). Use the simple past tense.**

CD 3, TR 23

Halina: Thanks for your advice about interviews, Dorota. Unfortunately[1],

I _____*didn't get*_____ the sales position. But I
(example: get)

_____ another interview this morning. It was
(1 have)

for a position in another company. I _____
(2 make)

any mistakes this time.

Dorota: That's good.

Halina: I was on time. And I was prepared. I _____ about
(3 learn)

the company on the Web first. I _____ the
(4 tell)

interviewers positive things about their company.

I _____ about my old job. I was lucky too. They
(5 complain)

_____ about Anna. I'm not sure about child
(6 ask)

care for her yet.

Dorota: Don't worry, Halina. They can't ask any personal questions in a

job interview. It's against the law.

Halina: Really? I _____ that.
(7 know)

[1]We use *unfortunately* to introduce bad news.

Grammar

The Simple Past Tense
Yes/No **Questions**
More Irregular Verbs
Information Questions
Subject Questions

Context

Choosing a Career

Jobs of the Future

Before
You Read

1. Do you know some people with interesting jobs? What kinds of jobs do they have?

2. In your opinion, what are some jobs of the future?

CD 3, TR 24

Read the following conversation. Pay special attention to *yes/no* and information questions in the simple past tense.

Matt is visiting Simon and Marta for the first time. Matt helped Marta's father in the hospital. Simon and Marta are talking about Matt's job.

Simon: So, Matt, you have an interesting career. You are a physical therapist, right?

Matt: Well, not exactly. I'm a PT assistant. I help the physical therapists in the hospital.

Marta: **Why did you choose** this career, Matt?

Matt: Well, I like physical activity. I like to help people. And a job in health services is a good job for the future. **Did you know** that?

Did You **Know?**

The U.S. population is getting older. Because of this, jobs in health care are increasing.

Simon: Yes. We read something about it last week.

Marta: **What did you do** to prepare for this job?

Matt: First, I took classes at a community college. I was in a special program for PT assistants.

Simon: **How long did it take?**

Matt: Two years. I got a certificate from the college.

Marta: **Did you have** on-the-job training also?

Matt: Yes. We had training at the hospital for some time. I worked with several physical therapists and their patients. I learned to help people with many different kinds of injuries. I was so busy in those days. I had another job too.

Marta: **What did you do?**

Matt: I was a part-time fitness instructor at an athletic club. I thought about a career in fitness.

Simon: **How long did you stay** there?

Matt: Only a year. It was temporary. Two jobs took too much time.

Vocabulary in Context

career	Matt studied for his **career.** He likes his job in health services.
on-the-job training	Companies often give new employees **on-the-job training.** The employees work and learn about the job at the same time.
patient	Marta's father was in the hospital. He was a **patient.**
injure (v.) injury (n.)	She fell and broke her leg. She **injured** her arm too. The **injuries** are very serious.
physical therapist (PT)	A **physical therapist** helps patients move and exercise after an accident or injury.
assistant	An **assistant** helps another person with his/her job.
fitness instructor	A **fitness instructor** works at a health club. He or she helps people with exercise and exercise machines.
athletic club (health club)	People go to an **athletic club** to exercise. Sometimes we call it a **health club** or gym.
temporary	Matt's job was **temporary.** He stayed for only one year.

Listening Activity 🔊
CD 3, TR 25

Listen to the sentences about the conversation. Circle *true* or *false*.

EXAMPLE   Matt works at a health club.   TRUE   (FALSE)

1. TRUE   FALSE   5. TRUE   FALSE
2. TRUE   FALSE   6. TRUE   FALSE
3. TRUE   FALSE   7. TRUE   FALSE
4. TRUE   FALSE

11.11 The Simple Past Tense—*Yes/No* Questions

The question pattern for regular and irregular verbs is the same. Use *did* + the base form.

DID	SUBJECT	VERB (BASE FORM)	COMPLEMENT	SHORT ANSWER
Did	I	**choose**	a good career?	Yes, you did.
Did	Matt	**visit**	Simon and Marta?	Yes, he did.
Did	they	**invite**	Matt to their home?	Yes, they did.
Did	you	**work**	last Saturday?	No, I didn't.
Did	we	**know**	about your last job?	No, you didn't.

Language Notes:

1. In fast, informal speech, we sometimes pronounce *did you* as /dɪdʒə/, and *did he* as /dɪdi/. Listen to your teacher pronounce the following sentences:

   Did you choose a career?   Did he get the job?
   Did you make a good choice?   Did he have any training?

2. Compare affirmative statements and questions.
   He **worked** on Saturday. **Did** he **work** on Sunday?
   She **got** the job. **Did** she **get** a good salary?

EXERCISE **1** Write *yes/no* questions with the words given. Answer them with a short answer. Use the ideas in the conversation on page 268.

EXAMPLE Matt / need / an education for his job

Did Matt need an education for his job? Yes, he did.

1. Matt / get / a bachelor's degree

   _____

2. Matt's employer / offer / on-the-job training

   _____

3. Simon and Marta / ask / about Matt's family

   _____

4. Simon / hear / about health careers on TV

   _____

5. Matt / help / Simon's father in the hospital

   _____

6. Simon and Marta / ask / Matt a lot of questions

   _____

11.12 More Irregular Verbs in the Simple Past Tense

BASE FORM	PAST FORM	BASE FORM	PAST FORM	BASE FORM	PAST FORM
eat	**ate**	spend	**spent**	come	**came**
choose	**chose**	keep	**kept**	meet	**met**
read	**read***	feel	**felt**	leave	**left**
write	**wrote**	think	**thought**	hear	**heard**

*Pronunciation Note: The past tense of **read** sounds like the color **red.**

EXERCISE **2**   **Fill in the blanks about the conversation on page 268 with the affirmative of a simple past tense verb. Choose verbs from the chart above and from the chart on page 262. Answers may vary.**

EXAMPLE   Matt _____ *spent* _____ two years at a community college.

1. Marta _____ Matt in the hospital.

2. Matt _____ to Simon and Marta's house.

3. Matt _____ a career in health services.

4. Matt _____ about a career as a fitness instructor.

5. Simon _____ about careers in health services last week.

6. It _____ Matt two years to get a certificate from college.

7. Then Matt _____ a full-time job at a hospital.

8. The hospital _____ him on-the-job training.

9. During his training, Matt _____ a temporary job at an athletic club.

10. Two jobs _____ too much of Matt's time.

11. He _____ his job at the athletic club for only a year. Then he _____ it.

12. Matt _____ Simon and Marta all about his training.

13. At the hospital, Matt _____ many people with injuries.

14. After his training, Matt _____ how to help people with injuries.

15. After the conversation, Matt _____ dinner with Simon and Marta.

11.13 The Simple Past Tense—Information Questions

QUESTION WORD(S)	DID	SUBJECT	VERB (BASE FORM)	COMPLEMENT	ANSWER
Why	**did**	I	**make**	mistakes?	Because you weren't prepared.
What kind of job	**did**	Matt	**find?**		A job as a PT assistant.
Where	**did**	you	**hear**	about the job?	From a friend.
How	**did**	you	**prepare**	for the job?	I took courses at a community college.
How many people	**did**	they	**interview**	today?	Five.
How long	**did**	they	**work**	at the hospital?	For five years.

Language Note: Compare affirmative statements and information questions.
Matt **got** his job last year. How **did** he **get** his job?
Matt **went** to Simon and Marta's house. Why **did** he **go** to their house?
He **worked** at an athletic club. When **did** he **work** at an athletic club?

EXERCISE **3**   Write an information question for each answer in the short conversations. The underlined words are the answers. Answers may vary.

EXAMPLE   **A:** _How many jobs did he apply for?_

   B: He applied for <u>three</u> jobs.

1. **A:** _____

   B: I took classes <u>at Newtown Community College</u>.

2. **A:** _____

   B: Simon read about <u>careers in health services</u>.

3. **A:** _____

   B: Matt met <u>four</u> PT assistants in that hospital.

4. **A:** _____

   B: They helped <u>people with injuries</u>.

5. **A:** _____

   B: Marta's father stayed in the hospital <u>for three weeks</u>.

6. **A:** _____

   B: Matt got a part-time job <u>as a fitness instructor</u>.

7. **A:** _____

   B: He kept that job <u>for a year</u>.

11.14 The Simple Past Tense—Subject Questions

In a subject question, use the past form of the verb.

QUESTION WORD(S)	VERB -*ED* OR IRREGULAR FORM	COMPLEMENT	ANSWER
What	**happened**	to the patient?	She went home.
Who	**helped**	the new patient?	Matt did.
How many students	**got**	a certificate in PT?	Thirty students did.
Which newspaper	**had**	information about health careers?	Last week's newspaper did.

EXERCISE **4** Make questions with the words given. Use the question word as the subject. Use regular and irregular past tense verbs.

EXAMPLE Who / take / those people to the hospital
Who took those people to the hospital?

1. What / happen / at the health club yesterday

2. Who / tell / you about that job

3. How many people / apply / for the job as a fitness instructor

4. Which patient / spend / two weeks at the hospital

5. Which student / choose / a job in health services

6. Who / write / about jobs of the future

7. What kinds of patients / need / help with their injuries

8. How many physical therapists / go / to community colleges

11.15 More Irregular Verbs in the Simple Past Tense

BASE FORM	PAST FORM	BASE FORM	PAST FORM	BASE FORM	PAST FORM
put	**put***	fall	**fell**	pay	**paid**
break	**broke**	hurt	**hurt***	cost	**cost***
find	**found**	understand	**understood**	buy	**bought**
drive	**drove**	lose	**lost**	sell	**sold**

Language Note: *For some verbs, the base form and the past form are the same.

EXERCISE 5   Write a question and an answer with the words given. Use the words in parentheses ( ) in the answer. Be careful. Some questions are about the subject.

EXAMPLE   Where / the patient / hurt her arm (at the health club)

Where did the patient hurt her arm?

She hurt it at the health club.

1. How / she / hurt her arm (fall and break)

   _____

   _____

2. Which arm / she / break (her right arm)

   _____

   _____

3. Who / drive / her to the hospital (her husband)

   _____

   _____

4. How long / the woman / stay in the hospital (only a few hours)

   _____

   _____

5. What kind of help / she / get later (from a good physical therapist)

   _____

   _____

6. Who / help / her in her house (she / pay for a service)

   _____

   _____

7. How much / this service / cost ($15 an hour)

_____

_____

8. Where / she / find this service (online)

_____

_____

9. How much work time / she / lose (only a week)

_____

_____

Editing Advice

1. Don't use the simple past tense after *to* (the infinitive).

       spend

He wanted to ~~spent~~ some time at the health club.

2. Use the base form after *did* and *didn't*.

       go

Where did they ~~went~~ after work?

       find

They didn't ~~found~~ good jobs.

3. Use the correct verb form and word order in questions.

     did your brother go

Where ~~your brother went~~ to college?

4. Don't use *did* in subject questions about the past. Use the past form.

     happened

What ~~did happen~~ at the interview today?

5. Use the correct spelling of the *-ed* forms.

     applied

She ~~applyed~~ for a job as a fitness instructor.

6. Use the correct verb form.

    hurt   *broke*

I ~~hurted~~ my leg.   He ~~breaked~~ his arm.

Editing Quiz

Some of the shaded words and phrases have mistakes. Find the mistakes and correct them. If the shaded words are correct, write C.

Matt is talking to a new patient, Tracy, about her injury.

Matt: Tracy, did your doctor ~~gave~~ *give* you a note for me?
(example)

Tracy: Yes. He gave *C* me this note.
(example)

Matt: Thanks. What happen? How you hurt your shoulder, Tracy?
                     (1)   *(2)*

Tracy: I falled during my exercise walk. I broke my shoulder. There was
        (3)   *(4)*

      something on the sidewalk and I didn't saw it.
                                        (5)

Matt: That's terrible! Did you called 911?
                          (6)

Tracy: I wanted to called 911 but I didn't have my cell phone.
         (7)   *(8)*

      But someone help me.
                 (9)

Matt: Who did help you?
            (10)

Tracy: A nice woman stoped her car to help me.
                  (11)

Matt: What the woman did? Did she took you to the hospital?
            (12)   *(13)*

Tracy: No. She call 911 and waited with me. Then the ambulance come
           (14)   *(15)*   *(16)*

      and taked me to the hospital.
          (17)

Matt: You were lucky. Did you know the woman?
          (18)   *(19)*

Tracy: No, I didn't. I wanted to thanked her later, but she didn't tell
                            (20)   *(21)*

      me her name.

Expansion

❶ What did you learn in this unit? Write three to five sentences about each topic:

- How Halina applied for a job at Baker's
- Halina's first job interview
- Halina's second job interview
- How Matt got a job as a physical therapist's assistant

❷ Write two questions you still have about each of the four topics above.

Writing
Activity

Rewrite the following conversation between Matt and his new patient, Tracy. Change *now* to *last year*. Make the necessary changes to the verbs.

Matt: Do you have a job now, Tracy?

Tracy: Yes, I do. I work in the employment services department at Baker's Department Store.

Matt: What do you do there?

Tracy: I keep information about employees. I help employees with their problems. And I write reports.

Matt: How do you get a job like that?

Tracy: Well, it isn't difficult. It takes two years to get a certificate in business. Then I have to send a lot of résumés to different companies.

Matt: Do you like your job?

Tracy: No, I don't. I don't want to work in business. I want to have a career in health services like you.

EXAMPLE

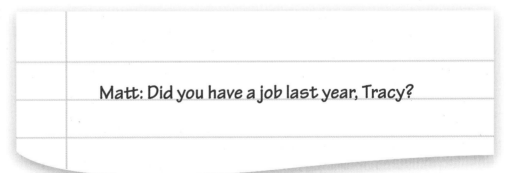

Matt: Did you have a job last year, Tracy?

 For more practice using grammar in context, please visit our Web site.

Giving Back

Lesson 1

Grammar
Review of Verb Tenses—Affirmative and Negative

Review of Infinitives

Review of Modal Verbs—Affirmative and Negative

Review of Time Expressions

Context
Volunteers

Helping Others

Before
You Read

1. What help did you need as a newcomer? Who helped you? How?
2. What do you do to help other newcomers?

Read the following conversation. Pay special attention to verb tenses and modals in the affirmative and negative.

Simon, Dorota, Victor, Lisa, and Halina are in a coffee shop.

Victor: Simon, thanks for your help on moving day. With your help, it **didn't take** us a long time. You **gave** me some good advice about used cars too. But I **don't have** a car yet. I'**m** still **looking**.

Simon: How'**s** your new apartment?

Lisa: We'**re** very comfortable there. It'**s** big and sunny. Our daughter **likes** her new school too. She **doesn't have to walk** far. We'**re** all **enjoying** life in the U.S. now. We **don't feel** like newcomers anymore. Thanks for all your help. We'**re not going to forget** it.

Simon: No problem.[1] Any time.

Halina: I **want to thank** you, Dorota. With your help, I **learned** about many important places in this city. Also, you **helped** me with my Social Security card. And your advice about job interviews **was** very helpful. I really **like** my new job. I'**m going to stay** with this company for a while.

Dorota: I **was** happy to help, Halina.

Halina: My life **is** easier now. I **don't feel** confused. I **feel** comfortable now. Maybe I **can help** you in your work with newcomers. I **can be** a volunteer. I'**m going to have** more time from now on.

Victor: You **can count on** my help too.

Simon: That'**s** good. Marta and I **are going to have** a meeting for volunteers next week. We **have to meet** in the evening. Many people **work** during the day. You **should come**. You **can learn** about other volunteer activities too. There **are** many opportunities to help others.

Did You **Know?**

In 2008, 61.8 million Americans volunteered a total of 8 billion hours.

---

[1]*No problem* is another way of saying "you're welcome."

Vocabulary in Context

yet	Victor has a driver's license, but he doesn't have a car **yet.**
comfortable	Halina feels **comfortable** here now. Her life here is easier for her.
newcomer	My friend just arrived in the U.S. He is a **newcomer.**
really	Halina **really** likes her new job. She likes it very much.
volunteer (n.) volunteer (v.)	Simon and Dorota are **volunteers.** They **volunteer** with newcomers. They do not get paid for their work.
from now on	Halina and Victor have an easier life now. **From now on,** they are going to have more time.
count on	You always help us. We can always **count on** you.
opportunity	There are many **opportunities** to help. You have a choice of many things.

Listening Activity

 Listen to the sentences about the conversation. Circle *true* or *false*.

CD 3, TR 27

EXAMPLE Simon, Dorota, and their friends are at Simon's house.

TRUE   (FALSE)

1. TRUE	FALSE	**5.** TRUE	FALSE
2. TRUE	FALSE	**6.** TRUE	FALSE
3. TRUE	FALSE	**7.** TRUE	FALSE
4. TRUE	FALSE	**8.** TRUE	FALSE

12.1 Review of Verb Tenses—Affirmative and Negative

The Simple Present Tense

	EXAMPLES	EXPLANATION
Be	a. Dorota **is** 40 years old. b. Halina **isn't** a manager now. c. Dorota **is** from Poland. d. The five friends **are** in a coffee shop. e. It **isn't** cold today. f. It **is** 3:00 P.M. g. Halina and Victor **are** happy. Their lives **aren't** as difficult now. h. It **is** hard to start life in a new country.	a. Age b. Occupation/work c. Place of origin d. Location e. Weather f. Time g. Description h. After *it* in impersonal expressions
There + Be	a. There **is** a need for volunteers. b. There **aren't** many people in the coffee shop	a. Use *there is* to introduce a singular subject. b. Use *there are* to introduce a plural subject.
Other Verbs	a. Halina **works** in an office. b. Dorota **doesn't work** every day.	a. Facts b. Habits, customs, regular activity

The Present Continuous Tense

EXAMPLES	EXPLANATION
Halina **is thanking** Dorota. They **are meeting** in a coffee shop.	Actions at the present moment
Halina **isn't looking** for a job at this time. She **is thinking** about volunteer activities.	Actions at a present time period

The Future Tense

	EXAMPLES	EXPLANATION
Be	Halina and Victor **are going to be** volunteers.	Future plans and predictions
There + Be	There **isn't going to be** a volunteer meeting tomorrow.	
Other Verbs	Halina **is going to help** newcomers. Halina **is going to have** more free time soon.	

(continued)

The Simple Past Tense

	EXAMPLES	EXPLANATION
Be	Halina **was** a department manager in Poland.	Actions completed in the past
There + Be	There **weren't** many people in the coffee shop yesterday.	
Regular Verbs	Victor **moved** to a new apartment two weeks ago. He **didn't move** far away.	
Irregular Verbs	Halina **got** a job in an office. She **didn't get** a job in a store.	

EXERCISE 1 Complete each sentence about the conversation on page 281 with the correct tense of the verb in parentheses ( ). Use affirmative verbs.

EXAMPLE   Halina _____is talking_____ to Dorota now.
                              (talk)

1. Simon, Dorota, Halina, Lisa, and Victor _____
                                                                (sit)

   together in a coffee shop.

2. Victor's family _____ a bigger apartment.
                          (find)

3. Lisa _____ the new apartment.
            (like)

4. Victor and Halina _____ American life now.
                              (enjoy)

5. Simon _____ Victor good advice about used cars.
             (give)

6. Victor _____ a used car soon.
              (buy)

7. Halina and Victor _____ newcomers several
                              (be)

   months ago.

8. Halina _____ a Social Security card.
              (have)

9. Dorota _____ Halina with her Social Security card.
              (help)

10. Halina _____ Dorota with other newcomers from
               (help)

    now on.

11. There _____ a volunteer meeting at Marta's house
              (be)

    soon.

EXERCISE 2 **Read each sentence. Write the negative form with the words in parentheses ( ).**

EXAMPLE   The five friends are having coffee now. (lunch)
<u>They aren't having lunch.</u>

1. Victor and Halina are talking about their lives now. (their problems)

   _____

2. Victor wanted to move. (stay in his old apartment)

   _____

3. His old apartment was too small. (big enough for his family)

   _____

4. Victor feels comfortable in the U.S. now. (strange anymore)

   _____

5. Simon gave Victor advice about cars. (about jobs)

   _____

6. Halina and Victor had a lot to do at first. (much free time then)

   _____

7. Victor and Lisa need a used car. (a new car)

   _____

8. Halina's going to work in the same company for a while. (look for another job soon)

   _____

12.2 Review of Infinitives

EXAMPLES	EXPLANATION
Halina started **to work** for a new company. She expects **to stay** there for a while. I'm happy **to help** you. It's fun **to be** a volunteer. It takes time **to learn** about a new country. Halina wants **to help** other people. Victor is trying **to buy** a used car.	The infinitive is *to* + the base form of the verb. The tense is always in the verb before the infinitive. Infinitives can go after: • verbs • adjectives • impersonal expressions with *it*

EXERCISE 3 Complete each sentence with an infinitive phrase. Use the ideas from the conversation on page 281. Answers will vary.

EXAMPLE   It's good _to help other people._

1. Victor wants _____

2. Halina needed _____

3. Halina is planning _____

4. It's not easy _____

5. Simon and Marta like _____

6. Simon and Marta are planning _____

7. Dorota was happy _____

12.3 Review of Modal Verbs—Affirmative and Negative

Can, Should, Must, Have To

EXAMPLES	EXPLANATION
a. Victor **can speak** Spanish. Dorota **can't speak** Spanish.	a. Ability—no ability
b. Simon has a license. He **can drive**. Ed **can't drive**.	b. Permission—no permission
c. Victor and Halina **can volunteer** now. Peter is too busy. He **can't volunteer** now.	c. Possibility—impossibility
a. We **should be** on time.	a. Advice or suggestion to do something
b. You **shouldn't arrive** late to an interview.	b. Advice not to do something
a. Workers **must have** a Social Security card.	a. Strong obligation because of a rule or law
b. You **must not drive** without a driver's license.	b. Strong obligation not to do something because of a rule or law
a. Victor's daughter **has to go** to school.	a. Necessity (by law, custom, rule, or personal obligation)
b. She **doesn't have to buy** her lunch at school. She can bring a lunch from home.	b. Not necessary

EXERCISE 4 **ABOUT YOU** Fill in the blanks. Make sentences that are true about you. Use the affirmative or negative of the modals in parentheses ( ).

EXAMPLES

_____I have to_____ work tonight.
     (have to)

_____I can't_____ read the newspaper without a dictionary.
    (can)

1. _____ speak English every day.
    (should)

2. _____ go to a meeting today.
    (have to)

3. _____ speak English like an American.
    (can)

4. _____ speak my native language in this class.
    (should)

5. _____ drive.
    (can)

6. _____ pay for classes at this school.
    (have to)

EXERCISE 5 Halina, Victor, Lisa, Simon, and Dorota continue their conversation. Fill in the blanks with the correct forms of the verbs in parentheses ( ). Use the different tenses, infinitives, and modals.

Part 1:

🔊
CD 3, TR 28

Dorota: We _____need_____ more volunteers this year.
    (example: need)

There's a lot to do. Sometimes we _____ enough
    (1 get, negative)

volunteers to help all the newcomers.

Victor: What else do volunteers do?

Simon: Well, many newcomers _____ how to drive in the
    (2 know, negative)

U.S. They _____ sure about the rules on American
    (3 be, negative)

roads. Volunteers _____ people with their driving
    (4 can / help)

practice. Tomorrow, Dorota

and I _____
    (5 meet)

with a group of newcomers.

One young man

_____ to
    (6 have to / drive)

work every day.

(continued)

I _____ with him yesterday. But
(7 practice)

I _____ busy next week.
(8 be)

Victor: I _____ him. But I _____ a car
(9 want / help)   (10 have, negative)

yet.

Simon: That's OK. This newcomer _____ a good
(11 buy)

used car last month. He _____ someone
(12 need / use, negative)

else's car.

Part 2:

Dorota: Next Thanksgiving, we _____ a holiday dinner
(1 prepare)

for newcomers. We _____ volunteers now. It's
(2 look for)

difficult _____ people right before a holiday.
(3 find)

Everyone is so busy then.

Halina: Peter and I _____ you. I _____ .
(4 want / help)   (5 can /cook)

Dorota: Thanks, Halina. I _____ my friend Nancy about
(6 tell)

you. Nancy _____ holiday meals every year in a
(7 prepare)

school in her neighborhood. Her holiday dinners are very popular

with newcomers. Last year, fifty newcomers _____ .
(8 come)

There _____ enough volunteers. Nancy
(9 be, negative)

_____ enough food. So I _____
(10 have, negative)   (11 volunteer / help)

her. I _____ the extra food from the deli.
(12 get)

Everyone _____ a wonderful time.
(13 have)

always	sometimes	this week	right away
never	hardly ever	in a few weeks	yesterday
from now on	rarely	next week	last year
often	right now	soon	two weeks ago
usually	at the moment	tomorrow	every week

EXERCISE 6 **Circle the time expressions in the following sentences. Then fill in the blanks in the sentences with an affirmative verb from the box. Use the correct tense. Answers may vary.**

help	move	tell	come	give	have
be	enjoy	teach	try to get	find	invite

EXAMPLE At the coffee shop (yesterday,) Dorota ___told___ Halina more about her friend Nancy.

1. Nancy often _____ newcomers.

2. These newcomers hardly ever _____ all the items necessary for their new life in America.

3. Nancy usually _____ them clothes and things for their house.

4. And she always _____ them about American life.

5. Last year, five new families from Africa _____ into Nancy's neighborhood.

6. In just a month, Nancy _____ them enough items for a comfortable home.

7. She _____ jobs for them later too.

8. These families _____ their new life in America now.

9. Nancy _____ all the newcomers to her famous holiday dinner later this year.

10. Last year, a city news reporter _____ to Nancy's dinner.

11. His report _____ on TV a week later.

12. A lot of people _____ her now.

13. Nancy _____ them to work with newcomers now.

EXERCISE 7 Look at the picture below. Write a paragraph about the picture. Use all the tenses you learned in this book: simple present, present continuous, future (*be going to*), simple past, and modal verbs. Use affirmative and negative sentences.

EXAMPLES   Newcomers are going to have an American Thanksgiving dinner.

There's a turkey on each table.

_____

_____

_____

_____

_____

_____

_____

_____

_____

_____

_____

Grammar
Review of *Yes/No* Questions
Review of Information Questions

Context
Volunteer Activities

Charity Work

Before
You Read

1. What volunteer activities do you know about?
2. Why do people volunteer?

🔊 **Read the following conversation. Pay special attention to *yes/no* questions and information questions.**

CD 3, TR 29

There's a volunteer meeting at Marta's house.

Marta: Good evening, everyone. These are my friends Rhonda, Val, and Elsa. They're volunteers. They're going to tell you about volunteer work. Rhonda, **are you** ready? **What's your volunteer group doing** this month?

Rhonda: Hello, everyone. My name is Rhonda and I work for an airline. We have a program to help poor children in other countries. This month we're planning a trip to South America. We're going to bring wheelchairs, eyeglasses, and medical supplies to people in small villages.

Marta: **Who gives** you these supplies, Rhonda?

Rhonda: Doctors give us medical supplies. Volunteers save their old eyeglasses for us. Charities help us too. And our airline pays for the flights.

Marta: **Do you bring** anything else to these people?

Rhonda: Yes. We bring clothing for children and adults too. And we also have special projects each year.

Marta: **What did your group do** last year, Rhonda? **Was it** a project for South Americans too?

Rhonda: Yes, it was. We brought a sick little boy from Colombia here to the U.S. He needed an operation. They didn't have medical care in his village. Two months later, I brought a healthy boy back to his parents. They were so happy. And I was too.

Marta: **Do volunteers have to work** for the airline?

Rhonda: Only airline workers can go on the trips. But you can help too.

Marta: **How can we help?**

Rhonda: You can collect supplies for us.

Marta: **What are you going to do** next?

Rhonda: Right now, we're collecting clothing and toys for a holiday party for Colombian kids.

Marta: Rhonda can answer your questions now. **Does anyone have a question for Rhonda?**

Did You Know?

Most volunteers in America are women between the ages of 35 and 44. But volunteers over age 60 give the most hours of their time.

Vocabulary in Context

wheelchair	Some people can't walk. They need a **wheelchair**.
village	Only 500 people live in his **village**.
collect	Rhonda **collects** eyeglasses to give to poor people.
fly (v.)/ flight (n.)	Rhonda is going to **fly** from New York to Colombia next week. Her **flight** leaves at 5 P.M.
airline	What **airline** is she going to use to fly to Colombia?
project	Rhonda's **project** is to collect clothing for poor people.
bring/ brought	A: What did you **bring** to the volunteer meeting? B: I **brought** some eyeglasses and clothes.
operation	A little boy was very sick. He needed an **operation** at a hospital.
toys	Children like to play with **toys**.

Listening Activity

🔊 **Listen to the sentences about the conversation. Circle *true* or *false*.**

CD 3, TR 30

EXAMPLE   Marta's asking Rhonda about her volunteer activities.   (TRUE)   FALSE

1. TRUE	FALSE		**5.** TRUE	FALSE
2. TRUE	FALSE		**6.** TRUE	FALSE
3. TRUE	FALSE		**7.** TRUE	FALSE
4. TRUE	FALSE		**8.** TRUE	FALSE

12.5 Review of *Yes/No* Questions

The Simple Present Tense

	YES/NO QUESTIONS	SHORT ANSWERS
Be	**Is** Rhonda a volunteer? **Are** the volunteers from South America?	Yes, she is. No, they aren't.
There + Be	**Is** there a meeting at Marta's house? **Are** there any Colombians at the meeting?	Yes, there is. No, there aren't.
Other Verbs	**Does** Dorota **work** for an airline? **Do** charities **help** with supplies?	No, she doesn't. Yes, they do.

The Present Continuous Tense

YES/NO QUESTIONS	SHORT ANSWERS
Is Rhonda **talking** about her career?	No, she isn't.
Are you **listening** to Rhonda?	Yes, I am.
Are the volunteers **asking** for money?	No, they aren't.
Are we **learning** about volunteer activities?	Yes, we are.

The Future Tense

YES/NO QUESTIONS	SHORT ANSWERS
Is Rhonda **going to need** help?	Yes, she is.
Is there **going to be** a party for the volunteers?	No, there isn't.
Are new volunteers **going to help**?	Yes, they are.

The Simple Past Tense

	YES/NO QUESTIONS	SHORT ANSWERS
Be	**Were** you a volunteer last year? **Was** Rhonda in South America last week? **Were** the volunteers helpful last year?	No, I wasn't. No, she wasn't. Yes, they were.
There + Be	**Was** there a problem with the volunteers? **Were** there enough volunteers to help?	No, there wasn't. Yes, there were.
Regular and Irregular Verbs	**Did** Rhonda **help** a sick boy? **Did** volunteers **go** to Mexico?	Yes, she did. No, they didn't.

Modal Verbs and *Have To*

	YES/NO QUESTIONS	SHORT ANSWERS
Should	**Should** we volunteer for that project?	Yes, we should.
Can	**Can** I volunteer?	Yes, you can.
Have To	**Did** Rhonda **have to** volunteer for this project?	No, she didn't.
	Do volunteers **have to** come to the meeting?	Yes, they do.

Language Note: Questions with *must* are not common. We use *have to* for questions.

EXERCISE 1 Ask a *yes/no* question about the conversation on page 292. Use the words given. Use the same tense as in the statement. Answer your question with a short answer.

EXAMPLE Rhonda has a job. (with an airline)

Does she have a job with an airline? Yes, she does.

1. Rhonda is talking. (about her job with the airline)

   _____

2. Rhonda brings medical supplies to poor children. (wheelchairs)

   _____

3. A little boy needed medical care last year. (an operation)

   _____

4. The sick boy was from a village. (from the U.S.)

   _____

5. Rhonda brought the boy to the U.S. (back to his parents)

   _____

6. The volunteers are going to have a party. (in the U.S.)

   _____

7. There are many people at Marta's house today. (any volunteers)

   _____

8. People should save their medical supplies for Rhonda's projects. (toys too)

   _____

9. People can ask Rhonda questions. (about other projects)

   _____

12.6 Review of Information Questions

The Simple Present Tense

	INFORMATION QUESTIONS	ANSWERS
Be	Who **is** Rhonda?	She's Marta's friend.
	Where **are** the volunteers?	They're at Marta's house.
There + Be	Why **is** there a meeting today at Marta's house?	To give information about volunteer work.
	How many people **are** there at the meeting?	About 20.
Subject Questions	Who **collects** eyeglasses?	Many people do.
	Which airline **helps** people?	Rhonda's airline does.
Other Questions	Where **does** Rhonda **work**?	At an airline.
	How **do** doctors **help**?	They give medical supplies.

The Present Continuous Tense

	INFORMATION QUESTIONS	ANSWERS
Subject Questions	How many volunteers **are speaking** at the meeting?	Three.
Other Questions	What kind of trip **is** Rhonda **planning**?	A trip to bring supplies to South America.
	What **are** volunteers **collecting** now?	Children's clothing and toys.

The Future Tense with *Be Going To*

	INFORMATION QUESTIONS	ANSWERS
Be	What **is** the new project **going to be**?	A holiday party for kids.
	When **are** you **going to be** a volunteer?	Next month.
There + Be	When **is** there **going to be** another meeting?	Next week.
	How many meetings **are** there **going to be**?	Only two more.
Subject Questions	Which children **are going to get** the gifts?	The children in one small village.
	Who **is going to be** at the next meeting?	Many new volunteers.
Other Questions	What **is** Rhonda **going to do** with the toys?	She's going to give them to kids.
	When **are** the volunteers **going to give** the toys to the children?	In December.

The Simple Past Tense

	INFORMATION QUESTIONS	ANSWERS
Be	Where **was** the last meeting?	We don't know.
	Why **were** the sick boy's parents worried?	Because there was no medical care in their village.
There + Be	Why **was** there a special project last year?	Because a little boy was sick.
	What kind of help **was** there for the boy?	Medical help.
Subject Questions	Which volunteers **brought** the boy to the U.S.?	Rhonda and her friends did.
	Who **came** to the meeting?	Victor and Lisa did.
Other Questions—Regular and Irregular Verbs	What kind of help **did** the boy **need**?	He needed an operation.
	When **did** the boy **have** his operation?	He had it last year.

Modal Verbs and *Have To*

	INFORMATION QUESTIONS	ANSWERS
Subject Questions	Who **can** help Rhonda?	All of us can help her.
	How many children **had to** get an operation last year?	One did.
Other Questions	When **can** we help Rhonda?	You can help right now.
	What **should** we bring to Rhonda?	You should bring her clothing and toys.
	When **does** Rhonda **have to** get the toys?	Before her next trip.

Language Note: Questions with *must* are not common. Use *have to* for questions.

EXERCISE **2**   **Write an information question about each sentence. Use the question words in parentheses ( ). Then write the answers. Use the ideas in the conversation on page 292.**

EXAMPLE   Rhonda has a job. (What kind)

What kind of job does she have?

She works for an airline.

1. Rhonda does volunteer work. (What kind)

_____

_____

2. Rhonda went to South America last year. (Why)

_____

_____

3. Someone pays for the flights to South America. (Who)

_____

_____

4. The volunteers are going to have a party for children. (When)

_____

_____

5. A sick boy had to come to the U.S. (Why)

_____

_____

6. People can help with the holiday project. (How)

_____

_____

7. We should collect things for Rhonda. (What)

_____

_____

8. Rhonda is explaining something to the new volunteers. (What)

_____

_____

EXERCISE **3** Look at the picture below. Rhonda is at the Christmas party for the children. Write six questions about the picture. Use *yes/no* questions and information questions. Use all the tenses: simple present, present continuous, future, and past. Use modal verbs too. Write the answers.

EXAMPLES Is there a Christmas tree at the party? Yes, there is.

Who is talking to Santa? A little girl is talking to Santa.

1. _____

   _____

2. _____

   _____

3. _____

   _____

4. _____

   _____

5. _____

   _____

6. _____

   _____

EXERCISE **4** Val, a second volunteer at Marta's meeting, is talking now. People are asking her questions. Complete each question with the words given. Use the answer to help you choose the tense.

EXAMPLE **Victor:** Where ___do you volunteer___ ?
(you / volunteer)

Val: I volunteer in my neighborhood. I work at a child-care center once a week. There are other volunteers too. We help with the children. We also plan projects for them.

1. Halina: How many _____ at the center?
(children / there)

Val: Every day is different. There are usually about 15 or 20 kids.

2. Simon: How many hours _____ ?
(each volunteer / have to / work)

Val: Usually four to six hours. But sometimes we work more. Last week was one of those weeks.

3. Victor: What _____ last week?
(happen)

Val: We had 10 new kids, so I worked an extra day to help.

4. Halina: What _____ ?
(you / do)

Val: I helped with the art activities, I served the meals, and I played with the children a lot.

5. Simon: How _____ about this day care center?
(you / learn)

Val: It was on our city's Web site. That's a good place to look for volunteer opportunities.

6. Marta: What project _____ now?
(the volunteers / plan)

Val: We're planning an art show and sale of the children's art.

7. Victor: What _____ for the show?
(children / learn / do)

Val: They're learning to paint with water colors.

8. Simon: When _____ ?
(the sale / be)

Val: In three months. I can tell you the date later.

9. Halina: What _____ with the money?
(center / do)

Val: We are going to buy books for the children's library.

EXERCISE **5** **Elsa, another volunteer, is talking now. People are asking Elsa questions. Complete each question with the words given. Use the answers to help you choose the tense.**

CD 3, TR 31

Marta: This is Elsa. She volunteers to help older people. She works with a neighborhood group. She works one week each month.

Woman: _Are you going to work_ this week, Elsa?
(example: you / work)

Elsa: Yes, I am. I'm going to help an older woman in my neighborhood. She can't see very well and she lives alone.

Man: How _____ her?
(1 you / help)

Elsa: I'm going to take her to a doctor's appointment tomorrow, and I'm going to take her to the supermarket on the weekend.

Woman: What _____
(2 this woman / do)
all day?

Elsa: She goes to the gym two days a week. She exercises in a swimming pool.

Woman: _____ the bus to the gym?
(3 she / have to / take)

Elsa: No, she doesn't. Another volunteer takes her.

Woman: _____ ?
(4 she / can swim)

Elsa: She doesn't exactly swim. She takes an exercise class for seniors. It's exercise in the water.

Woman: When _____ these classes?
(5 she / start)

Elsa: She started the classes 20 years ago. She says, "This class is responsible for my long life." She's 90 years old!

Man: How _____ this job, Elsa?
(6 find)

Elsa: I heard about it from a friend in the neighborhood. We need more volunteers. Who _____ us?
(7 want/help)

Editing Advice

1. Use the base form after *doesn't*, *don't*, *didn't*, *have to*, and modals.

   go
   Peter didn't ~~went~~ to the meeting last Saturday.

   work
   He had to ~~worked~~ last Saturday.

   go
   Volunteers should ~~to go~~ to the meetings.

2. Don't forget to use the base form in an infinitive.

   help
   They wanted to ~~helped~~ us with the project.

3. Don't use a form of *be* with the simple present or past tenses.

   goes
   Elsa's neighbor ~~is go~~ to the store every week.

   walked
   She ~~was walk~~ to the store yesterday.

4. Don't use statement word order in a question.

   did he work
   Where ~~he worked~~ last year?

   is Elsa going to drive
   When ~~Elsa is going to drive~~ her neighbor to the supermarket?

5. Don't use *do*, *does*, or *did* in a subject question.

   works
   Who ~~does work~~ as a volunteer?

6. Be sure each verb is in the correct tense and form for the context.

   left
   Everyone ~~leaved~~ Marta's meeting at 10:00 last night.

   goes
   The older woman ~~is going~~ to the gym two days a week.

7. Use the correct form in a short answer.

   I'm not.
   Are you a volunteer? ~~No, I don't.~~

Editing Quiz

Some of the shaded words and phrases have mistakes. Find the mistakes and correct them. If the shaded words are correct, write C.

Marta is interviewing another volunteer, Sam, at her meeting.

Marta: What kind of volunteer job ^do you have?
(example)

Sam: I ^C work at a nature museum. I teach children's groups about animals, birds, and plants. Last month a group come to do a school project.
(1)

I help them. They had to wrote a report about the birds in our museum.
(2)   *(3)*

They didn't knew about these birds before.
(4)

Marta: That's interesting. Where did you heard about this job?
(5)

Sam: I finded it on the Internet. There's a great Web site for volunteers.
(6)   *(7)*

It's www.serve.gov.

Marta: How this site works?
(8)

Sam: You fill in your city and your interests. The site give you many
(9)

opportunities. It's easy use. You doesn't have to look at many
(10)   *(11)*

different sites.

Marta: It's just for young people?
(12)

Sam: No, it doesn't. There are opportunities for older people too. They
(13)

can go to Senior Corps for information.

Marta: I'm have an idea for a volunteer project. What should I do?
(14)   *(15)*

Sam: You should to put your idea on the site and ask for volunteers. Many
(16)

people are volunteering these days. And more people going to volunteer
(17)   *(18)*

in the future.

Marta: Why?

(continued)

Sam: There's a new law in October 2009, the Serve America Act.
(19)

Because of this law, student volunteers can get money for their

education. And the number of older people is going up. So
(20)

we going to have more older volunteers too.
(21)

Marta: Thank you for your time Sam. We hope all of you can stay for coffee

and cake. Sam, you're going to stay for coffee with us?
(22)

Sam: Yes, thank you. But I have to leave by 4:30.
(23)

Expansion

Learner's Log

❶ Write three sentences about each topic. Use a different tense in each sentence.

- Val's volunteer job
- Elsa's volunteer job
- Rhonda's volunteer job

❷ Write three questions you still have about volunteer work.

Writing Activities

❶ Answer one of the following questions. Use affirmative and negative statements in the correct tense. Write 6–8 sentences.

- Do you know a volunteer in the U.S.? What does he/she do?
- Do you want to be a volunteer? What are you going to do? Why?
- Were you (or was someone you know) a volunteer in your country? Write about your (or the person's) volunteer activity.
- Did a volunteer help you? How?

EXAMPLE My neighbor Tom is a volunteer. He builds and repairs houses for low income people. . . .

2 Write five to six true sentences about the picture of Val in the child-care center. Write at least one sentence with each tense you learned in this book: the present continuous, simple present, future, past, and a modal verb.

EXAMPLE

Val is talking to a little boy.

 For more practice using grammar in context, please visit our Web site.

Appendices

Appendix A

The Calendar

Months	Days	Seasons
January (Jan.) February (Feb.) March (Mar.) April (Apr.) May June (Jun.) July (Jul.) August (Aug.) September (Sept.) October (Oct.) November (Nov.) December (Dec.)	Sunday (Sun.) Monday (Mon.) Tuesday (Tues.) Wednesday (Wed.) Thursday (Thurs.) Friday (Fri.) Saturday (Sat.)	Winter Spring Summer Fall or Autumn

Dates

January 6, 1999
Jan. 6, 1999
1/6/1999
1/6/99
1-6-99

March 27, 2010
Mar. 27, 2010
3/27/2004
3/27/10
3-27-10

(continued)

Numbers

Cardinal Numbers	Ordinal Numbers
1 = one	first
2 = two	second
3 = three	third
4 = four	fourth
5 = five	fifth
6 = six	sixth
7 = seven	seventh
8 = eight	eighth
9 = nine	ninth
10 = ten	tenth
11 = eleven	eleventh
12 = twelve	twelfth
13 = thirteen	thirteenth
14 = fourteen	fourteenth
15 = fifteen	fifteenth
16 = sixteen	sixteenth
17 = seventeen	seventeenth
18 = eighteen	eighteenth
19 = nineteen	nineteenth
20 = twenty	twentieth
21 = twenty-one	twenty-first
30 = thirty	thirtieth
40 = forty	fortieth
50 = fifty	fiftieth
60 = sixty	sixtieth
70 = seventy	seventieth
80 = eighty	eightieth
90 = ninety	ninetieth
100 = one hundred	hundredth
1,000 = one thousand	thousandth
1,000,000 = one million	millionth

Peter Thomas
17 Cherry Tree Lane
New York, NY 10001

6-38/542   7024

DATE _September 6, 2010_

PAY TO THE ORDER OF _Teresa Jones_ $ _950 00/100_

Nine Hundred Fifty and 00/100   DOLLARS

Summerville Bank

FOR _rent_   _Peter Thomas_

⑈01234567⑈ 012345678910 ⑈ 7024

Appendix B

Spelling Rules for Verbs and Nouns

Spelling of the -s Form of Verbs and Nouns

Verbs	Nouns	Rule
visit—visits need—needs like—likes spend—spends see—sees	chair—chairs bed—beds truck—trucks gift—gifts bee—bees	Add -s to most words to make the -s form.
miss—misses wash—washes catch—catches fix—fixes	dress—dresses dish—dishes match—matches box—boxes	Add -es to base forms with ss, sh, ch, and x at the end.
worry—worries try—tries study—studies	party—parties city—cities berry—berries	If the word ends in a consonant + y, change y to i and add -es.
pay—pays play—plays enjoy—enjoys	boy—boys day—days key—keys	If the word ends in a vowel + y, do not change the y. Just add -s.
	leaf—leaves knife—knives	If the noun ends in f or fe, change f or fe to ves.

Irregular -s Forms of Verbs

have—has
go—goes
do—does

Irregular Plural Forms of Nouns

man—men woman—women child—children mouse—mice	foot—feet tooth—teeth person—people (or persons) fish—fish

(continued)

Spelling of the *-ing* Forms of Verbs

Verbs	Rule
go—go**ing** eat—eat**ing** spend—spend**ing**	Add *-ing* to most verbs to make the *-ing* form.
tak<u>e</u>—tak**ing** writ<u>e</u>—writ**ing** mak<u>e</u>—mak**ing**	If a verb ends in silent *e*, drop the *e* and add *-ing*. Do NOT double the final consonant. WRONG: writting
pa<u>y</u>—pa**ying** bu<u>y</u>—bu**ying** worr<u>y</u>—worr**ying** stud<u>y</u>—stud**ying**	If a verb ends in a *y*, just add *-ing*. WRONG: studing
st<u>op</u>—sto**pping** r<u>un</u>—ru**nning** spl<u>it</u>—spli**tting**	If a one-syllable verb ends in consonant + vowel + consonant, double the final consonant and add *-ing*.
begín—begi**nning** permít—permi**tting** occúr—occu**rring**	If a two-syllable word ends in consonant + vowel + consonant, double the final consonant and add *-ing* only if the last syllable is stressed.
ópen—open**ing** háppen—happen**ing** devélop—develop**ing**	If a multi-syllable word ends in consonant + vowel + consonant and the final syllable is not stressed, do NOT double the final consonant. Just add *-ing*.

Spelling of the *-ed* Forms of Regular Past Tense Verbs

Verbs	Rule
listen—listen**ed** look—look**ed**	Add **-ed** to most regular verbs to form the past tense.
ba<u>k</u>e—bake**d** smi<u>l</u>e—smile**d** sa<u>v</u>e—save**d**	If a verb ends in silent *e,* just add **-d.**
wor<u>ry</u>—worr**ied** stu<u>dy</u>—stud**ied**	If a verb ends in a consonant + *y*, change the *y* to *i* and add **-ed.**
en<u>joy</u>—enjoy**ed** de<u>lay</u>—delay**ed**	If a verb ends in a vowel + *y*, just add **-ed.**
s<u>top</u>—sto**pped** d<u>rag</u>—dra**gged** s<u>lam</u>—sla**mmed**	If a one-syllable verb ends in consonant + vowel + consonant, double the final consonant and add **-ed.**
per<u>mít</u>—permi**tted** oc<u>cúr</u>—occu**rred**	If a two–syllable word ends in consonant + vowel + consonant, double the final consonant and add **-ed** only if the last syllable is stressed.
<u>ó</u><u>pen</u>—open**ed** h<u>áp</u><u>pen</u>—happen**ed** de<u>vé</u><u>lop</u>—develop**ed**	If a multi-syllable word ends in consonant + vowel + consonant and the final syllable is not stressed, do NOT double the final consonant. Just add **-ed.**

Appendix C

Spelling Rules for Comparative and Superlative Forms

Simple Form	Comparative Form	Superlative Form	Rule
old cheap	old**er** cheap**er**	old**est** cheap**est**	Add **-er** and **-est** to most adjectives.
big hot	big**ger** hot**ter**	big**gest** hot**test**	If the adjective ends with consonant + vowel + consonant, double the final consonant before adding **-er** or **-est.**
ni<u>c</u>e la<u>t</u>e	nic**er** lat**er**	nic**est** lat**est**	If the adjective ends in *e*, add **-r** or **-st** only.
bus<u>y</u> eas<u>y</u>	bus**ier** eas**ier**	bus**iest** eas**iest**	If the adjective ends in *y*, change *y* to *i* and add **-er** or **-est.**

Alphabetical List of Irregular Past Forms

Base Form	Past Form	Base Form	Past Form
be	was/were	lend	lent
become	became	let	let
begin	began	lie[1]	lay
bend	bent	light	lit (or lighted)
bet	bet	lose	lost
bite	bit	make	made
blow	blew	mean	meant
break	broke	meet	met
bring	brought	mistake	mistook
build	built	pay	paid
buy	bought	put	put
catch	caught	quit	quit
choose	chose	read	read[2]
come	came	ride	rode
cost	cost	ring	rang
cut	cut	run	ran
do	did	say	said
draw	drew	see	saw
drink	drank	sell	sold
drive	drove	send	sent
eat	ate	shake	shook
fall	fell	shoot	shot
feed	fed	shut	shut
feel	felt	sing	sang
fight	fought	sit	sat
find	found	sleep	slept
fit	fit	speak	spoke
fly	flew	spend	spent
forget	forgot	spread	spread
get	got	stand	stood
give	gave	steal	stole
go	went	swim	swam
grow	grew	take	took
have	had	teach	taught
hear	heard	tear	tore
hide	hid	tell	told
hit	hit	think	thought
hold	held	throw	threw
hurt	hurt	understand	understood
keep	kept	wake	woke
know	knew	wear	wore
lead	led	win	won
leave	left	write	wrote

[1]When *lie* means to not tell the truth, the past form is *lied*. When it means to place something down, the past form is *lay*.

[2]We pronounce the past tense of *read* like the color red.

Appendix E

Capitalization Rules

- The first word in a sentence: My friends are helpful.

- The word "I": My sister and I took a trip together.

- Names of people: Julia Roberts; George Washington

- Titles preceding names of people: Doctor (Dr.) Smith; President Lincoln; Queen Elizabeth; Mr. Rogers; Mrs. Carter

- Geographic names: the United States; Lake Superior; California; the Rocky Mountains; the Mississippi River

  NOTE: The word "the" in a geographic name is not capitalized.

- Street names: Pennsylvania Avenue (Ave.); Wall Street (St.); Abbey Road (Rd.)

- Names of organizations, companies, colleges, buildings, stores, hotels: the Republican Party; Heinle Cengage; Dartmouth College; the University of Wisconsin; the White House; Bloomingdale's; the Hilton Hotel

- Nationalities and ethnic groups: Mexicans; Canadians; Spaniards; Americans; Jews; Kurds; Eskimos

- Languages: English; Spanish; Polish; Vietnamese; Russian

- Months: January; February

- Days: Sunday; Monday

- Holidays: Christmas; Independence Day

- Important words in a title: *Grammar in Context*; *The Old Man and the Sea*; *Romeo and Juliet*; *The Sound of Music*

  NOTE: Capitalize "the" as the first word of a title.

Glossary of Grammatical Terms

- **Adjective** An adjective gives a description of a noun.

  It's a *tall* tree.   He's an *old* man.   My sisters are *nice*.

- **Adverb** An adverb describes the action of a sentence or an adjective or another adverb.

  She speaks English *fluently*.   I drive *carefully*.
  She speaks English *extremely well*.   She is *very* intelligent.

- **Affirmative** means yes.

- **Apostrophe** ' We use the apostrophe for possession and contractions.

  My *sister's* friend is beautiful.   Today *isn't* Sunday.

- **Article** The definite article is *the*. The indefinite articles are *a* and *an*.

  I have *a* cat.   I ate *an* apple.   *The* teacher is helpful.

- **Base Form** The base form, sometimes called the "simple" form, of the verb has no tense. It has no ending (-*s* or -*ed*): *be, go, eat, take, write*.

  I didn't *go* out.   He doesn't *know* the answer.
  You shouldn't *talk* in the library.

- **Capital Letter** A B C D E F G . . .

- **Comma** ,

- **Comparative Form** A comparative form of an adjective or adverb is used to compare two things.

  My house is *bigger* than your house.
  Her husband drives *faster* than she does.

- **Complement** The complement of the sentence is the information after the verb. It completes the verb phrase.

  He works *hard*.   I slept *for five hours*.   They are *late*.

- **Consonant** The following letters are consonants: *b, c, d, f, g, h, j, k, l, m, n, p, q, r, s, t, v, w, x, y, z*.

  NOTE: *y* is sometimes considered a vowel, as in the word *syllable*.

- **Contraction** A contraction is made up of two words put together with an apostrophe.

  He's my brother.   *You're* late.   *What's* your name?
  (*He's = He is*)   (*You're = You are*)   (*What's = What is*)

- **Count Noun** Count nouns are nouns that we can count. They have a singular and a plural form.

    1 pen – 3 pens   1 table – 4 tables

- **Frequency Words** Frequency words are *always, usually, often, sometimes, rarely, seldom, hardly ever,* and *never.*

    I *never* drink coffee.   We *always* do our homework.

- **Imperative** An imperative sentence gives a command or instructions. An imperative sentence omits the word *you.*

    Come here.   *Don't* be late.   Please *sit* down.

- **Infinitive** An infinitive is *to* + the base form.

    I want *to leave.*   You need *to be* here on time.

- **Modal** The modal verbs are *can, could, shall, should, will, would, may, might,* and *must.*

    They *should* leave.   I *must* go.

- **Negative** means no.

- **Nonaction Verb** A nonaction verb has no action. We do not usually use a continuous tense (*be* + verb *-ing*) with a nonaction verb. The nonaction verbs are: *believe, cost, care, have, hear, know, like, love, matter, mean, need, own, prefer, remember, see, seem, think, understand, want,* and sense-perception verbs.

    She *has* a computer.   We *love* our mother.   You *look* tired.

- **Noncount Noun** A noncount noun is a noun that we don't count. It has no plural form.

    She drank some *water.*   He ate some *rice.*
    I need *money.*   We had a lot of *homework.*

- **Noun** A noun is a person (*brother*), a place (*kitchen*), or a thing (*table*). Nouns can be either count (*1 table, 2 tables*) or noncount (*money, water*).

    My *brother* lives in California.   My *sisters* live in New York.
    I get *money* from my parents.   Everyone needs *love.*

- **Object** The object of the sentence follows the verb. It receives the action of the verb.

    He bought *a car.*   I saw *a movie.*   I met *your brother.*

- **Object Pronoun** Use object pronouns (*me, you, him, her, it, us,* and *them*) after the verb or preposition.

    He likes *her.*   I saw the movie. Let's talk about *it.*

- **Parentheses** ( )

- **Participle, Present** The present participle is verb + *-ing.*

    She is *sleeping.*   They are *laughing.*

(continued)

- **Period** .
- **Phrase** A phrase is a group of words that go together.

    Last month my sister came to visit.
    There is a red car *in front of my house.*

- **Plural** Plural means more than one. A plural noun usually ends with *-s.*

    She has beautiful *eyes.*   Please wash the *dishes.*

- **Possessive Form** Possessive forms show ownership or relationship.

    Mary's coat is in the closet.   *My brother* lives in Miami.

- **Preposition** A preposition is a connecting word: *about, above, across, after, around, as, at, away, before, behind, below, by, down, for, from, in, into, like, of, off, on, out, over, to, under, up,* and *with.*

    The book is *on* the table.   I live *with* my parents.

- **Pronoun** A pronoun takes the place of a noun.

    Dorota bought a new car. *She* bought *it* last week.
    John likes Mary, but *she* doesn't like *him.*

- **Punctuation** Period . Comma , Colon : Semicolon ; Question Mark ? Exclamation Mark !

- **Question Mark** ?
- **Regular Verb** A regular verb forms its past tense with *-ed.*

    He *worked* yesterday.   We *listened* to the radio.

- **-s Form** The *-s* form is a present tense verb that ends in *-s* or *-es.*

    He *lives* in New York.   She *watches* TV a lot.

- **Sentence** A sentence is a group of words that contains a subject[1] and a verb (at least) and gives a complete thought.

    SENTENCE: She came home.
    NOT A SENTENCE: When she came home

- **Simple Form of Verb** The simple form of the verb, also called the "base" form, has no tense; it never has an *-s, -ed,* or *-ing* ending.

    Did you *see* the movie?   I can't *find* his phone number.

- **Singular** Singular means one.

    She ate a *sandwich.*   I have one *television.*

- **Subject** The subject of the sentence tells who or what the sentence is about.

    My *sister* bought a new car.   *The car* is beautiful.

---

[1]In an imperative sentence, the subject *you* is omitted: *Sit down. Come here.*

- **Subject Pronouns** Use subject pronouns (*I, you, he, she, it, we, you,* and *they*) before a verb.

    They speak Japanese.   *We* speak Spanish.

- **Superlative Form** A superlative form of an adjective or adverb shows the number-one item in a group of three or more.

    January is the *coldest* month of the year.
    You have the *best* seat in the room.

- **Syllable** A syllable is a part of a word that has only one vowel sound. (Some words have only one syllable.)

    change (one syllable)   after (af·ter = two syllables)
    look (one syllable)   responsible (re·spon·si·ble = four syllables)

- **Tense** A verb has tense. Tense shows when the action of the sentence happened.

    SIMPLE PRESENT: She usually *drives* to work.
    FUTURE: She *is going to drive* tomorrow.
    PRESENT CONTINUOUS: She *is driving* now.
    SIMPLE PAST: She *drove* yesterday.

- **Verb** A verb is the action of the sentence. The verb *be* connects.

    He *runs* fast.   I *speak* English.   You *are* late.

- **Vowel** The following letters are vowels: *a, e, i, o, u.* Y is sometimes considered a vowel (for example, in the word *mystery*).

Appendix G

The United States of America: Major Cities

AL	Alabama	HI	Hawaii	MA	Massachusetts	NM	New Mexico	SD	South Dakota
AK	Alaska	ID	Idaho	MI	Michigan	NY	New York	TN	Tennessee
AZ	Arizona	IL	Illinois	MN	Minnesota	NC	North Carolina	TX	Texas
AR	Arkansas	IN	Indiana	MS	Mississippi	ND	North Dakota	UT	Utah
CA	California	IA	Iowa	MO	Missouri	OH	Ohio	VT	Vermont
CO	Colorado	KS	Kansas	MT	Montana	OK	Oklahoma	VA	Virginia
CT	Connecticut	KY	Kentucky	NE	Nebraska	OR	Oregon	WA	Washington
DE	Delaware	LA	Louisiana	NV	Nevada	PA	Pennsylvania	WV	West Virginia
FL	Florida	ME	Maine	NH	New Hampshire	RI	Rhode Island	WI	Wisconsin
GA	Georgia	MD	Maryland	NJ	New Jersey	SC	South Carolina	WY	Wyoming
								DC*	District of Columbia

*The District of Columbia is not a state. Washington, D.C., is the capital of the United States.
Note: Washington, D.C., and Washington state are not the same.

Vocabulary in Context Index

(continued)

Vocabulary Word(s)	Page Number	Vocabulary Word(s)	Page Number
depend (on)	236	grain	121
deposit	189	guideline	121
desk job	88	gym	88
difference between	166	hard	15
different	3	hardware store	157
difficult	260	have fun	65
dirty	9	headache	148
do errands	178	health club	269
don't worry	9	help/helpful	3
downstairs	157	high chair	200
drive-through	189	hire	211
during	88	hold/hold hands	178
each other	65	holiday	27
early	16	home supply store	157
economical	236	hungry	82
education	225	hurt	110
elevator	157	identity document	50
employer/employee	250	immigrant	3
empty	9	in a hurry	100
enjoy	65	income/low-income	121
enough	157	infant	110
enter	56	information	50
everything	3	injure	269
excited	200	injury	269
exercise	88	inside	32
expect	73	instead	260
expensive	56	interested	157
extra	73	interview	250
extras	236	invite/invitation	65
fast	27	item	9
fat	121	job	73
favorite	128	keep	73
fee	211	kid	27
fill out	50	lamp	157
financial aid	56	laundromat	3
fitness instructor	269	law	100
fly/flight	293	learner's permit	100
for a while	200	less than	121
forget	50	let	50
free	16	life	3
free time	65	like	236
from now on	282	lightbulb	157
fuel economy	236	look up	56
full-time	73	lunch box	128
furniture	200	mailing supplies	178
get paid	73	make a decision	236
get some sleep	200	make mistakes	260
get (to a place)	260	make money	73
gift	200	meal	82
go shopping	148	mean	73

Vocabulary Word(s)	Page Number	Vocabulary Word(s)	Page Number
mechanic	236	pound	16
messenger	88	practice	100
microphone	189	prefer	157
middle initial	56	prepared	260
mileage	236	prepared food	82
move/mover	211	price	16
necessary	9	print	50, 178
neighborhood	211	probably	189
nervous	260	product	16
never	32	program	148
newcomer	282	project	293
news	148	public school	136
next door	88	pump	110
note	136	really	282
nutrition	121	reference	250
of course	39	relative	200
offer	225	relax	73
on (my, your, etc.) mind	32	rent	211
on sale	16	repair	236
on the way	110	resale shop	200
on time	27	résumé	260
online	56	return	136
on-the-job training	269	ride a bicycle/bike	88
operation	293	right	9
opportunity	282	roll	189
order	82	rule	100
ounce	166	safety	100
out of	39	salary	73
outdoor concert	65	sales position	260
outlet mall	110	sample	16
outside	32	save	100
over	100	scale	178
overtime	73	school supplies	136
pack	211	seat belt	110
package	16, 178	secret	39
park	88	security guard	39
part-time	73	self-service	178
pass a test	100	serious	32
passenger	110	serve	121
patient	269	service	157
permit	100	several	110
pharmacy	148	shampoo	166
physical therapist (PT)	269	shelf/shelves	16
pick up	178	shop	148
PIN	39	shopping cart	157
polite	32	sign	50
popular	65	sneakers	88
position	250	son	27
positive	260	spend time	65
postage	178	stamp	178

(continued)

Index

Photo Credits